LECTURES ON DON QUIXOTE

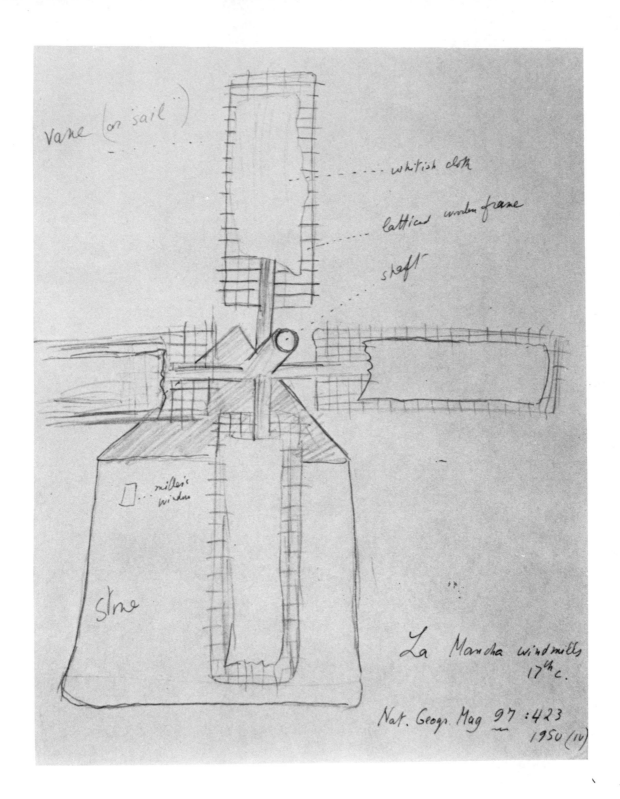

Vane (or 'sail')

whitish cloth

latticed wooden frame

shaft

miller's window

stone

La Mancha windmills
17th c.

Nat. Geogr. Mag 97 : 423
1950 (IV)

Nabokov's rendering of a seventeenth-century windmill

Vladimir Nabokov

LECTURES ON DON QUIXOTE

EDITED BY Fredson Bowers

INTRODUCTION BY Guy Davenport

HARCOURT BRACE JOVANOVICH

BRUCCOLI CLARK   SAN DIEGO   NEW YORK   LONDON

Other books in this series:
LECTURES ON LITERATURE
LECTURES ON RUSSIAN LITERATURE

DESIGNED BY BARBARA DUPREE KNOWLES

Library of Congress Cataloging in Publication Data
Nabokov, Vladimir Vladimirovich, 1899-1977.
Lectures on Don Quixote.
1. Cervantes Saavendra, Miguel de, 1547-1616.
Don Quixote—Addresses, essays, lectures. I. Title.
PQ6352.N25 1983   863'.3   82-21314
ISBN 0-15-14595-5

HBJ Printed in the United States of America   First Edition   BCDE

Contents

Editor's Preface
by Fredson Bowers

When Vladimir Nabokov entered the United States in 1940 to begin his new life in this country, he brought with him, according to his own account,* a number of lectures for the academic career that faced him. The present series on Cervantes's *Don Quixote*, however, was especially written when he was given leave of absence from his regular position on the Cornell University faculty so that he could accept a visiting appointment at Harvard University in the spring semester of the academic year 1951-52.

Among the Harvard General Education courses inaugurated about five years earlier was Humanities 1, 2, the first semester devoted to the epic taught by the classicist John H. Finley, Jr., and the second, to the novel taught by Professor Harry Levin. Both had been influential in setting up the General Education program, in which Humanities 1, 2 had become a showpiece. From time to time Professor Levin was forced to meet commitments in other departments that required a substitute for Humanities 2: I. A. Richards, Thornton Wilder, and Vladimir Nabokov were to fill in for him as occasion served. According to Professor Levin's memory, he gave it as his opinion in talking with Nabokov about the works to be taught that *Don Quixote* was the logical starting point for discussing the development of the novel. Nabokov agreed with this opinion so strongly that he set about preparing a series of lectures on Cervantes specifically for the course, to be followed by his already prepared Cornell

* Vladimir Nabokov, *Strong Opinions*, New York: McGraw-Hill, 1973, p. 5.

lectures on Dickens, Gogol, Flaubert, and Tolstoy. No evidence is preserved to show that the Cervantes lectures were given later at Cornell on Nabokov's return.*

Nabokov prepared for his Harvard duties, and the new Cervantes lectures, with especial care. His first act, it would seem, was to write out an extensive chapter-by-chapter summary of the entire work. Since his teaching methods relied heavily on quotation from the author under discussion, this summary consisted in part of his own narrative and in part of copied-out or noted quotations, both punctuated by various personal comments on the action, the dialogue, the characters, and the themes. The text he used was the translation of *Don Quixote* by Samuel Putnam, published by the Viking Press in 1949 and subsequently reprinted by Random House in the Modern Library. Almost all page references in the manuscripts were keyed to this edition (not to be confused with the abridged Viking Portable against which Nabokov specifically warned his students). However, he suggested that the paperback *Don Quixote*, translated by J. M. Cohen for Penguin Books in England (1950), would be acceptable.

The copy of the Putnam translation Nabokov utilized for his own written-out notes and lectures has not been preserved, but his Penguin paperback is in the possession of the Nabokov family. This copy contains pencil lines drawn in the margins against a number of passages but, disappointingly, only a notation or two, such as the query "Victory? Defeat?" against part one, chapter 9, or "Ducal theme Begins" against part two, chapter 30. The evidence is not clear whether this was actually Nabokov's teaching copy (there could have been problems with the quotations in his lectures keyed to the Putnam page numbers); but fortunately the matter is of small concern owing to its almost complete lack of annotation, of no use here to an editor.

The Narrative-Commentary section, which in the present volume follows the six formal lectures, reproduces Nabokov's original summary of the novel, written out and then typed in a form that could be mined as necessary. After Nabokov had thus familiarized himself thoroughly with the novel by constructing this Narrative-Commentary, he made his first attempt at the active preparation of the lectures themselves. Here the

---

* At one time or another in his literature courses at Cornell University Nabokov lectured severally on Jane Austen, Dickens, Stevenson, Joyce, Flaubert, Proust, Kafka, Tolstoy, Gogol, Turgenev, Chekhov, Dostoevski, and Gorki. For the texts of these lectures, see *Lectures on Literature* (New York and London: Harcourt Brace Jovanovich/Bruccoli Clark, 1980) and *Lectures on Russian Literature* (New York and London: Harcourt Brace Jovanovich/Bruccoli Clark, 1981).

evidence of the manuscripts suggests that initially he conceived of a narrative analyzing the structure of *Don Quixote* on the basis of the comprehensive theme of Victories and Defeats. The evidence further confirms that he wrote out a preliminary version of such a lecture series at considerable length.

In working up this study, he abstracted numerous pages from the original typed Narrative-Commentary and considerably altered their chronological order to fit the new central theme. Handwritten pages of elaboration, extension, and more detailed commentary linked the rearranged typed pages to fit them into the imposed thematic Victories and Defeats discussion. Only later, after this draft had been completed did the more varied thematic subjects for the present six lectures form in his imagination as a structural concept superior both to the chronological survey of his original notes and to the simple opposition of Victories and Defeats as a peg on which to hang the narrative.

For the final form of these six lectures, then, as they were delivered and are now preserved in their six folders, Nabokov made a further rewriting in which he abstracted—as he needed the material—various pages from the Victories and Defeats draft, as well as additional pages from the original Narrative-Commentary notes to add to his new lecture pages. He deleted the material on the typed pages that was not to be used, and thus worked these pages into his handwritten final manuscript. The sixth chapter, on Victories and Defeats, was completely rewritten according to a new formula. Only some forty-odd pages, about a fifth of the original Narrative-Commentary notes, remained segregated in a folder, unused either in the draft or in the final lectures. To reconstitute the original Narrative-Commentary for this volume its typed pages (identifiable by their pagination) have been recovered from the discarded manuscript of the Victories and Defeats draft, and the handwritten portions of this manuscript have been added, as appropriate, to the lectures or else inserted in the Narrative-Commentary. Additional pages have been utilized in part from the manuscript of the six lectures to recover the typed material that had been deleted after Nabokov had inserted what he wanted from these pages in the final six-lecture manuscript. The scattered pages of this Narrative-Commentary, thus assembled and added to the forty or so unutilized pages of the original that had been set aside, now comprise the Narrative-Commentary section, with only a few pages missing from the whole.

The reconstruction of the original of this section produced a certain amount of repetition both of comment and of quotation earlier abstracted for use in the six lectures: such material has been removed so that any covering of the same ground in the Narrative-Commentary is in the nature of an expansion or fitting-in of the discourse as found in the lectures. This necessary editing of the material has entailed various editorially inserted bridge passages to link quotations that were for Nabokov but suggestive notes for possible elaboration; moreover, various quotations have been expanded because of their intrinsic interest and a few new ones added for the pleasure of the reader. To replace the few leaves that have been lost, a limited number of plot summaries have been inserted to preserve the continuity.

The preserved manuscripts consist of Nabokov's original six folders, each folder holding a lecture and occasionally loose pages of notes that must be regarded as early accumulation of background material. (As many as possible of these notes have been worked into the body of the lectures.) The length of the lectures differs markedly, in part dependent upon the optional cutting that he did in the text by means of minatory brackets (for Nabokov was meticulous about the timing of his read lectures). But also since each lecture took the same length of time in delivery, the highly variable number of leaves was in part owing to the limited use he might make (perhaps only a few sentences from a page) of the earlier written material that he was working into the lectures' final form. The final lectures are all in Nabokov's handwriting except for these typed interspersed leaves drawn from the early draft version of the Victories and Defeats form of the lectures. Many of these draft leaves had, of course, originated as the typed version of his original summary notes when he was first investigating the novel on a systematic basis. The first lecture consists of some twenty pages; the second of thirty-five; the third expands to seventy-one; the fourth is reduced to twenty-nine; the fifth to thirty-one; and the final version of the sixth, with a conclusion, to about fifty. In addition to these folders which represent chiefly the lectures as delivered, the file contains about 175 pages of discarded synopsis, loose pages, and a folder containing fifteen pages of very rough notes on Avellaneda's spurious *Second Volume of Don Quixote.*

The editorial problem resolved itself into an attempt to present the maximum of Nabokov's conception of *Don Quixote*, with his commentary, on a scale larger than the arbitrary confines of the six classroom lectures to which he was bound. Within the lectures themselves Nabokov would delete truly rejected material so thoroughly as to make it illegible. But he was also in the habit of enclosing material within brackets that he might or might not read depending upon the time, the passage of minutes often

VLADIMIR NABOKOV

being indicated by marginal notes. Also, when he utilized pages from his early Narrative-Commentary, he might draw a diagonal line through material that could not be used either because of time limitation, or because it lacked pertinence to the point that he was at the moment engaged in making. The editor has consistently restored the bracketed text since it formed part of the original writing-out, was usually pertinent, and might well have been delivered if the clock had warranted. Additional material deleted from the interspersed typed leaves has been included in context, particularly if quotation from *Don Quixote* would prove helpful; but most of this discarded material has been restored to the Narrative-Commentary section where it had originally belonged.

Nabokov usually wrote out quotations that he intended to read, but occasionally he did no more than indicate their page numbers in the Putnam translation. One cannot be sure in this latter case whether, time permitting, he opened his book and read to the class, or whether he merely referred his students to the passage for their private reading. (All are fully quoted in the present text.) The editor has treated quotations with some freedom in that when appropriate he may extend a briefer Nabokov quoted passage or else add appropriate quotations either in the text or in footnotes further to illustrate Nabokov's remarks in the lecture. In general, the lectures follow the structure and order of Nabokov's final form except for the expansions detailed, especially those authorized by his own bracketed holograph. However, the first chapter, although far from synthetic in its present form, was in looser structural shape than the others and has been assembled not only from the original but also by the inclusion of notes and remarks on separate pages distributed among the folders but not integral with their content.

Since the finally arrived-at lectures concentrate on various themes and hence do not treat the events of the plot in any fixed chronological order, the Narrative-Commentary may serve to bring together a coherent view of the novel as Cervantes wrote it, interspersed with a number of Nabokov's expositions and analyses that found no place in the lectures. As a result this section must be considered an integral part of the present volume, not alone for an understanding of Nabokov's total view of *Don Quixote* as a work of art but also for the more mundane purpose of recalling to distant readers the events to which Nabokov may merely allude in his lectures. One may hope that its narrative summary will not deter first readers, stimulated by the lectures, from introducing themselves to the novel itself as a new experience in the world's great literature.

Finally, the brief appendix of extracts from *Le Morte d'Arthur* and

Amadis of Gaul reproduces the typescript used for the preparation of mimeographed sheets distributed to Nabokov's students in order to acquaint them with some typical passages in the sort of chivalric romances that Don Quixote was reading and endeavoring to imitate.

VLADIMIR NABOKOV

Foreword
by Guy Davenport

I remember with delight," Vladimir Nabokov said in 1966 to Herbert Gold, who had traveled to Montreux to interview him, "tearing apart *Don Quixote*, a cruel and crude old book, before six hundred students in Memorial Hall, much to the horror and embarrassment of some of my more conservative colleagues." Tear it apart he did, for good critical reasons, but he also put it back together. Cervantes's masterpiece was not in Nabokov's syllabus at Cornell, he was apparently not fond of it, and when he began preparing his Harvard lectures on it (Harvard having insisted that he not omit it) his first discovery was that American professors had over the years gentrified the cruel and crude old book into a genteel and whimsical myth about appearance and reality. So first of all he had to find the text for his students under all the prissy humbug a long tradition of misreading had sifted over it. Nabokov's new reading is an event in modern criticism.

Nabokov's intention to polish these lectures given at Harvard in 1951-1952 and at Cornell from 1948 to 1959 was never realized, and those of us who were not among "the 600 young strangers" enrolled in Humanities 2 at Harvard, spring semester 1951-1952, must read Nabokov on Cervantes from notes that survived in manila folders, scrupulously and splendidly edited by Fredson Bowers, the most distinguished of American bibliographers.

Memorial Hall, where Nabokov read these lectures, is as symbolic a place for them as the most fastidious ironist could wish. It is a gaudy Victorian pile that Mark Twain's Connecticut Yankee could assure us is precisely the bamboozled composite of medieval architecture he saw in his dream. It was designed as a pilot example of Collegiate Gothic in 1878 by William Robert Ware and Henry Van Brunt, to memorialize the soldiers slain by quixotic Confederates in the Civil War. In this building precipitated from the imagination of Sir Walter Scott and John Ruskin, in this consummately quixotic architectural rhetoric, what could be more fitting than that a connoisseur of ridiculous postures and keen nuances should jolt us awake in the matter of the ingenuous old gentleman from La Mancha.

Once, when I was teaching *Don Quixote* at the University of Kentucky, a student raised his long Baptist arm to say that he had come to the conclusion that the hero of our book is crazy. That, I said, is something that has been discussed for 400 years and now we, snug in this classroom on an autumn afternoon, get to have our shot at it. "Well," he muttered with some querulousness, "I find it hard to believe that they would write a whole book about a crazy man." His *they* is correct. The book Nabokov took apart so deftly at Harvard was a book evolved from Cervantes's text, so that when one brings up *Don Quixote* in any discussion, the problem of whose Quixote arises. Michelet's? Miquel de Unamuno's? Joseph Wood Krutch's? For Cervantes's character, like Hamlet, Sherlock Holmes, and Robinson Crusoe, began to stray from his book almost as soon as he was invented.

Not only has there been a steady sentimentalization of the Don and his sidekick, Sancho Panza—sweet, charmingly befuddled Don Quixote! comic Sancho, so picturesquely a levelheaded peasant!—but a displacement as well of the text by its illustrators, especially Gustave Doré, Honoré Daumier (and nowadays Picasso and Dalı), its celebrators, imitators, dramatizers, and users of the word *quixotic*, which means anything you want it to mean. It should mean something like *hallucinated, self-hypnotized,* or *play in collision with reality.* How it came to mean *admirably idealistic* is an explanation Nabokov undertakes in these lectures.

To put Cervantes's Don Quixote back into Cervantes's text Nabokov (encouraged by the need to do so after looking into a batch of American critics and their laughably irresponsible accounts of the book) first wrote out a chapter-by-chapter summary—which Professor Bowers helpfully includes. The diligence of this summary can only shame those teachers who still have a week's go at *Don Quixote* in sophomore survey courses all over the Republic without having read the book since they themselves were sophomores, without ever having read Part II, or (I know of one) not having read the book at all. For *Don Quixote*, as Nabokov knew with some

VLADIMIR NABOKOV

pain and annoyance, is not the book people think it is. Far too many interpolated *novelle* (of the kind we cheerfully forget mar *The Pickwick Papers*) impede the plotless plot. We all rewrite the book in our heads so that it is a picaresque succession of events: the appropriation of the barber's basin as Mambrino's helmet, the tilt at the windmills (which became the archetypal quintessence of the book), charging the sheep, and so on. Many people wholly innocent of the text can supply you with a plausible plot summary.

What Nabokov's eyes kept seeing as he prepared his lectures was the accurately perceived fact that the book elicits cruel laughter. Cervantes's old man who had read himself into insanity and his smelly squire were created to be the butt of mockery. Quite early readers and critics began to sidestep this Spanish fun and to interpret the story as another kind of satire: one in which an essentially sane, humane soul in a crass and unromantic world can only appear as insane.

The problem is not simple. Spain, which has traditionally rejected outsiders, has no talent (like China or the USA, for example) for accommodating them. In Cervantes's lifetime there was the hysterical expulsion of Jews, Moors, and converts of Jewish and Islamic origins. Spain kept the gladiatorial slaughters in an arena (for the amusement of the populace) long after all the rest of the Roman Empire had abandoned them. The national entertainment, the bullfight, sets Spain aside among civilized people even today. The historical moment in which *Don Quixote* was written, the reign of Felipe II, that paranoid fanatic who styled himself the Most Catholic King, is one we have silvered over with a moonlight of Romance. Nabokov was lecturing in the hotbed of Spanish romanticizing. Lowell and Longfellow had invented a Spain which has stuck in the American imagination (as witness the musical *Man from La Mancha*) and which, pitifully, American tourists flock to Spain to find.

And yet, in its way, the Spain of Felipe II was quixotic. Its nobles owned suits of armor in which no cavalryman would dare try to conduct a battle. Felipe, practical nattering fussbudget of a king, used to stand his empty suit of armor at attention to review his troops. He himself was inside the palace, among his voluptuous Titians, doing the accounts, reading and annotating every letter sent and received in his network of embassies and spies as wide as from the New World to Vienna, as deep as from Rotterdam to Gibraltar. He, if any model is to be found, is Don Quixote, but an anti-Quixote. Like the Don, he lived in a dream whose illusory fabric kept tearing. He burnt heretics, but how do you know a heretic is a heretic? Was he not in the same epistemological hot spot as Don Quixote seeing sheep as sheep but also as Moors? Felipe's cruel spies were forever hauling people who said they were good Catholics to the torturer on the suspicion that they were (if you knew how to find out) insincere converts, Humanists, Protestants, Jews, Muslims, atheists, witches, or God knows what.

Europe was going through a time in which reality began to flip-flop. Hamlet teased Polonius with the ambiguous shapes of clouds. Don Quixote's abilities to fool himself are a focus of the age's anxieties. Identity, for the first time in European history, became a matter of opinion or of conviction. Chaucer's laughter at "pigges bones" was not skepticism of authentic relics to be venerated. But in *Don Quixote* the confusion of a horse trough with a baptismal font seriously opens the question (whether Cervantes intended to or not) as to whether what we call a baptismal font isn't a water trough innocent of all the quixotic magic we assign to it.

Over the years, I think, the meaning of *Don Quixote* has skewed into the winds of the Enlightenment and sailed brightly under false colors which we have all too willingly wished upon it. This is what brought Nabokov's gaze into such stringency. He wanted the book to be itself alone, to be a fairy tale, to be an imaginative construct independent of the myth "real life." And yet *Don Quixote* is precisely a book that plays games with "real life." In its way it is a kind of treatise about how meaning gets into things and lives. It is a book about enchantment, the inappropriateness of enchantment in a disenchanted world, and the silliness of enchantment in general. Despite this, it enchants. It became, with much misreading and cooperation on our part, what it mocked.

Nabokov, astute observer of the American psyche, knew that all 600 Harvardlings and Cliffies in his audience believed in knights, just as they believed in the Old West with its cowboys errant, and in the Gothic architecture of Memorial Hall. He wasted no time disabusing them; in fact, cheerfully told them they would hear nothing of Cervantes, his times or his missing left hand (lost at Lepanto) from *him*. Instead, he insisted that they know what a windmill was, and drew them one on a blackboard, and instructed them in the names of its parts. He told them why a country gentleman might mistake them for giants—they were an innovation in seventeenth-century Spain, the last country to hear of anything new in all Europe.

He is very clear, and very funny, about Dulcinea del Toboso. But he does not scatter his students' attention by digressing on Courtly Love, its strange metamorphic history, and its curious survival today. If, as he delivered these carefully wrought revisionist lectures, part of his mind was surely over at the University Museum four minutes walk away, where he spent eight years of the preceding decade as research fellow in entomology studying the anatomy of butterflies, another part must have been on a project concerning Courtly Love, its madnesses and follies, which would mature three years hence as *Lolita*. That diminutive of a Spanish name, Dolores, raises our curiosity. *Lolita* is too logically a progression of Nabokovian themes (the other as the self, the generative power of delusions, the interplay of sense and obsession) to have been influenced by a close and tedious reading of the *Quixote*. And yet there's the picaresque journey as the "harmonizing intuition" of the two works. And there's the sprite Lolita. She began as a seductive child in the first appearance of romantic love in the West, boy or girl, Sappho's darlings or Anakreon's striplings. Plato philosophized these hopeless loves into something called the love of Ideal Beauty. The theme became salacious and overbearing in the leaden hands of the Romans, melted almost away in the early Middle Ages, to emerge again in the tenth century as Romance. By Cervantes's time Courtly Love had saturated literature (it still does), and in his satire of it and of its new context Chivalry, he found it obvious enough to transmute the stock paragon of virtue and beauty into a country girl with big feet and a prominent wart.

Don Quixote had no effect whatsoever on the health of the Romance; it simply invented a robust and parallel tradition which has moved alongside ever since. A Richardson would now have a Fielding. We would keep the ideal beauty, but in the house next door lives Madame Bovary. Scarlet O'Hara and Molly Bloom, spirited Irish women both, have equal claim on our imagination. Even in the old romances, from early on, the virtuous beauty is balanced by a sorceress, Una by Duessa. After *Don Quixote* the false beauty began to be interesting in herself, an Eve claiming her old prerogatives as temptress. By the late seventeenth and eighteenth centuries she had set up shop both in literature and real life. To get at a French king, Michelet observed, you had to wiggle your way through a wall of women. The mistress became a kind of social institution; literature said she was demanding and dangerous, but more interesting and gratifying than a wife: a ritual detail of the Romance *Don Quixote* supposedly laid by the heels. In the overripe Decadence the mistress became a spicy Lilith, the primeval feminine in a lacy nightie, reeking of doom, damnation, and death. Lulu, Benjamin Franklin Wedekind called her. Molly, said Joyce. Circe, said Pound. Odette, said Proust. And out of. this chorus Nabokov plucked his Lulu, Lolita, whose real name was more Swinburnian, Dolores, blending her with her cousins Alice (Nabokov is the translator of *Alice in*

Wonderland into Russian), Ruskin's Rose, and Poe's Annabel Lee. But her Grandmama was Dulcinea del Toboso. And Humbert Humbert's memoirs, we remember, are offered to us by a professor as the ravings of a madman.

So these lectures are not without their interest to admirers of Nabokov's novels. Both Cervantes and Nabokov recognize that playing can extend beyond childhood not as its natural transformation into daydreaming (which psychiatrists find so suspicious, and discourage) or creativity of all sorts, but as play itself. That's what Don Quixote is doing: playing knight-errant. Lolita's side of her affair with Humbert Humbert is play (she is surprised that grown-ups are interested in sex, which to her is just another game), and the psychology of Humbert (meant to elude the theories of Freud) may be that he is simply stuck in the playtime of childhood. In any case, whenever a critic considers the picaresque novel, or literary treatments of illusion and identity, he will find himself thinking of Cervantes and Nabokov together.

These lectures on Cervantes were a triumph for Nabokov in that I think he surprised himself in his final opinion of *Don Quixote*. He approached his task conscientiously despite thinking of this old wheeze of a classic as a white elephant and something of a fraud. It was the suspicion of fraud that propelled his interest. Then, I think, he saw that the fraud was in the book's reputation and epidemic among its critics. Here was a state of affairs that Nabokov liked to go at *bec et ongle*. He began to find symmetry, of sorts, in the sprawling mess. He begins to suspect that Cervantes is unaware of the book's "disgusting cruelty." He begins to like the Don's dry humor, his engaging pedantry. He accepts the "interesting phenomenon" that Cervantes created a character greater than the book from which he has wandered—into art, into philosophy, into political symbolism, into the folklore of the literate.

Don Quixote remains a crude old book full of peculiarly Spanish cruelty, pitiless cruelty that baits an old man who plays like a child into his dotage. It was written in an age when dwarfs and the afflicted were laughed at, when pride and haughtiness were more arrogant than ever before or since, when dissenters from official thought were burnt alive in city squares to general applause, when mercy and kindness seem to have been banished. Indeed, the first readers of the book laughed heartily at its cruelty. Yet the world soon found other ways of reading it. It gave birth to the modern novel all over Europe. Fielding, Smollett, Gogol, Dostoevski, Daudet, Flaubert shaped this fable out of Spain to their own ends. A character who started out in his creator's hands as a buffoon has turned out in the course of history to be a saint. And even Nabokov, always quick to detect and expose the cruelty at the core of all sentimentality, lets him have his way. "We do not laugh at him any longer," he concludes. "His blazon is pity, his banner is beauty. He stands for everything that is gentle, forlorn, pure, unselfish, and gallant."

Write required books on blackboard.

Lecture One

Introduction to "Don Quixote"

I shall devote to day's talk to the following seven points:
(1) Required Reading, (2) The connection between Real Life and Fiction
(3) The "where" of Don Quixote (4) The "when" of the book
(5) What people think of the book (6) ~~pattern~~ general remarks (on form)
(7) The long shadow of Don Quixote. Do not be distressed
by ~~initial~~ obscurities — I shall try to clear up everything as we go along; and do
not fume at my metaphors; they have some mnemonic value.
There are three ways of pronouncing that name (in sun) Кишóть, Кихóть
and Кюксóт. The last has a glitter of crossed swords in
the middle which compels my choice.

(1)

Required reading

In your hands has been placed or will to place a (приход. ор.)
~~Please, ~~ is the list of ~~our~~ five novels, ~~in that order.~~
"Don Quixote" ~~a~~ is - God bless it - a longish book consisting
of two parts in one volume, Penguin edition. Also recommended
to those who can afford is the Viking Press edition, in two vol. with entertaining notes.
~~Those~~ "Don Quixote" is almost a thousand pages long and can
be read in twenty-four hours. The problem is to spread these
twenty four hours rationally. I think you could manage it within
a fortnight and then ~~these decide~~ use another week to the re-reading of certain
passages, in the light of accumulated class-notes

Nabokov's notes for his opening remarks to his Harvard students

Introduction

"REAL LIFE" AND FICTION

We shall do our best to avoid the fatal error of looking for so-called "real life" in novels. Let us not try and reconcile the fiction of facts with the facts of fiction. *Don Quixote* is a fairy tale, so is *Bleak House*, so is *Dead Souls*. *Madame Bovary* and *Anna Karenin* are supreme fairy tales.* But without these fairy tales the world would not be real. A masterpiece of fiction is an original world and as such is not likely to fit the world of the reader. On the other hand, what is this vaunted "real life," what are these solid "facts"? One is suspicious of them when one sees biologists stalking each other with loaded genes, or battling historians locked in each other's arms as they roll in the dust of centuries. Whether or not his newspaper and a set of senses reduced to five are the main sources of the so-called "real life" of the so-called average man, one thing is fortunately certain: namely, that the average man himself is but a piece of fiction, a tissue of statistics.

The notion of "real life," then, is based on a system of generalities, and it is only as generalities that the so-called "facts" of so-called "real life" are in contact with a work of fiction. The less general a work of fiction is, then, the less recognizable it is in terms of "real life." Or to put it the other way around, the more vivid and new details in a work of fiction, then the more it departs from so-called "real life," since "real life" is the generalized epithet, the average emotion, the advertised multitude, the commonsensical world. I am deliberately plunging at once into rather icy waters, which is inevitable if one wishes to break the ice. There is no use, therefore, looking

* At the end of his prefatory remarks to his first class about assignments and requirements, VN remarked, "*Don Quixote* is, among other things, our training ground for learning methods of approach to Dickens, Flaubert, et cetera."

1

I   Introduction to Don Quixote   50 mnts.   1

II   Don Quixote and Sancho Panza   40 "   } 2

III   Remarks on Structure _____   15 "
        Arcadian theme   20   } 3
        The Inset novella theme
        Chivalry theme   30 "

IV   Cruelty of the Book ~~~~~~~   15 "
        Mystification Theme   15 "   } 4
        (The Ducal Enchantments)   20 "

V   Beauty of the book
        Altisidora   20 "
                                               } 5   320/50
        The Chroniclers _____   25 "
        Dulcinea and death   15

VI   Don Quixote's Victories
                and Defeats   40 "
                                               } 6
        Altisidora and Death ~~~~~   15

        Conclusion   15 "

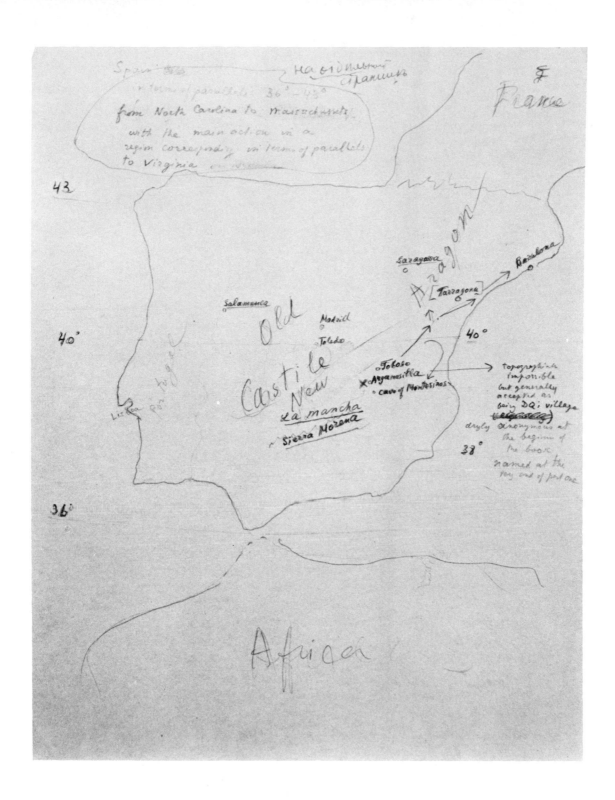

Nabokov's map of Spain, locating the action of the novel

in these books for detailed factual representation of so-called "real life." On the other hand, between certain generalities of fiction and certain generalities of life there is some correspondence. Take physical or mental pain, for instance, or dreams, or madness, or such things as kindness, mercy, justice—take these general elements of human life, and you must agree that it should be a profitable task to study the way they are transmuted into art by masters of fiction.

THE "WHERE?" OF DON QUIXOTE

Let us not kid ourselves. Cervantes is no land surveyor. The wobbly backdrop of *Don Quixote* is fiction—and rather unsatisfactory fiction at that. With its preposterous inns full of belated characters from Italian storybooks and its preposterous mountains teeming with lovelorn poetasters disguised as Arcadian shepherds, the picture Cervantes paints of the country is about as true and typical of seventeenth-century Spain as Santa Claus is true and typical of the twentieth-century North Pole. Indeed, Cervantes seems to know Spain as little as Gogol did central Russia.

However, it is still Spain; and here is where the generalities of "real life" (in this case geography) may be applied to the generalities of a work of fiction. In a general way Don Quixote's adventures, in the first part, take place around the villages of Argamasilla and El Toboso in La Mancha, in the Castilian parched plain, and to the south in the mountains of the Morena range, Sierra Morena. I suggest that you look at these places on the map that I have drawn. Spain as you will see spreads in terms of platitudes (sorry, latitudes), degrees 43 to 36, from Massachusetts to North Carolina, with the book's main action taking place in a region corresponding to Virginia. You will find the university town of Salamanca in the west, near the border of Portugal; and you will admire Madrid and Toledo in the middle of Spain. In the second part of the book the general drift of the ramble takes us north toward Saragossa in Aragon but then for reasons I shall discuss later the author changes his mind and sends his hero to Barcelona instead, on the eastern coast.

If, however, we examine Don Quixote's excursions topographically, we are confronted by a ghastly muddle. I shall spare you its details and only mention the fact that throughout those adventures there is a mass of monstrous inaccuracies at every step.* The author avoids descriptions that

* See Paul Groussac, *Une Énigme littéraire: Le DON QUICHOTTE d'Avellaneda* (Paris: A. Picard, 1903), pp. 77-78 and note. VN

VLADIMIR NABOKOV

would be particular and might be verified. It is quite impossible to follow these rambles in central Spain across four or six provinces, in the course of which until we reach Barcelona in the northeast one does not meet with a single known town or cross a single river. Cervantes's ignorance of places is wholesale and absolute, even in respect of Argamasilla in the La Mancha district, which some consider the more or less definite starting point.*

THE "WHEN?" OF THE BOOK

So much for space. Now about time.

From 1667, the publication year of Milton's *Paradise Lost*,** we now slide back into a sunshot hell, back to the first two decades of the seventeenth century.

Odysseus in a blaze of bronze leaping from the threshold upon the wooers; Dante shuddering at Virgil's side as sinner and snake grade into one; Satan bombing the angels—these and others exist within a form or phase of art that we call epic. Great literatures of the past seem to have to be born on the periphery of Europe, along the rim of the known world. We are aware of such southeastern, southern, and northwestern points as, respectively, Greece, Italy, and England. A fourth point is now Spain in the southwest.

What we shall witness now is the evolution of the epic form, the shedding of its metrical skin, the hoofing of its feet, a sudden fertile cross between the winged monster of the epic and the specialized prose form of entertaining narration, more or less a domesticated mammal, if I may pursue the metaphor to its lame end. The result is a fertile hybrid, a new species, the European novel.

So the place is Spain and the time is 1605 to 1615, a very handy decade easy to pocket and keep. Spanish literature flourishes, Lope de Vega writes 500 plays which today are as dead as the armful of plays by his contemporary, Miguel de Cervantes Saavedra. Our man comes very softly out of his corner. I can devote only a slanting minute to his life, which, however, you will easily find in various introductions to his work. We are

* At the end of this sentence, Nabokov notes in reference to Argamasilla, "Don Quixote's village mentioned in the last pages of Part One." That Argamasilla was the village is more a reasonable tradition than an established fact, based on its being the residence of each of the six fictive academicians whose epitaphs and other verses end part one. The opening sentence of chapter 1 of part one starts, in Putnam's translation, "In a village of La Mancha the name of which I have no desire to recall, there lived not so long ago. . . ." In the narrative itself Cervantes never provides its name.

** VN adds to his students, "which most of you have *regained* under Prof. Finley's guidance," an allusion to the distinguished Hellenist John H. Finley, who in Humanities I (the first semester) lectured on five epics including *Paradise Lost*.

interested in books, not people. Of Saavedra's maimed hand you will learn not from me.

Miguel de Cervantes Saavedra (1547-1616); William Shakespeare (1564-1616). The Spanish Empire was at the height of its power and fame when Cervantes was born. Its worst troubles and its best literature began at the end of the century. Madrid in the days of Cervantes's literary apprenticeship, from 1583 onward, was alive with needy rhymesters and producers of more or less polished Castilian prose. There was, as I have already said, Lope de Vega, who completely overshadowed the playwright Cervantes and could write an entire play within twenty-four hours with all the jokes and deaths necessary. There was Cervantes himself—a failure as a soldier, as a poet, as a playwright, as an official (he was paid sixty cents a day for requisitioning wheat for the luckless Spanish Armada)—and then, in 1605, he produced the first part of *Don Quixote*.

It may be worthwhile to cast a rapid glance over the world of letters between 1605 and 1615, in which years both parts of *Don Quixote* were published. One thing catches the fancy of this observer: it is the almost pathological orgy of sonnet-making throughout Europe, in Italy, Spain, England, Poland, France; the queer but not wholly contemptible urge to cage an emotion, an image, or an idea within a cell of fourteen lines, behind the gilt bars of five or seven rhymes, five in the Latin countries, seven in England.

Let us glance at England. In the tremendous afterglow of the Elizabethan period the great series of Shakespeare's incomparable tragedies—*Hamlet* (1601), *Othello* (1604), *Macbeth* (1605), *King Lear* (1606)—were or had just been produced. (Indeed, while Cervantes was making his mad knight, Shakespeare might have been making his mad King.) And in Shakespeare's oakshade Ben Jonson and Fletcher and a number of other dramatists grew—a dense undergrowth of talent. Shakespeare's sonnets, the ultimate reach of this type of thing, were published in 1609 and that influential monument in prose, King James's version of the Bible, came out in 1611. Milton was born in 1608, between the publication dates of the first and the second part of *Don Quixote*. In England's Virginia colony Captain John Smith produced his *A True Revelation* in 1608 and *A Map of Virginia* in 1612. He was the teller of the tale of Pocahontas, a rude but robust narrator, this country's first frontier writer.

For France this decade was a short period of slump between two great eras, immediately after the admirable colorful era of Ronsard the poet and of Montaigne the essayist. Poetry was dying a decorous death at the hands

6   VLADIMIR NABOKOV

of pale perfectionists, perfect rhymesters but impotent visionaries, such as the famous and influential Malherbe. Such inept sentimental novels as *L'Astrée* by Honoré d'Urfé were the fashion. The next really great poet, La Fontaine, was not yet born, and neither Racine nor Molière the playwrights were yet on the scene.*

In Italy, in an age of oppression and tyranny beginning in the middle of the sixteenth century, with all thought under suspicion and all expression of thought fettered, the decade we are discussing is one of inflated poetry with nothing worth mentioning beyond the extravagant metaphors and far-fetched conceits of Giovanni Marini and his followers. Torquato Tasso the poet had completed his tragically botched life ten years before, and Giordano Bruno, the great independent thinker, had just been burned at the stake (1600).

As for Germany, no great writers are present during the decade under discussion, which corresponds to the threshold of the so-called German Renaissance (1600-1740). French literature was strongly influencing various minor poets, and there were numerous literary societies modeled on Italian ones.

In Russia between the fiery pamphlets of Ivan the Terrible (end of the sixteenth century) and the birth of the greatest of all Muscovite writers (before the nineteenth-century Renaissance) the Archpriest Avvakum (1620-1681), all we can distinguish in a protracted era of oppression and isolation are anonymous fairy tales, narrated unrhymed poems intoned by reciters singing the exploits of legendary heroes (the oldest text of these Bwilinas was written down in 1620 for an Englishman, Richard James). In Russia, as in Germany, literature was still fetal.

THE GENERAL COMMENTS OF CRITICS

Some critics, a very vague minority long dead, have tried to prove that *Don Quixote* is but a stale farce. Others have maintained that *Don Quixote* is the greatest novel ever written. A hundred years ago one enthusiastic French critic, Sainte-Beuve, called it "the Bible of Humanity." Let us not fall under the spell of these enchanters.

The translator Samuel Putnam in the Viking edition recommends books by Bell and by Krutch** on *Don Quixote*. I strongly object to many things

---

* To his class VN added (inserted in his handwriting in what is at this point a typescript) the minatory "You will check your knowledge of these names in Webster."

** The Putnam translation in the Viking edition was taken over by the Modern Library. Readers should avoid the Viking Portable edition, in which large portions of the text are summarized. The critics VN refers to are Aubrey F. G. Bell, *Cervantes* (Norman: University of Oklahoma Press, 1947), and Joseph Wood Krutch, *Five Masters:*

in those books. I object to such statements as "[the] perception [of Cervantes] was as sensitive, his mind as supple, his imagination as active, and his humor as subtle as those of Shakespeare." Oh no—even if we limit Shakespeare to his comedies, Cervantes lags behind in all those things. *Don Quixote* but squires *King Lear*—and squires him well. The only matter in which Cervantes and Shakespeare are equals is the matter of influence, of spiritual irrigation—I have in view the long shadow cast upon receptive posterity of a created image which may continue to live independently from the book itself. Shakespeare's plays, however, will continue to live, apart from the shadow they project.

It has been noted that both writers died on St. George's Day, 1616, "after having joined to slay the dragon of false appearances," as Bell (p. 34) puts it whimsically but incorrectly: far from slaying the dragon, Cervantes and Shakespeare each in his own way paraded the lovely beast, leading it on a leash to have its iridescent scales and melancholy eye enjoyed through the eternity of letters. (Incidentally, although the twenty-third of April is taken to be the date of both men's deaths—and is my birthday—Cervantes and Shakespeare died by different calendars; there is a ten-day gap between the two dates.)

Around *Don Quixote* we hear a plangent clash of opinions—sometimes with the ring of Sancho's sturdy but pedestrian mind and sometimes reminding us of Don Quixote's fury in attacking windmills. Catholics and Protestants, lean mystics and fat statesmen, well-meaning but verbose and stonedead critics of the Sainte-Beuve, Turgenev, or Brandes type, and quadrillions of quarrelsome scholars have expressed their conflicting views about the book and the man who made it. There are those like Aubrey Bell, who thinks that no great masterpiece can be composed without the help of a universal church; he praises "the broad-minded tolerant spirit of the ecclesiastical censors in Spain" (p. 166) and maintains that Cervantes and his hero were good Catholics in the bosom of the good Counter Reformation. There are others—crusty Protestants—who on the contrary insinuate that Cervantes may have been in touch with the Reformers.* Bell also holds that the lesson of the book is Don Quixote's presumption—the folly of aiming at the general good, a field of endeavor that belongs to the

---

A Study in the Mutations of the Novel (New York: Cape & Smith, 1930). The quotation that follows is drawn from Bell's *Cervantes*, p. 35.

* In a bracketed note VN wrote, "See Duffield, who points out that a certain quotation from the Bible in *Don Quixote* coincides with the wording not of the standard Catholic text (the Vulgate, 1592, based on St. Jerome's Latin version, fourth century) but with the Spanish Reformers' Bible of 1569." Alexander James Duffield translated *Don Quixote* with notes by various hands, 3 volumes, 1881. The reference is to his book DON QUIXOTE, *His Critics and Commentators* (London: C. K. Paul, 1881), p. 44.

Church alone. The same school maintains that Cervantes bothered as little about the Inquisition as did the playwright Lope de Vega or the painter Velázquez so that whatever fun is poked at the priests in the book is good-natured, family fun, strictly an internal affair, cloister quips, jollities in the rose garden. But other critics harshly adopt a directly opposite point of view and try to prove, not very successfully, that Cervantes in *Don Quixote* fearlessly expressed his scorn for what a harsh Protestant commentator, Duffield, calls "Romish ritual" and "priestly tyranny";* and the same critic concludes that not only was Don Quixote a monomaniac but that the whole of "Spain in the sixteenth century was overrun with madmen of the same [pathological] type, men of one idea"—since "the king, the Inquisition, the nobles, the cardinals, priests, and nuns . . . were all dominated," as that critic violently puts it, "by one mastering and overbearing conviction that the way to heaven was through a door, the keys of which were in their keeping."**

We shall not follow in the dusty path of these pious or impious, impish or solemn, generalizations. It does not really matter very much whether Cervantes was a good Catholic or a bad one; it does not even matter whether he was a good or a bad man; nor do I deem very important his attitude, whatever it was, to the conditions of his day. Personally, I am more inclined to accept the view that he did not much bother about these conditions. What, however, does concern us is the book itself, a certain

* Duffield, p. 66n: "I do not contend that Cervantes was tilting at the Christian faith; it would be a gross libel to say so; but that he did fearlessly express his scorn for Romish ritual and priestly insolence, arrogance, and tyranny, would be folly to deny. One of the methods by which our great and sunny satirist abolished for ever the sham sages and mock knights was bringing them into the light of nature and common sense, making myth and fiction and lie to come in contact with reality; and when he makes rosaries out of shirt-tails, puts holy water into porringers, mitres and *sambenitos* on asses' backs, and the bones of saints and the holiness of friars into Sancho's mouth, it is to bring all these to a like test."

** Duffield, pp. 94-95: "I say that Don Quixote was mad.

"His madness was not the result of an injured or a weakened brain; he does not become ferocious like Cardenio, nor was he an idiot like Anselmo; he was a monomaniac, mad on one idea, and perfectly sane, even wondrous wise, on all others. His madness was seated, not so much in his head, as in his stomach, and he could, any day he chose, have cured himself. This is not a fancy of mine: it is a statement of the distinctive and discriminating knowledge of the author of *The Ingenious Hidalgo, Don Quixote de la Mancha.*

"Spain in the sixteenth century was overrun with madmen of the same type, men of one idea. The country was ruled by madmen—the king, the Inquisition, the nobles, the cardinals, priests, and nuns, who were all dominated by one mastering and overbearing conviction that the way to heaven was through a door, the keys of which were in their keeping. It was this belief, which in some assumed the force of a fierce infatuation, that inflamed the minds of such men as Charles V., Philip II., Ignacio Loyola, Torquemada, the Duke de Avila, Cisneros, with the holy woman Santa Teresa, and almost every other leading spirit in arms, in the Church, even in literature, and in every department of the State; and so far as these were under the influence of monomania, so far did they resemble Don Quixote. It is therefore of the greatest interest to us to be assured that Cervantes knew what he was about when he began to make his map of the human mind. He was perhaps the first to navigate its darkest region, to tell us of the quality of this terrible darkness, and to show how it could be shined upon with the healing blessedness of light. There is as much pleasure to be obtained in proving this statement as in following the adventures of Don Quixote in his native land." Ed.

Spanish text in a more or less adequate English translation. Proceeding from the text, we do come, of course, across certain moral implications that have to be considered in a light that perhaps transcends the world of the book itself, and we shall not wince when we come to those thorns. *"L'homme n'est rien—l'oeuvre est tout"* (the master is nothing, the masterpiece is everything) said Flaubert. In many an art-for-art man there dwells a frustrated moralist—and there is something about the ethics of the book *Don Quixote* that casts a livid laboratory light on the proud flesh of some of its passages. We are going to speak of its cruelty.

GENERAL REMARKS ON FORM

Novels can be divided into *one-track* novels and *multi-track* novels.

> *One-track*—in which there is only one major line of human existence.
> *Multi-track*—in which there are two such lines, or many.

The one or many lives may be present all the time in every chapter, or else the author may use what I call the *switch*, minor or major.

> *Minor*—when the chapters in which the major life or lives are actively present but alternate with chapters in which minor characters discuss those main lives.
> *Major*—when in multi-track novels the author switches completely from the account of one life to the account of another, then back again. The many lives may be kept apart for long stretches, but one of the features of the multi-track novel as a literary form is that the many lives are bound to come into contact at this or that point.

Madame Bovary, for instance, is a one-track novel, with hardly any switches. *Anna Karenin* is a multi-track novel with major switches. What is *Don Quixote*? I should call it a one-and-a-half track novel, with a few switches. Knight and squire are really one, and anyway the squire only plays up to his master; however, at a certain point in the second part they get separated. The switches are very crude, as the author shuttles self-consciously between Sancho's island and Don Quixote's castle, and it is a positive relief to everybody concerned—author, characters, and reader—when the two get together again and revert to their natural knight-and-squire combination.

From another point of view directed at questions of matter rather than manner, modern novels can be divided into such types as family novels, psychological novels (which are often written in the first person), mystery novels, and so on. Major works are generally a combination of various such types. Anyway, we should try not to be too pedantic in this. The whole thing may become extremely boring and the question of type really loses all interest when we are forced to tackle pretentious works of little or no artistic value, or on the other hand, to try to cram a stuffed eagle of a masterpiece into a pigeonhole.*

Don Quixote belongs to a very early, very primitive type of novel. It is closely allied to the picaresque novel—from *picaro*, meaning rogue in Spanish—a type of story as old as the vineclad hills, which has a slyboots, a bum, a quack, or any more or less droll adventurer for hero. And this hero pursues a more or less antisocial or asocial quest, moving from job to job or from joke to joke in a series of colorful, loosely strung episodes with the comic element factually predominating over any lyrical or tragic intent. It is also significant that by selecting a bum for his hero, the author in times of political oppression when a moral message is enforced by the government or the church—it is significant that by making such a selection the author slyly sheds any dangerous responsibility for his hero's social-religious-political background since the tramp, the adventurer, the madman is fundamentally asocial and irresponsible.**

Of course, in the adventures of our visionary Don we see much more than the tribulations of two grotesque characters, one lean and the other fat, but still the book belongs essentially to a primitive form, to the loosely strung, higgledy-pickled, variegated picaresque type and was accepted and enjoyed as such by the primitive reader.

THE LONG SHADOW OF DON QUIXOTE

Through the other novelists that we shall read, *Don Quixote* will, in a way, remain with us all the time. We shall recognize his most significant and memorable characteristic, namely, *whimsical nobility*, in the quixotic owner of the anything but bleak house—John Jarndyce, one of the most appealing and appetizing characters in all fiction. When we come to Gogol's novel *Dead Souls* we shall easily discern in its pseudo-picaresque

---

* In a deleted passage that follows VN wrote, "Thus, it does not really matter a hoot to what categories we assign the novels of—sorry, I told myself I would not name any modern names." The apology after the dash is interlined above bracketed (for optional omission) "Galsworthy or Mannworthy, or Upton Lewis, or Jules Rolland." This twisting of names was one of VN's favorite devices. Thomas Mann, Upton Sinclair, Sinclair Lewis, Jules Romains, and Romain Rolland were not among his favorite authors.

** In a deleted passage VN continues: "Times of oppression in Russia under Nicolas the First or under Lenin and Stalin have also seen the production of picaresque novels. I submit that Cervantes in his brutal and utilitarian day chose the picaresque form because it was the safest; and for further safety he attached to it the very first moral that occurred to him, which in modern terms would be: some comic strips lead a fellow astray."

pattern and in the strange quest that its hero undertakes a freakish echo and a morbid parody of Don Quixote's adventures. In regard to Flaubert's novel *Madame Bovary* we shall not only find that the lady herself is almost as crazily immersed in romantic meanders as our gaunt hidalgo, but we shall also discover something more interesting, namely, that Flaubert, in pursuing with the utmost tenacity the grim adventure of composing his book, can be termed a very Don Quixote in that most telling feature of the very great writers: honesty of unflinching art. And finally in Tolstoy's *Anna Karenin* we shall dimly recognize the earnest knight again in one of the main characters, Lyovin.

We should, therefore, imagine Don Quixote and his squire as two little silhouettes ambling in the distance against an ample flaming sunset, and their two huge black shadows, one of them especially elongated, stretching across the open country of centuries and reaching us here. In my second lecture we shall look at those two figures through some glasses I have made: and *in vitro*. In my third lecture I shall discuss various points of structure—structural devices—especially the Arcadian theme, the Inset Novella Theme, the Books of Chivalry Theme. My fourth lecture will be devoted to Cruelty, Mystifications, Enchantments. My lecture number five will deal with the theme of Fake Chroniclers and Mirrors, and will also take care of little Altisidora, and of Dulcinea, and of Death. My last Quixotic lecture will be a play-by-play account of Don Quixote's victories and defeats.

VLADIMIR NABOKOV

Two Portraits: Don Quixote
And Sancho Panza

THE MAN DON QUIXOTE

Even if allowance be made for the fading away of the Spanish in the twilight of translation, even so Sancho's cracks and proverbs are not very mirth provoking either in themselves or in their repetitious accumulation. The corniest modern gag is funnier. Nor do the horseplay scenes in our book really convulse modern diaphragms. The Knight of the Mournful Countenance is a unique individual; with some reservations, Sancho of the matted beard and tomato nose is the generalized clown.

Now, tragedy wears better than comedy. Drama endures in amber; the guffaw is dispelled in space and time. The nameless thrill of art is certainly closer to the manly shudder of sacred awe, or to the moist smile of feminine comparison, than it is to the casual chuckle; and of course in that line there is something still better than the roar of pain or the roar of laughter—and that is the supreme purr, of pleasure produced by the impact of sensuous thought—*sensuous thought*—which is another term for authentic art. Of this there is in our book a small but infinitely precious supply.

Let us examine the mournful man. Before he dubs himself Don Quixote, his name is plain Quijada or Quesada. He is a country gentleman, owner of a vineyard, master's house, and two acres of arable land; a good Catholic (who will later evolve a bad conscience); a tall, lanky gentleman around fifty. In the middle of his back he has a brown bristly mole, which according to Sancho is the sign of a strong man; so is the abundant hair on his chest. However, there is but little flesh on those big bones of his; and just as his mental state appears as a checkerboard of lucidity and insanity, so is his bodily condition a crazy quilt of vigor, fatigue, endurance, and twinges of

The man Don Quixote

Even if allowance be made for the frittering away fading away of the Spanish in the twilight of translation, even so Sancho's cracked and proverbs are not very mirth provoking either in themselves or in their (surreptitious accumulation. The corniest modern gag is funnier. Nor do the horseplay scenes in our book really convulse modern diaphragms. We know that mine stays as hard as a boxcar. The knight of the mournful countenance is a unique individual; Sancho with some reservations, of the mottled beard and tomato nose is the generalized clown.

Now, tragedy wears better than comedy. (Drama endures in amber; the guffaw is dispelled in space and time.) The nameless thrill of art is certainly closer to the manly shudder of sacred awe, or to the moist smile of feminine compassion than it is to the casual chuckle; and of course, in that line there is something still better than the roar of pain or the roar of laughter — and that is the supreme pure of pleasure produced by the impact of sensuous thought — sensuous thought — which is another form for authentic art. Of this there is in our book sufficient for a small but infinitely precious supply.

The opening of Nabokov's remarks on Don Quixote

hopeless pain. The pathetic pangs of defeat poor Quixote suffers are perhaps worse than the bathetic bangs he gets on the head; but we should not forget the one awful, constant physical discomfort which his nervous energy and his grim passion for sleeping in the open may surmount but can hardly cure: the poor fellow has suffered for many years from a serious kidney ailment.

I shall have a good deal to say, later, about the brutality of the book and about the curious attitude toward that cruelty on the part of experts and laymen alike, who view it as a kindly humane work.

Now and then, for the purpose of coarse medieval farce, Cervantes shows us his hero in nothing but his shirt, which is described in detail as not long enough to cover his thighs completely. I must apologize for listing these gruesome details—but we need them so as to refute the champions of wholesome fun, of humane titters. His legs are very long, lean, and hairy, and anything but clean; however, his dried-up unprofitable hide does not, apparently, attract the parasites that afflict his fleshy companion. Let us now proceed to clothe our patient. Here is his doublet, a close-fitting jacket of chamois skin, with missing or mismatching buttons, and all stained with rust from the rain and sweat that has bathed his leaky armor. His soft collar, of the Salamanca student type, has no lace; his tight brown breeches are patched with tawny; his green silk stockings are latticed with falling stitches; and his shoes are the color of dates. Over all this comes his fantastic assortment of arms that makes him look in the moonlight like an armed phantom—an armed phantom that would not be out of place on the battlements of Elsinore, in the kingdom of Denmark, had Hamlet's boon companions wished to play a prank on the moody student from Wittenberg.

Don Quixote's suit of armor, then, is old, black, and moldy. In the first chapters his improvised helmet is tied on with green ribbons, the knots of which take several chapters to undo. At one time this helmet of his is a barber's basin, a bowl of bright brass with a circular incurvation, a dent in the rim for the chins of customers—for the bee in his bonnet. With his buckler on his lean arm and a tree-bough for lance he straddles his Rocinante, which is as lean and as long-necked and as intrinsically gentle as he, endowed with the same pensive eyes, with the same phlegmatic demeanor and raw-boned dignity that his master reveals when not actually about to fight; for when Don Quixote does start going, anger makes his brow twitch and twist, he puffs his cheeks, he glares all around, he stamps the ground with his right foot, acting, as it were, the additional part of a charger while Rocinante stands beside with drooping head.

When Don Quixote raises his pasteboard visor, he discloses a withered dust-covered face with a somewhat crooked eagle nose, deep-sunken eyes, gaps in his front teeth, and a big melancholy mustache still quite black in contrast with the sparse grayish hair of his head. It is a solemn face, long and gaunt; its complexion is sallow at first; eventually the torrid sun of the Castilian plain tans it a yeoman's brown. So lean is that face, so hollow its cheeks, so few molars remain, that those cheeks of his appear (as his creator has it) "to be kissing each other in the inside of the mouth."

His manners are a kind of transition from his physical appearance to the mystery of his dual nature. His composure, his gravity, his beautifully calm demeanor and self-control are oddly in contrast with his mad fits of belligerent rage. He loves silence and decorum. His choice of expressions is exquisitely careful without being mannered. He is a perfectionist, a purist: he cannot hear a churl mispronounce words or use a wrong expression. He is chaste, enamored with a veiled dream, persecuted by enchanters; and above all he is a gallant gentleman, a man of infinite courage, a hero in the truest sense of the word. (This important point should be kept in mind.) Although extremely courteous and ready to please, there is one thing that he will never stand and that is any shadow of criticism of Dulcinea, his dream lady. As his squire correctly marks, his attitude toward Dulcinea is religious. Don Quixote's thoughts never go beyond rendering her homage for her own sake, with no expectance of any reward other than being accepted as her champion. "That," observes Sancho, "is the kind of love I have heard the preacher say we ought to give to our Lord, for Himself alone, without being moved by any hope of eternal glory or fear of Hell."

I am thinking especially of the first part of the work, for there are some curious changes that Don Quixote's character undergoes in the second part: with lapses of lucidity come gaps of fear. Thus we should stress again the point of his absolute courage, forgetting, as it were, a certain scene in the second part when he quakes with fear because his room is suddenly full of cats. But all in all he is, among knights, the bravest, the most lovelorn of any in this world. There is no malice in him; he is as trustful as a child. In point of fact, his childishness is sometimes more prominent than perhaps his creator had intended it to be. When at a certain turn of the novel, chapter 25 of the first part, he suggests performing "mad things" as a penance—additional deliberate "mad things" on the top of his normal madness, so to speak—he shows a rather limited schoolboyish imagination in the way of pranks.

" 'There is one thing at least that I should like to ask of you, Sancho,' the knight said [as Sancho is about to leave the Sierra Morena with the letter to

Dulcinea], 'and if I do ask this, it is because it is necessary. I should like you to see me stripped and performing a couple of dozen acts of madness, which I can get through with in less than half an hour; for having seen them with your own eyes, you can safely swear to the other things that you may care to add, and I assure you I mean to do more than you will be able to relate.' . . . With this, he hastily slipped off his breeches and, naked from the waist down, leaped into the air a couple of times, falling heels over head and revealing things that caused Sancho to give Rocinante the rein, that he might never see them again. The squire was satisfied now [Cervantes concludes the chapter]; he could swear that his master was quite mad."

Now for that basic madness of his. He had been a quiet country gentleman, Señor Alonso, who looked after his own estates, was an early riser, and was fond of hunting. At fifty he plunged into the reading of books of chivalry and took to eating heavy suppers, including what one translator (Duffield) renders as "resurrection pie" (*duelos y quebrantos*—literally, pains and breakage), a "pot made of the flesh of animals who have died accidental deaths by falling down precipices and getting their neck bones broken." The "pains" refer not to the pain experienced by these animals— that was inessential—but to the feelings of the sheep owners and shepherds upon discovering their loss. A nice point, this. Whether due to this diet of adventurous heroic pork, of adventurous cows and sheep so catastrophically converted into beef and mutton, or whether he had never been quite sane in the first place, the fact is that Don Quixote takes the noble resolution to revive and restore to a drab world the colorful calling of knight-errantry with its special rigid technique and with all its brilliant visions, emotions, and acts. With grim determination he chooses for his destiny "toil, anxiety and arms."*

Henceforth he appears as a crazy sane man, or an insane one on the verge of sanity; a striped madman, a dark mind with lucid interspaces. This is how he appears to others; but to him, too, things appear in this dual form. Reality and illusion are interwoven in the pattern of life. "How," he remarks to his squire, "how is it possible for you to have accompanied me all this time without coming to perceive that all the things that have to do with knight-errantry appear to be mad, foolish, and fantastic. . . . Not that they are so in reality: it is simply that there are always a lot of enchanters going about among us, changing things and giving them a deceitful appearance, directing them as suits their fancy, depending upon whether they wish to favor or destroy us."

* VN adds, first bracketed and then crossed-out, "or 'sweat, tears and blood' as another much fatter gentleman put it on another much more tragic occasion."

In the *Odyssey*, as you remember, the adventurer has mighty supporters. In the scenes of stealth and disguise we are only half-afraid that Odysseus by some false move may reveal too soon his strength, whereas in Don Quixote's case it is the poor knight's intrinsic and lovable weakness that we fear may be divulged to his brutal friends and foes. Odysseus is essentially safe; he is like a healthy man in a healthy dream who, whatever happens to him, shall awake. The star of the Greek's destiny glows with a level light despite all hardships and dangers. His companions may disappear one by one, swallowed by monsters or toppling from roofs in their cups—but he is guaranteed a serene old age in the blue remoteness of the future behind him. Kindly Athena—not the idiotic Dorotea or the devilish duchess of *Don Quixote*—kindly Athena keeps the glaucous beam of her shimmering eye (now gray, now sea-green, varying with scholars) upon the wanderer; wary and wily, he steps in her wake. But in our book the melancholy Don is on his own. To his tribulations the God of Christians is singularly indifferent—being busy elsewhere, perhaps, being nonplussed, we may assume, by the ungodly activities of his professional followers in that thumbscrew age.

When Don Quixote recants at the end of the book, in its saddest scene, it is neither from gratitude to his Christian God, nor is it under divine compulsion—but because it conforms to the moral utilities of his dark day. An abrupt surrender, a miserable apostasy, this, when on his deathbed he renounces the glory of the mad romance that made him what he was. This surrender is not quite comparable to the robust recantation of testy old Tolstoy when he disavowed the admirable illusion of *Anna Karenin* for the alphabetic platitudes of Sunday school. Nor am I thinking of Gogol crouching in penitent tears before a stove to burn the second part of *Dead Souls*. Don Quixote's situation is more akin to the plight of that French poet of unique genius, Rimbaud, who in the eighties of the last century gave up poetry because he had come to the conclusion that poetry was a synonym of sin. With mixed feelings I notice that the otherwise wise *Webster's New Collegiate Dictionary* in its biographical section does not list Rimbaud while giving space to Radetzky, Austrian field marshal; Raisuli, Moroccan brigand; Henry Handel Richardson, pseudonym of Ethel Florence Lindesay Richardson, Australian novelist; Rasputin, holy man and politician; and good old Ramsay, James Andrew Broun, 1812-1860, tenth Earl and first Marquis of Dalhousie, British colonial administrator.

Sancho Panza must have compiled that list.

VLADIMIR NABOKOV

The Man Sancho Panza

(the pig belly on crane legs)

Twenty minutes

Who is he? Here.

A poor farmer who had been a shepherd in his youth; He is a family man but a vagabond at heart.

Sancho Panza is not described physically when introduced — except that he is shown sitting on his donkey like a patriarch — which conveys a sense of stupid dignity and ripe years. A little later his image becomes clearer, and his mind ... Sancho wears a thick, unkempt beard. Although small in stature (for better contrast with his tall lanky master) he has a huge belly. He is short of body but his long shanks — in fact his name Sancho seems to be derived from Zancas = shanks. ... Readers and illustrators are apt to play down these thin legs ... In the second part of the novel Sancho is, if anything, fatter than he was at first, and the sun has tanned him the same brown as his master.

There is one moment in his life when we see him with the utmost lucidity — but that moment is brief — this is when he sets out for the continental island he is to govern. He is now dressed like a man of the law. His cloak is of camel hair, and he wears a cap of the same material. He is mounted on a mule (a glorified donkey); but the grey donkey itself, a kind of part or attribute of Sancho's personality, comes behind, decked out in brilliant silver trappings. Thus Sancho's little fat figure rides by with the same foolish dignity as had marked his first appearance

---

The opening of Nabokov's remarks on Sancho Panza

THE MAN SANCHO PANZA
(The Pig Belly on Crane Legs)

Who is he? A laborer who had been a shepherd in his youth, and then, at one time, a beadle to a brotherhood. He is a family man but a vagabond at heart, Sancho Panza, sitting on his donkey like a patriarch—which conveys a sense of stupid dignity and ripe years. A little later his image and his mind become clearer; but he is never as detailed as Don Quixote and this difference is in keeping with the fact that the character of Sancho is a product of generalization while that of Don Quixote is the result of an individual approach. Sancho wears a thick, unkempt beard. Although small in stature (for better contrast with his tall, lanky master) he has a huge belly. He is short of body but has long shanks—in fact his name Sancho seems to be derived from Zancas—shanks, or the long thin legs of birds. Readers and illustrators are apt to play down those thin legs of his so as not to interfere with the contrast between him and Don Quixote. In the second part of the novel Sancho is, if anything, fatter than he was at first, and the sun has tanned him the same brown as his master. There is one moment in his life when we see him with the utmost lucidity—but this moment is brief: this is when he sets out for the continental island he is to govern. He is now dressed like a man of the law. His cap and his cloak are of camel hair. His mount is a mule (a glorified donkey); but the gray donkey itself, a kind of part or attitude of Sancho's personality, comes behind, decked out in brilliant silken trappings. Thus Sancho's little fat figure rides by with the same foolish dignity as had marked his first appearance.

It would seem that, at first, Cervantes intended to give his lionhearted lunatic a witless coward for squire, in manner of contrapuntal contrast: lofty madness and low stupidity. However, Sancho proves to have too much mother wit to be considered a perfect fool, although he may be the perfect bore. He is no fool in chapter 10 of part one when after the fight with the Biscayan he reveals a clear perception of Don Quixote's courage: " 'The truth is,' said Sancho, 'I have never read any history whatsoever, for I do not know how to read or write; but what I would wager is that in all the days of my life I have never served a more courageous master than your Grace' "; and he shows a deep respect for his master's literary style in chapter 25 when he hears the letter to Dulcinea that he is to carry: " 'Why, damn me, how your Grace does manage to say everything here just the way it should be said, and how well you work that Knight of the Mournful Countenance into the signature! To tell the truth, your Grace is the very devil himself, and there's nothing you don't know.' "* This has a special implication since it is Sancho himself who dubbed Don Quixote the Knight of the Mournful Countenance. On the other hand, there is a streak of the enchanter in Sancho: he deceives his master at least three times; and when Don Quixote is on his deathbed Sancho still eats and drinks heartily and is much consoled by the inheritance coming to him.

He is a thorough rogue but a witty one, composed of the odds and ends of countless rogues in literature. The only thing that does give him some kind of personality is the grotesque echo in him to certain notes in his master's dignified music. For the benefit of a servant girl he sums up very neatly the definition of a knight-errant: a beaten bum and a king, which is not far from what could be said in relation to another fantastic apparition, with a longer beard, in a bleaker land—King Lear. Of course, Kent's noble heart and the curious lyrical strain in King Lear's fool cannot be said to be represented in Sancho Panza, who with all his vague virtues is after all a fat-buttocked creature of farce; but he is a faithful companion, and the epithet "noble" is used by Cervantes in all seriousness when speaking of Sancho's resolve to stay by the side of his master at a moment of special danger. This love for his master and his love for his gray are his most human traits. And when the otherwise coarse and selfish Sancho kindheartedly gives money to a galley slave, one does get a little thrill as one realizes that Sancho may be prompted by the fact that the slave is like Sancho's master, an old man suffering from an affection of the bladder. And if he is not a fool, neither is he a typical coward. Although of a peaceful disposition, he enjoys a fight when he is really aroused; and when drunk he looks upon dangerous and fantastic adventures as excellent sport.

This leads me to the (artistically speaking) vulnerable points in Sancho's mental set-up. There is for example his attitude toward Don Quixote's delusions. At first Cervantes stresses the lucid quality of the fat squire's common sense, but we soon discover in chapter 26 that Sancho is curiously absentminded, a dreamer in his own right: witness his forgetting a certain letter that would have given him three ass-colts. He persistently tries to correct Don Quixote's delusions, but suddenly in the beginning of part two plays the part of an enchanter himself and in a most cruel and grotesque

* We may also compare the passage about the Don's learning in part two, chapter 22: "Listening to all this [Don Quixote's discourse with Basilio], Sancho was talking to himself. 'This master of mine, when I say something that has some pith and body to it, is in the habit of telling me that I ought to take a pulpit in hand and go through this world preaching fine sermons; and I will say of him that when he begins stringing sayings together and

manner helps to deepen his master's main delusion—the one referring to Dulcinea. But then he becomes confused about his responsibility for that delusion.

It has been stressed by various commentators that both Don Quixote's madness and Sancho's common sense are mutually infectious, and that while, in the second part of the book, Don Quixote develops a sanchoid strain, Sancho, on the other hand, becomes as mad as his master. For example, he tries to convert his wife to a belief in islands and earldoms just as Don Quixote's efforts are directed to make him believe that windmills are giants and inns are castles. While a certain famous but very pedestrian critic, Rudolph Schevill,* stresses the contrast between the unselfish old-fashioned hidalgo and his practical unromantic squire, the subtle and inspired Spanish critic Salvador de Madariaga** sees Sancho as a kind of

---

giving advice, he not only could take a pulpit in hand, but two of them by each finger and go through the market places talking his head off. The devil take you for a knight-errant, what a lot of things you know! I thought in my heart that he knew only those things that had to do with chivalry, but he has a finger in everything and is always putting in his spoonful." Or later, in chapter 58 after Don Quixote has discoursed on the four carvings the workmen uncover for his inspection: "Once again, Sancho was amazed at his master's erudition; it was as if he had never known him before. There surely was not a story in the world, he thought to himself, not a single event that the knight did not have at his fingertips and firmly fixed in his memory." Nor should we forget Sancho's splendid apostrophe to Don Quixote's courage when the knight is about to descend into the Cave of Montesinos: " 'May God be your guide,' exclaimed Sancho, 'and the Rock of France, along with the Trinity of Gaeta, O flower, cream, and skimming of knights-errant! There you go, daredevil of the earth, heart of steel, arms of brass! Once more, may God be your guide and bring you back safe, sound, and without a scratch to the light of this world which you are leaving to bury yourself in the darkness that you go to seek.' " Ed.

* "Don Quixote and Sancho have now been launched together in the world, all highways are theirs, and in the character of Don Quixote alone they carry the essentials which will enable them to come victorious out of any adventure that may arise. The bonds and laws of actual society no longer exist, the limitations imposed by narrow conceptions and perverted customs are definitely thrust aside; henceforth all decisions on good and evil, on right and wrong, are to be made by the visionary hero. For, as Don Quixote himself says: 'Knights-errant are independent of all jurisdiction, their law is their sword, their charter their prowess, and their edicts their will.' But as life invariably restores a balance between extremes, so the idealism of the new knight unwittingly finds a corrective lens in the squire who is destitute of any imagination or vision. This contrast is wrought out, as we shall see, in numberless details. . . . The contrast is naturally bound to endure through their entire association, because of the irreconcilable contradiction which exists not only between the two minds of Don Quixote and Sancho, but, by the essence of life itself, between our body and spirit, our demerits and virtues, our illusions and achievements." *Cervantes*, Master Spirits of Literature series (New York: Duffield, 1919), pp. 215-216. Ed.

** "Superficial tradition has reduced its marvellous psychological fabric to a line of simplest melody. Don Quixote, a valiant knight and idealist; Sancho, a matter-of-fact and cowardly rustic. What tradition does not see is that this design which, on a first impression, is based on contrast, resolves itself into a complicated and delicate parallel, the development of which is one of the subtle achievements of this book of genius. *Sancho is, up to a point, a transposition of Don Quixote in a different key.* Such cases of parallelism are seldom lacking in great works of art. Like Laertes and Fortinbras to Hamlet, or Gloucester to King Lear, Sancho is a parallel to Don Quixote, bringing out the main figure and enriching the design of the whole.

"Both are men endowed with abundant gifts of reason, intellectual in Don Quixote, empirical in Sancho, who at a certain moment become possessed of a self-delusion which unbalances their mind and life. But while in Don Quixote this self-delusion gathers round a nucleus of glory symbolized in Dulcinea, in Sancho it gradually takes form around a kernel of material ambition, symbolized in an island. The Curate's words were not empty:

transposition of Don Quixote in a different key. Indeed, the two seem to swap dreams and destinies by the end of the book, for it is Sancho who returns to his village as an ecstatic adventurer, his mind full of splendors, and it is Don Quixote who drily remarks, "Drop those fooleries." Vigorous and virile by temperament, easily angered, made prudent by experience, Sancho may thus be said to avoid unequal and useless combat not because he is a poltroon but because he is a more cautious warrior than Don Quixote. Childish and simple by nature and ignorance (while Don Quixote remains childish despite all his knowledge), Sancho trembles before the unknown and the supernatural, but his shudder is only one step removed from his master's quiver of gallant delight—and thus he is a worthy brother of the knight he accompanies. In the second part "while Sancho's spirit rises from reality to illusion, Don Quixote's descends from illusion to reality. And the two curves cross in that saddest of adventures, one of the cruelest in the book, when Sancho enchants Dulcinea, bringing the most noble of knights, for love of the purest illusion, to his knees before the most repulsive of realities: a Dulcinea coarse, uncouth, and reeking of garlic."* Another critic speaks piously of the author's "sympathy for the peasant," and in order to explain the burlesque in Sancho Panza makes the extraordinary statement that Cervantes was aware that his more sophisticated readers would expect that if low figures were introduced they should be treated satirically. (Why this is sophistication and why Cervantes should toady to it is not clear.) The same critic goes on: the "wise and lovable" Sancho (who is neither very wise nor very lovable) as secretly known to Cervantes (and to the critic in question) had to be partially sacrificed to the demands of literature since he had to serve as foil to the gravity and high aspirations of Don Quixote.** Yet another funny commentator thinks that in the development of Sancho Panza's mind and character (far more than in the delineation of Don Quixote) Cervantes gave expression to a type of wisdom and eloquence, and to a shrewd analysis of life, which constitute the essence of humanism.† Big words, little sense.

... we shall see a drift of this machine of absurdities, of such a knight and such a squire, who, one would think, were cast in the same mould; and indeed the madness of the master, without the follies of the man, would not be worth a farthing.

"For indeed Don Quixote and Sancho are true brothers and their maker planned them after the same pattern." *Don Quixote: An Introductory Essay in Psychology* (Oxford at the Clarendon Press, 1935), pp. 96-97. Ed.
* Madariaga, p. 120.
** The reference is to Bell, *Cervantes*, pp. 138-139.
† Nabokov refers to Krutch's "Miguel de Cervantes," in *Five Masters*, pp. 86-101.

The explication of the curious difference of critical attitudes toward the two heroes lies, I suspect, in the fact that all readers can be separated into Don Quixotes and Sancho Panzas. When I find in a library copy of Schevill's book passages marked, thickly and slovenly, with blue ink and when the inkmarked passage is "Cervantes gives a realistic picture of the middle class something or other," then I know for sure whether the reader is a Sancho or a Quixote.

We have departed a little from the body of the book in the direction of the spirit of readerdom, so let us return to the novel.

Sancho Panza's main characteristic is that he is a sackful of proverbs, a sack of half-truths that rattle in him like pebbles. I believe that there *are* strange and subtle interechoes between the knight and his squire, but I also contend that so-called broad humor swamps in Sancho's case whatever personality can be made out after the grease has been washed off the bones. Scholars who speak of sidesplitting episodes in the book do not reveal any permanent injury to their ribs. That in this book the humor contains, as one critic puts it, "a depth of philosophical insight and genuine humanity, in which qualities it has been excelled by no other writer"* seems to me to be a staggering exaggeration. The Don is certainly not funny. His squire, with all his prodigious memory for old saws, is even less funny than his master.

So here are the two heroes, their shadows merging in one and overlapping, forming a certain unity that we must accept.

During Don Quixote's first sally, during his first four adventures (counting as fourth the dream that crowns his first three battles), Sancho is absent. His appearance on the scene, his becoming Don Quixote's squire, is the Don's fifth adventure.

The two main characters are ready. I now propose to study the ways and means that Cervantes will think up to keep the story going. I intend to study the book's ingredients, its structural devices, ten all told.

* Bell, *Cervantes*, p. 200: "Thus Cervantes is never irresponsible and defends himself beforehand against the charge of being a mere jester, a *'lustiger Geselle.'* He might have been as serious as Tasso and Racine, he might have been as reckless as Rabelais or Ariosto; he preferred, with his customary discretion, to steer a middle course, and in the humor which resulted from this compromise he was rewarded by a depth of philosophical insight and genuine humanity, in which qualities it has been excelled by no other writer." Ed.

Miguel Cervantes Saavedra, 1547-1615.

1547   Birth at Alcalá de Henares, Castille.

1568   Elegies and other verses on the death of the Queen.

1569-75 In Italy

1571   At Battle of Lepanto

1575   Captured by the Turks

1575-80 Ransom and return to Spain.

1584   Marriage.

1587-94 Commissionary in Andalusia

1590   Application for post in the West Indies

1592   Arrested for debt

1597   Jailed at Seville

1605   Again arrested.

1605   Don Quixote I

1615   Don Quixote II

1616   (23.IV New Style) Death at Madrid (10 days after Shakespeare)

Lecture 3

I listed last time DQ's physical features such as the iron tendons and the ailing kidneys the big bones, the mole on the back, his lanky limbs, his mournful gaunt, sun-tanned face, his fantastic assortment of rusty in the somewhat old moth moonlight arms. I listed his spiritual traits — such as his gravity, his dignified manner, and his infinite courage, his madness, the chequerboard of his mental condition, squares of lucidity and squares of lunacy, with the a kind of Knight's move gear-shifting from mad logic to man logic and back again I have mentioned his pathetic help-genule helpers of which I shall have more to say wings sum to the caught of the rook I have likewise listed Sancho's and features, his quixotic lean legs, and the belly of an is the name "august" which in modern circus slang for the bum type of clown. I have picked out mentioned some points at which his otherwise farcical personality is connected with the dramatic shadow of his master I shall have more to say of Sancho in the role of enchanter.

I am now going to take up and examine some of the structural pegs on which our book loosely hangs — the most scarecrow masterpieces among masterpieces but forming [risin with outspreadflid eyes] against the backdrop of time a marvelous photopia of folds, f, o, l, d, s.

The opening of Nabokov's lecture on structure

Structural Matters

I have listed Don Quixote's physical features such as the big bones, the mole on the back, the iron tendons and the ailing kidneys, his lanky limbs, his mournful, gaunt, sun-tanned face, his fantastic assortment of rusty arms in the somewhat old molish moonlight. I listed his spiritual traits—such as his gravity, his dignified manner, his infinite courage, his madness, the checkerboard of his mental condition, squares of lucidity and squares of lunacy, with a kind of knight's move gear-shifting from mad logic to man logic and back again.* I have mentioned his pathetic gentle helplessness, of which I shall have more to say when we come to the beauty of the book. I have likewise listed Sancho's features, his quixotic lean legs and the belly and face of an "August," which in modern circus slang is the name for the bum type of clown. I have mentioned some points at which his otherwise farcical personality is connected with the dramatic shadow of his master. I shall have more to say of Sancho in the role of enchanter.

I am now going to take up and examine some of the structural pegs from which our book loosely hangs—the most scarecrow masterpiece among masterpieces but forming against the backdrop of time a marvelous photopia (vision with light-adjusted eyes) of folds, f, o, l, d, s.

But first a few general considerations. *Don Quixote* has been called the greatest novel ever written. This, of course, is nonsense. As a matter of fact,

---

* For VN's application of the phrase "knight's move" and its significance, see his lecture on Jane Austen's *Mansfield Park* in *Lectures on Literature* (1980), p. 57: "Especially in dealing with Fanny's reactions, Austen uses a device that I call the *knight's move*, a term from chess to describe a sudden swerve to one or the other side on the board of Fanny's chequered emotions."

it is not even one of the greatest novels of the world, but its hero, whose personality is a stroke of genius on the part of Cervantes, looms so wonderfully above the skyline of literature, a gaunt giant on a lean nag, that the book lives and will live through the sheer vitality that Cervantes has injected into the main character of a very patchy haphazard tale, which is saved from falling apart only by its creator's wonderful artistic intuition that has his Don Quixote go into action at the right moments of the story.

I think there can hardly be any doubt as to the fact that *Don Quixote* was originally intended by Cervantes to be a long short story, providing amusement for an hour or two. The first sally, the one from which Sancho is still absent, is obviously conceived as a separate novella: it reveals a unity of purpose and accomplishment, capped with a moral.* But then the book grew and expanded and came to include matters of all kinds. The first part of the work divides into four sections—eight chapters, then six, then thirteen, and then twenty-five. The second part does not divide into sections. Madariaga remarks that the rapid and bewildering succession of episodes and inset tales which suddenly breaks into the main narrative toward the end of the first part, long before the second part was conceived, is the padding of a tired author who disperses in minor tasks an effort no longer sufficient for his main creation. In part two (without sections) Cervantes regains full control over his central theme.

In order to give the work some crude unity, Sancho is made, here and there, to recall former incidents. But in the evolution of literature the seventeenth-century novel—especially the picaresque novel—had not yet evolved consciousness, conscious memory permeating the whole work, when we feel that the characters remember and know events that we remember and know about them. This is a development of the nineteenth century. But in our book even the artificial recalls are haphazard and are half-hearted.

Cervantes, in writing his work, seems to have had alternate phases of lucidity and vagueness, deliberate planning and sloppy vagueness, much as his hero was mad in patches. Intuition saved Cervantes. As Groussac remarks, he never saw his book in front of him as a perfect composition, standing aloof, completely separate from the chaos of matter from which it had grown. Not only that, not only did he never foresee things, but also he never looked back. One has the impression that when he was in the act of writing the second part, he did not have a copy of the first part on his

---

* "Ce petit pavillon isolé existait par lui-même, et rien ne faisait prévoir qu'il deviendrait le vestibule d'un château." Paul Groussac, *Une Énigme littéraire: Le DON QUICHOTTE d'Avellaneda*, p. 61. VN. ("This small isolated pavilion existed by itself and nothing indicated that it would become the vestibule of a mansion.")

writing desk; never thumbed through it: he seems to remember that first part as an average reader would, not as a writer, not as a student. Otherwise it is impossible to explain how he managed, for instance, while in the very act of criticizing the errors committed by the author of the spurious continuation of *Don Quixote* to make even worse blunders in the same connection, in regard to the same characters. But, I repeat, the intuition of genius saved him.

STRUCTURAL DEVICES

I shall now list and briefly describe the following ten structural devices, some of the ingredients of our meat pie.

(1) Snatches of old ballads which echo in the corners and crannies of the novel, adding here and there a quaint melodious charm to pedestrian matter. Most of these popular ballads, or references to them, are inevitably dimmed in translation. Incidentally, the very first words of the book, "In a certain village of La Mancha" ("*En un lugar de la Mancha*"), are those of an old ballad. I cannot go into this matter of ballads in any detail for lack of time.

(2) Proverbs: Sancho, of the second part especially, is a bursting bag of old saws and sayings. To the readers of translations this Breughelian side of the book is as dead as cold mutton. So there again—I am not going to pursue this line of inquiry.

(3) Wordplay: alliterations, puns, mispronounced words. All this is lost in translation, too.

(4) Dramatic dialogue: Let us keep in mind that Cervantes was a frustrated playwright who found his medium in a novel. The natural tone and rhythm of the conversations in the book are marvelous even in translation. The theme is obvious. You will enjoy by yourselves in the solitude and silence of your dormitories the various conversations of the Sancho family.*

---

* Part one, chapter 52: "At news of the knight's return, Sancho Panza's wife had hurried to the scene, for she had some while since learned that her husband had accompanied him as his squire; and now, as soon as she laid eyes upon her man, the first question she asked was if all was well with the ass, to which Sancho replied that the beast was better off than his master.

" 'Thank God,' she exclaimed, 'for all his blessings! But tell me now, my dear, what have you brought me from all your squirings? A new cloak to wear? Or shoes for the young ones?'

" 'I've brought you nothing of the sort, good wife,' said Sancho, 'but other things of greater value and importance.'

" 'I'm glad to hear that,' she replied. 'Show me those things of greater value and importance, my dear. I'd like a sight of them just to cheer this heart of mine which has been so sad and unhappy all the centuries that you've been gone.'

(5) The conventional poetical, or more correctly pseudo-poetical, description of nature enclosed in paragraph form and never mingling organically with the story or the dialogue.

(6) The invented historian: I shall devote half a lecture to the examination of this magic device.

(7) The novella, the inset story of the *Decameron* (ten-a-day) type, an Italian collection of a hundred tales by Boccaccio, fourteenth century. I shall return to this in a moment.

(8) The Arcadian (or Pastoral) theme is closely allied to the Italian novella and to the chivalry romance, merging with them at various points. This Arcadian slant is derived from the following odd combination of notions: Arcadia, a mountainous district of legendary Greece, had been the abode of a simple contented people; so let us disguise ourselves as shepherds and spend sixteenth-century summers wandering in idyllic bliss or romantic distress about the mollified mountains of Spain. The special theme of distress pertained to chivalry stories of penitent, unhappy, or insane knights who would retire to the wilderness to live like fictitious shepherds. These Arcadian activities (minus the special distress) were later transferred to other mountainous parts of Europe by eighteenth-century writers of the so-called sentimental school, in a kind of back-to-nature movement, though actually nothing could be more artificial than the tame and coy kind of nature visualized by Arcadian writers. In point of fact, sheep and goats stink.

(9) The Chivalry theme, allusions to books of chivalry, parodies of various situations and devices in them; in a word, a continuous awareness of romances of knight-errantry. In your eager hands will be placed

---

" 'I will show them to you at home, wife,' said Sancho. 'For the present be satisfied that if, God willing, we set out on another journey in search of adventures, you will see me in no time a count or the governor of an island, and not one of those around here, but the best that is to be had.'

" 'I hope to Heaven it's true, my husband, for we certainly need it. But tell me, what is all this about islands? I don't understand.'

" 'Honey,' replied Sancho, 'is not for the mouth of an ass. You will find out in good time, woman; and you're going to be surprised to hear yourself called "my Ladyship" by all your vassals.'

" 'What's this you are saying, Sancho, about ladyships, islands, and vassals? . . .

" 'Do not be in such a hurry to know all this, Juana [later *Teresa*],' he said. 'It is enough that I am telling you the truth. Sew up your mouth then; for all I will say, in passing, is that there is nothing in the world that is more pleasant than being a respected man, squire to a knight-errant who goes in search of adventures. It is true that most of the adventures you meet with do not come out the way you'd like them to, for ninety-nine out of a hundred will prove to be all twisted and crosswise. I know that from experience, for I've come out of some of them blanketed and out of others beaten to a pulp. But all the same, it's a fine thing to go along waiting for what will happen next, crossing mountains, making your way through woods, climbing over cliffs, visiting castles, and putting up at inns free of charge, and the devil take the maravedi that is to pay.' " Ed.

specimens—copies of passages from two books of that kind—the best.* After reading these passages you will not rush out in search of rusty armor and old polo ponies, but you may get a faint whiff of the charm that Don Quixote found in those tales. You will also note the similarity of certain situations.

Being by nature a storyteller and a magician, but not a preacher, Cervantes is anything but a fiery adversary of a social evil. He does not really give a hoot whether or not books of chivalry are popular in Spain; and, if popular, whether or not their influence is pernicious; and, if pernicious, whether or not it may actually drive crazy a virgin gentleman of fifty. Although Cervantes makes a great show of being morally concerned with these matters, the only thing about this chivalry or antichivalry affair that interests him is firstly its most convenient use as a literary device to propel, shift, and otherwise direct his story; and secondly its no less convenient use as a righteous attitude, a purpose, a flutter of indignation which in his pious, utilitarian, and dangerous day a writer had better take. It would be a loss of my labor and of your attention if we were to fall for the deception and seriously probe this perfectly artificial and indeed fatuous moral, if any, of *Don Quixote*; but the structural use Cervantes makes of the chivalry theme as a literary device—this is a fascinating and important matter and I shall discuss it amply.

Finally (10) The mystification theme, the cruel burlesque jest (the so-called *burla*), which can be defined as a sharp-petaled Renaissance flower on a hairy medieval stem. The mystification practiced upon the dignified madman and his simple squire by the ducal pair in the second part of the work are good examples of this kind of thing. I shall discuss the dignified madman and his simple squire by the ducal pair in the second part of the work are good examples of this kind of thing. I shall discuss the mystification theme later on in connection with a general account of the cruelty of the book.

I shall now proceed to discuss some of these ten points, with additional details and illustrations.

DIALOGUE AND LANDSCAPE

If we follow the evolution of literary forms and devices from the remotest antiquity to our times we notice that the art of dialogue was developed and perfected much earlier than the art of describing, or better say expressing, nature. By 1600 the dialogue with great writers in all

* See Appendix for mimeographed material distributed to the students. Ed.

countries is excellent—natural, supple, colorful, alive. But the verbal rendering of landscapes will have to wait until, roughly speaking, the beginning of the nineteenth century to reach the same level as the dialogue had reached 200 years before; and it is only in the second part of the nineteenth century that descriptive passages referring to outside nature were integrated, were merged with the story, ceased to stick out in separate paragraphs, and became organic parts of the whole composition.

No wonder then that in our book the dialogue is so vivid and the landscape so dead. I direct your attention especially to the charmingly supple conversation Sancho has with his wife in chapter 5 of part two.

" 'What do you bring with you, friend Sancho,' she asked, 'that makes you so merry?'

" 'Wife,' he replied, 'if it was God's will, I'd be glad not to be as happy as I am.'

" 'I don't understand you, husband,' said she. 'I don't know what you mean by wishing you were not as happy as you are. I may be a fool, but I fail to see how you can find pleasure in not having it.'

" 'Look here, Teresa,' said Sancho, 'I am happy because I have made up my mind to go back to serving my master Don Quixote, who wants to go out a third time in search of adventures, . . . although, naturally, it makes me sad to have to leave you and the young ones. If God would only let me eat my bread at home, dryshod, without dragging me through the byways and crossroads—and it would not cost Him anything, all He has to do is will it—it goes without saying that my happiness would be more solid and lasting than it is, whereas now it is mixed up with my sorrow at leaving you. That is what I meant when I said that I'd be glad if, God willing, I was not so happy.'

" 'Listen to me, Sancho,' his wife replied. 'Ever since you joined up with a knight-errant, you've been talking in such a roundabout way that there's no understanding you.'

" 'It is enough, wife, if God understands me; for He understands everything, and that is good enough for me. . . .

" '. . . I promise you, wife, . . . that if God only sees to it that I get hold of any kind of an island at all, I will get Mari-Sancha a husband so high up in the world that no one will be able to come near her without calling her "my Ladyship." '

" 'No, Sancho,' said his wife. 'Marry her to someone who is her equal; that's the best way. If you take her out of wooden shoes and put her into pattens, if you take her out of her gray flannel petticoat and put her into silken hoop skirts, . . . the poor girl will not know where she is and every step she takes she will be making a thousand blunders and showing the thread of the coarse homespun stuff she's made of.'

" 'Be quiet, foolish woman,' said Sancho. 'All she will need is two or three years to get used to it, and, after that, dignity and fine manners will fit her like a glove; and if not, what does it matter? Let her be "your Ladyship" and come what may.' . . .

" 'Husband,' said Teresa, 'are you sure you know what you are talking about? For I am very much afraid that if my daughter becomes a countess it will be her ruination. You can do what you like, you can make a duchess or a princess of her, but I want to tell you it will be without my will or consent. . . .

" 'You, brother, go ahead and govern your island and strut all you like, but I tell you in the name of my sainted mother that neither my daughter nor I is going to stir one step from our village. . . . Go, then, to look for adventures with that Don Quixote of yours, and leave us to our misadventures; for God will make things better for us if we deserve it. . . .

" 'What I say is, if you are determined to be a governor, take your son Sancho with you so that you can teach him how to govern also; for it is a good thing for sons to learn and follow their father's trade.'

" 'As soon as I have a government,' said Sancho, 'I will send for him posthaste. I will send you some money too; for there are always plenty of people to lend it to governors that do not have it. And I want you to dress him up in such a way as to hide what he is and make him look like what he is not.'

" 'You send the money,' Teresa replied, 'and I'll see to that.'

" 'So, then, it's understood, is it, that our daughter is to be a countess?'

" 'The day that I see her a countess,' was Teresa's answer, 'I'll feel that I am laying her in her grave. But I tell you again: do as you like; for we women are born with the obligation of obeying our husbands, however stupid they may be.'

"Saying this, she began weeping in earnest, as though she already saw her Sanchica dead and buried."

Cervantes's love of nature is typical of the so-called Italian Renaissance in letters—a tame world of conventional brooks and invariable green meadows and pleasant woods, all made to man's measure or improved by man. It will stay with us through the eighteenth century; you may find it in the England of Jane Austen. A good example of the dead, artificial, and trite descriptions of nature in our book is the one referring to dawn in chapter 14 of part 2, with the thousands of birds and their joyful songs saluting the dawn, and the liquid pearls, and the laughing springs, and the murmuring brooks and the rest of this dismal devise.* Those brooks and rivers murmured against man and rebelled in the nightmare riparian revolution of *Finnegans Wake*.

My goodness, to think of the wild, bitter, sunstunned, frozen, parched, tawny, brown pinedark mountains of Spain and then to read of those dew pearls and birdies! It is as if after visiting the sagebrush plateaus of our own West, or the mountains of Utah or Colorado with their aspens and pines and granite and gulches and bogs and glaciers and grim peaks—the visitor would describe all this in terms of a New England rock garden, with imported shrubs trimmed like poodles and a rubber hose painted a mimetic green.

THE INSET STORY

In chapter 44 of the second part Cervantes introduces an ironic defense of the inset *Decameron*-like stories that cluster toward the end of the first part.

"They say that in the original version of the history it is stated that the interpreter did not translate the present chapter as Cid Hamete had written it,** owing to a kind of grudge that the Moor had against himself for having undertaken a story so dry and limited in scope as is this one of Don Quixote. For it seemed to him he was always having to speak of the knight and of Sancho, without being able to indulge in digressions of a more serious and entertaining nature. He remarked that to go on like this, pen in hand, with his mind fixed upon a single subject and having to speak through the mouths of a few persons only, was for him an intolerable and unprofitable drudgery.

"By way of relieving the monotony, in the first part of the work he had employed the artifice of introducing a few *novelas*, such as the *Story of the*

---

* The passage VN refers to reads as follows: "At that moment gay-colored birds of all sorts began warbling in the trees and with their merry and varied songs appeared to be greeting and welcoming the fresh-dawning day, which already at the gates and on the balconies of the east was revealing its beautiful face as it shook out from its hair an infinite number of liquid pearls. Bathed in this gentle moisture, the grass seemed to shed a pearly spray, the willows distilled a savory manna, the fountains laughed, the brooks murmured, the woods were glad, and the meadows put on their finest raiment." A less heightened but no less conventional passage can be quoted from chapter 25 of part one: "Conversing in this manner, they reached the foot of a tall mountain, which, standing alone amid a number of surrounding peaks, had almost the appearance of a rock that had been carved out of them. Alongside it flowed a gentle brook, while all about was a meadow so green and luxuriant that it was a delight for the eyes to behold. There were many forest trees and a number of plants and flowers to add to the quiet charm of the scene." Ed.
** For the fiction that the Moor, Cid Hamete Benengeli, had written *Don Quixote*, see chapter 9 of part one. Ed.

One Who Was Too Curious for His Own Good and *The Captive's Story*, tales that, so to speak, had nothing to do with the narrative proper, the other portions being concerned with things that had happened to Don Quixote himself, such as could not be omitted. He also felt, he tells us, that many readers, carried away by the interest attaching to the knight's exploits, would be inclined to pass over these novelettes either hastily or with boredom, thereby failing to note the fine craftsmanship they exhibited, which, however, would be plainly evident when they should be published by themselves instead of appearing as mere adjuncts to Don Quixote's madness and Sancho's foolishness."

In his notes to this passage the translator Samuel Putnam remarks first the humorless comment of the earlier translator John Ormsby to the effect that "The original, bringing a charge of misinterpretation against its translator, is a confusion of ideas that it would not be easy to match." He then adds: "Cervantes is here alluding to those who had criticized him for the introduction of these stories in Part I, and in a manner is justifying their presence there. That he took these tales seriously is indicated by the remark concerning their craftsmanship in the next sentence. In the introduction to his translation of *Don Quixote*, Ormsby observes: " 'He [Cervantes] had these stories ready written, and it seemed a good way of disposing of them; it is by no means unlikely that he mistrusted his own powers of extracting from Don Quixote and Sancho material enough to fill a book; but, above all, it is likely that he felt doubtful of his venture. It was an experiment in literature . . . he could not tell how it would be received; and it was well, therefore, to provide his readers with something of the sort they were used to, as a kind of insurance against total failure. The event did not justify his diffidence. The public . . . skimmed the tales hastily and impatiently, eager to return to the adventures of Don Quixote and Sancho; and the public has ever since done much the same.' "* Spanish critics have been more blunt: Cervantes may have simply run out of Quixotic adventures at the end of the first part, they say. Hence the inset tales.**

---

* VN adds an interlined comment: "Harvard students, of course, do *not* skim."

** In a detached fragment VN notes that in chapter 3 of part two, when the publication of part one is being discussed, "Carrasco, the bachelor, says that one of the faults that is found with the book is that the author has inserted in it a novella ('The One Who Was Too Curious') that has nothing to do with the story of Don Quixote. The latter declares 'that the author of this book was not a sage but some ignorant prattler who at haphazard and without any method set about the writing of it, being content to let things turn out as they might.' And Don Quixote mentions a painter who when asked what he was painting would reply, 'Whatever it turns out to be.' It is curious to note that further in the book, in chapter 65, Cervantes repeats this anecdote, forgetting that he has already told it. This seems to confirm in a very amusing way that indeed there is not much 'method' about the book."

Except for the goatherd's story, an insipid episode that introduces the Arcadian theme in various conversations and verses in chapters 12-14, the other inset stories concern the persons who form a character grouping in the final episode of the novel before the return of Don Quixote in an ox cart to his home. Setting aside the story of the "One Who Was Too Curious," which is read by the curate from papers provided by the innkeeper, the tale of the Captive Captain* and his Zoraida-Maria accounts for their presence, as—with more justification for the action—does the narrative of Don Luis and Doña Clara. But most intimately connected with a denouement of sorts is Dorotea's story completed by Cardenio's. This protracted episode involves two sets of lovers (Cardenio's bride Luscinda is kidnapped by Dorotea's lover Don Fernando). Cardenio tells his tale and Dorotea tells hers, and eventually they all meet at the truly enchanted *venta* (roadside inn) and are shuffled in a so-called *recognition scene* (a degenerate descendant of the *Odyssey*) to form the initial happy pairs—a preposterous and tedious business, especially since an additional set of lovers (Don Luis and Doña Clara) arrives at the same venta, with various other characters, so that the inn becomes as crowded as a certain ship cabin in a certain old Marx Brothers movie. The whole episode starts in chapter 23 with a valise of gold and some poems by Cardenio discovered by Don Quixote and Sancho in the Sierra Morena and is not resolved until chapter 36 when the four lovers are brought together at the inn and unmasked and reunited in the recognition scene. But then Dorotea and the rest, under the guidance of the curate and the barber, evolve an elaborate hoax in order to have Don Quixote proceed homeward, and so the characters continue to bob about till chapter 47 when they go their different ways after leaving Don Quixote in his ambulant cage.

CHARACTER GROUPING

This big scene before the book comes to an end takes place at the inn where, much earlier, Sancho had been tossed in a blanket, and involves as resident characters the landlord, his wife, his daughter, and his servant girl Maritornes. The characters who arrive at the inn are the following ten parties:

First Party: Don Quixote, Sancho Panza, the curate, the first barber, Cardenio, Dorotea (chapter 32).

---

* VN in a side comment: "Cervantes himself had been a prisoner in Algiers, but the story is no better than the other inset tales and its artificial conventional setting is not graced by any live color as one might have hoped."

Second Party: Don Fernando, kidnapper of Luscinda, with her and three attendants on horseback and two servants on foot (chapter 36).

Third Party: Captain Pérez de Viedma from Africa and Zoraida-Maria. At this point (chapter 37), with Don Quixote presiding, they sit down to supper, Don Quixote and twelve table fellows, Don Quixote's Last Supper in part one. After supper the following arrive:

Fourth Party: On their way to America, of all places, a judge (who turns out to be the Captain's brother) and his daughter Clara, with several (say four) attendants (chapter 42).

Fifth Party: At least two mule lads, who put up in the stable, of whom one is young Don Luis in disguise, Clara's admirer (chapter 62).

Sixth Party: Four horsemen arrive in the middle of the night, servants of Don Luis, who have come to take him home (chapter 63).

Seventh Party: Two travelers leave who have been staying all along and had spent the night there but had not been present at the supper. They now try to sneak out without paying,* but are intercepted by the landlord (chapter 44).

Eighth Party: Barber number two from whom (in chapter 21) Don Quixote and Sancho had taken a brass basin ("Mambrino's helmet") and a packsaddle (chapter 44).

Ninth Party: Three troopers of the Holy Brotherhood arrive, highway police who patrol the roads (chapter 65).

Tenth Party: A wagoner stops at the inn with a team of oxen whom the curate will hire to take Don Quixote home (chapter 46).

Some thirty-five people in all.

This grouping having been arranged in our book, it is high time to wind up the main thread of the linked inset stories, the Cardenio-Luscinda-Fernando-Dorotea affair which threatens to get thoroughly displaced in the reader's mind. For let us not forget that we have at this time three levels of narration:—(1) Don Quixote's adventures, (2) the Italianate novella read by the curate, which has come to a hasty end, and (3) the Cardenio et cetera affair, which in degree of acceptable artistic reality stands somewhere between the characters of the Anselmo-Lotario trash of the inset novella and the Don Quixote masterpiece—much nearer to the former than to the latter, in fact. So, Cardenio recognizes Luscinda while Dorotea recognizes Fernando. Look at the hurry in which the author is to settle this unfortunate matter:

* VN adds a pencil-note comment: "The reader is inclined to follow their example and quit, too."

"The curate then came over to remove her veil and throw water on her face [Dorotea had fainted at the sight of Fernando], and as soon as he saw her features Don Fernando recognized her even as he held the other woman [Luscinda] in his arms, and at the sight of her his own face turned deathly pale. He could not, however, release his hold on Luscinda, who was struggling to free herself from his grasp, she and Cardenio having recognized each other by their voices. For Cardenio also had heard the cry that Dorotea gave as she fainted, and believing it to be his Luscinda, he had rushed out terror-stricken. The first thing he saw was Don Fernando with Luscinda in his arms, and Fernando now recognized him, while the three of them—Luscinda, Cardenio, and Dorotea—remained silent and bewildered, scarcely knowing what had happened. They all gazed at one another without saying a word: Dorotea at Don Fernando, Fernando at Cardenio, Cardenio at Luscinda, and Luscinda at Cardenio" (chapter 36).

This is a very lame chapter. Despite the author's skill, it hopelessly blends with the Italian interpolation. And we still have the "Princess Micomicona" (as seen by Don Quixote) and her giant on our hands.

The two friends of Don Quixote, a curate and a barber, with the help of Dorotea as the "Princess" who preempts Don Quixote's quest to restore her to her throne, had planned to trick him into going back to his native village with them; but the loves of Luscinda and Dorotea being solved, and Don Luis and Doña Clara having settled themselves, there is still time for a few merry pranks. Knowing well the peculiarities of his nature, they encourage the Don's craziness and by carrying this or that joke further, they grant some good laughs to the large company at the inn. At one point here, in chapter 45, the adventures of the various secondary characters get into a terrific tangle, and here is the climax: When Don Quixote hears one of the Holy Brotherhood troopers maintaining that what he, Don Quixote, took for a noble steed's harness was really the packsaddle of a donkey, he attacks the troopers with his lance, aiming "such a blow at the trooper's head that if the officer had not dodged, it would have left him stretched out on the ground. [Incidentally, this is a tediously frequent turn of phrasing in the book, during its various encounters.] The pike as it struck the ground was shattered to bits; whereupon the other officers, seeing their companion assaulted in this manner, cried out for help in the name of the Holy Brotherhood. The innkeeper, who was one of the band, at once ran to get his staff of office and his sword and, returning, took his place alongside his comrades. Don Luis' servants surrounded their master that he might not escape amid the excitement; and the [second] barber, perceiving that the household was turned upside down, once more seized his packsaddle as Sancho did the same.

"Drawing his sword, Don Quixote attacked the officers, while Don Luis cried to his servants to release him and go to the aid of the knight and of Cardenio and Don Fernando, both of whom were lending their support.* The curate shouted, the landlady screamed, her daughter wailed, Maritornes wept, Dorotea was dumfounded, Luscinda terrified, and Dona Clara ready to faint. The barber cudgeled Sancho, and Sancho mauled the barber. Don Luis, when one of his servants seized his arm to keep him from running away, gave the fellow a punch that bloodied his mouth, and the judge came to the lad's defense. Don Fernando had a trooper down and was kicking him vigorously, and the innkeeper was again raising his voice to call for help for the Holy Brotherhood. In short, the entire hostelry was filled with shouts, cries, screams, with tumult, terror, and confusion, with sword slashes, fisticuffs, cudgelings, kickings, bloodshed, and mishaps of every sort." A chaos of pain, inflicted or received.

Let me draw your attention to a point of style. We see here—and in other similar passages of general participation in this or that conflict—we see a forlorn attempt on the author's part to group his characters according to their natures and emotions—to bring them in a group, but also keep them as individuals before the reader's eyes, so as to remind him all the time of their special features and have them act all together, without leaving anybody out. All this is quite clumsy and inartistic, especially as in a minute they all forget their quarrels. (We shall see, when we get to Flaubert's *Madame Bovary*, two and a half centuries later how, in the course of the evolution of the novel, the crude method of Cervantes is brought to a point of most delicate perfection when Flaubert wishes to group or pass in review his characters and this or that turn of his novel.)

THE CHIVALRY BOOKS THEME

The vogue of chivalry books in Spain has been described as a kind of social plague which had to be fought and which, it is further said, Cervantes did fight—and destroy forever. My impression is that all this has been dreadfully exaggerated and that Cervantes did not destroy anything; in fact, today damsels in distress are saved and monsters are slain—in our pulp literature and in our movies—as lustily as they were centuries ago. And of

* VN's interlined comment at this point is: "Is anybody following? I'm not."

course the great Continental novels of the nineteenth century, full of adulteries and duels and crazy quests, are the direct descendant of chivalry books, too.

But if we take chivalry books in the literal sense of the term, then I think we shall find that by 1605, the time of *Don Quixote*, the chivalry romances fad had almost faded away; and their decline had been noticeable for the last twenty or thirty years. Cervantes, in fact, is thinking of books that he had read as a youth and had not glanced at afterward (there are lots of blunders in his references)—so that to draw a modern parallel, he is rather like an author of today who would attack Foxy Grandpa or Buster Brown instead of lunging against Li'l Abner or the fellows in infra-red tights. In other words, composing a book of a thousand pages in order to give an additional push in a matter that was neither worthwhile nor urgent (being taken care of by time itself), this would have been on Cervantes's part an action as crazy as any windmill adventure of Don Quixote. The masses were illiterate, and the picture drawn by some commentators of a literate shepherd reading aloud Lancelot's romance to a group of illiterate but entranced muledrivers is merely silly. Among gentlefolks or the scholars the fashion had passed, although off and on archbishops, kings, and saints may have still read the books with pleasure. By 1600 odd volumes, well thumbed and dusty, might still be found in a country gentleman's attic, but that's all.

Cervantes's critical attitude toward fantastic novels is based—insofar as he speaks his own mind—on what he considered their lack of truth—and by truth he seemed to have meant not much more than the data obtained by common sense, which of course is a very lowbred kind of truth. Through his various representatives in his own book he deplores the absence of historical truth in romances because, he contends, they deceive simple souls who believe those stories to be true. But Cervantes completely confuses the issue by doing three odd things in his own book. Firstly, by inventing a chronicler, an Arab historian, who supposedly kept track of the life of a historical Don Quixote—which is just the kind of device that the authors of the most ridiculous romances employed in order to bolster their tales with respectable truth, with acceptable pedigrees. Secondly, he confuses the issue by having his curate, his man of common sense, or supposed common sense, praise or exempt from destruction half a dozen chivalry books—among these the very book *Amadis of Gaul* that is constantly in the limelight throughout Don Quixote's adventures and seems to be the main source of his madness. And, thirdly (as Madariaga has pointed out*), he confuses the issue by committing the very mistakes—mistakes against taste and truth—that he, Cervantes the critic, laughs at when discussing books of chivalry; for just as the people in those books, so his own madmen and maidens, sundry shepherds, et cetera, run wild in the Sierra Morena and compose poems in a most artificial and ornate style that makes the reader's gorge rise. The final impression one gets when this matter of chivalry books is inspected closely is that if Cervantes selected a certain subject to be derided in various ways, he did so not because he felt any special urge to improve the morals of his day but partly because in his moral utilitarian day in the stern eye of the Church a moral was necessary, and mainly because a satire on romances dealing with knights-errant was a convenient and innocent gadget to keep his picaresque novel going—the kind of peg that made the winged horse Clavileño fly to remote kingdoms.

Let us now see how the chivalry-book device affects the structure of the novel.

The book seems to start as a skit on the stories of chivalry, and on the readers of such tales who "became so immersed in" their reading that they, like Don Quixote, "spent whole nights from sundown to sunup and his days from dawn to dusk in poring over his books, until, finally, from so little sleeping and so much reading, his brain dried up and he went completely out of his mind." The brain, organ of reason, is distinguished by Cervantes from the soul, region of the imagination, which those insane persons filled "with everything that [they] had read, with enchantments, knightly encounters, battles, challenges, wounds, with tales of love and its torments, and all sorts of impossible things, and as a result had come to

* Madariaga, _Cervantes_, pp. 51-53: "Thus Cervantes the author fell into the very faults derided in Books of Chivalry by Cervantes the critic. For indeed this seems to be a constant feature of his criticism that he is unable to generalize his views into a principle and that in practice he often presents, though in a slightly different form, the same defects which he condemns in theory. This is true of his matter no less than of his style. . . . He made himself responsible for a good half-dozen of those wandering maidens whom he ridiculed when he met them with whip and palfrey in the hills and dales of Chivalry Books ['those maidens who, with whip and palfrey, and with all their maidenhood about them, wandered from hill to hill, from dale to dale, so that unless a rogue or a villain in axe and helmet, or a boisterous giant ravished them, maidens there were in past ages who, after eighty years during which they never had slept under a roof, went to their grave as pure virgins as the mothers who bore them.' Part I, Chapter 9], but who seem quite acceptable to him when, clad in pastoral attire, they bewail their fate to the winds in the solitary haunts of the Sierra Morena, or when, after many a perilous adventure, they are caught red-handed disguised as pirates in command of a Turkish brigantine. . . . Thus the two forces—unbridled imagination and weight of reality—which oppose each other in this book, have not yet achieved a state of balance. . . . But how often, in true imitation of Don Quixote, does he gallop through the fields of imagination and lose sight of earth! Pastoral scenes in particular are his King Charles's head, just as Chivalry Books are Don Quixote's. . . . There is indeed good ground for the view that much of the popularity which _Don Quixote_ instantly gained was due precisely to the spirit of wild romance which it retained from the enchanted lands of chivalry and pastoral books whence it came." Ed.

believe that all these fictitious happenings were true"; or, more exactly, that they present a higher reality than the reality of everyday life. Our crazy country gentleman, Quijada or Quesada, but most likely Quejana or Quijano, (1) polished some old pieces of armor, (2) attached a visor of cardboard and iron strips to a visorless helmet, (3) found a high-sounding name for his nag, "Rocinante," (4) found a name for himself, "Don Quixote de la Mancha," and (5) a name for his lady, "Dulcinea del Toboso," who in vague reality was a peasant girl called Aldonza Lorenzo in the village of El Toboso.

Then, without delay, on a hot summer day he sallied out in quest of adventures. He mistakes a humble inn for a castle, two whores for highborn damsels, a swineherd for a trumpeter, the innkeeper for the governor of the castle, cod for trout. The only thing that distresses him is that he has not yet been dubbed a knight in a formal legitimate way. Don Quixote's dream comes true only because the innkeeper is a rogue and a sport with a sense of brutal humor who plays up to Quixote the dreamer: "the castellan brought out the book in which he had jotted down the hay and barley for which the mule drivers owed him, and, accompanied by a lad bearing the butt of a candle and the two aforesaid damsels, he came up to where Don Quixote stood [at his vigil] and commanded him to kneel. Reading from the account book—as if he had been saying a prayer—he raised his hand and, with the knight's own sword, gave him a good thwack upon the neck and another lusty one upon the shoulder, muttering all the while between his teeth. He then directed one of the ladies to gird on Don Quixote's sword, which she did with much gravity and composure . . ." (chapter 3). Note the description of the ceremonial vigil: "For a while the knight-to-be, with tranquil mien, would merely walk up and down; then, leaning on his lance, he would pause to survey his armor, gazing fixedly at it for a considerable length of time. As has been said, it was night now, but the brightness of the moon, which well might rival that of Him who lent it, was such that everything the novice knight did was plainly visible to all." It is here that the parody of chivalry becomes for the first time in the book lost in the pathetic, poignant, divine element which radiates from Don Quixote. It is interesting to recall in connection with the phrase "of Him who lent it" at this point—the ceremonial vigil—that Ignatius of Loyola on the eve of founding the order of the Society of Jesus in 1534 spent the night in front of the altar of the Virgin as he had read in chivalry books knights used to keep vigil.

After being badly battered in a battle with the servants of some merchants, Don Quixote is succored by a neighbor, who brings him home.

The curate proposes to condemn to the flames the books that have driven the Don mad. We are haunted by the creeping feeling that tables are being gently turned, and that these books and those dreams and that madness are of a finer quality—and, in a word, ethically better—than the curate's and the housekeeper's so-called common sense.

It is a commonplace of commentary to say that Cervantes attacked—if he attacked anything at all—second-rate romances of chivalry and not the institution of chivalry itself. Glancing for a moment at the generalities of life in connection with the generalities of fiction, we might go further and say that there is a link between the most subtle and sophisticated rules of knight-errantry and the rules of what we call democracy. The real link is in the element of sportsmanship, fair play, and brotherhood found in true chivalry. And this was stressed in the books that Don Quixote had read, bad as some of them were.

The chivalry theme and the Arcadian theme often mingle in Don Quixote's mind, as they do in the books he read. In chapter 11 Don Quixote outlines his concept of the Golden Age, the backdrop of ancient times: *Food and drink*—jumbo acorns, honey, spring water; *habitation*—the bark of cork oaks (*quercus suber*) of which a roof for a hut is made; *animal husbandry*—completely replaces agriculture, which "wounds the bosom of the earth." (As if those damned sheep with their razor-sharp teeth did not destroy grasslands to the roots.) Also note very carefully that the shepherd-esses became the inevitable ornaments of novels in the eighteenth century, in the period of so-called sentimentalism, or budding romanticism of which a typical exponent was the French philosopher Rousseau (1712-1778). And it never occurred to those advocates of the simple life that at times the work of a sheepman—or sheepgirl—may be more nerve-racking than that of a city executive. Let us go on with our list. *Clothes for women*—a few leaves of burdock or of ivy. And in the *moral domain*—(1) all things held in common, (2) universal peace and friendship, (3) then truth, frankness, honesty, (4) maidenly modesty, (5) absolute justice. And, of course, as a kind of inspired and inspiring police force, (6) the institution of knight-errantry.

After Don Quixote had eaten heartily of a meal of meat and cheese, with plenty of wine, Cervantes relates in chapter 11 that he held up an acorn and fell into the following soliloquy: "Happy the age and happy those centuries to which the ancients gave the name of golden, . . . In that blessed era all things were held in common, and to gain his daily sustenance no labor was required of any man save to reach forth his hand and take it from the sturdy oaks that stood liberally inviting him with their sweet and seasoned fruit.

The clear-running fountains and rivers in magnificent abundance offered him palatable and transparent water for his thirst; while in the clefts of the rocks and the hollows of the trees the wise and busy honey-makers set up their republic so that any hand whatever might avail itself, fully and freely, of the fertile harvest which their fragrant toil had produced. The vigorous cork trees of their own free will and grace, without the asking, shed their broad, light bark with which men began to cover their dwellings, erected upon rude stakes merely as a protection against the inclemency of the heavens.

"All then was peace, all was concord and friendship; the crooked plowshare had not as yet grievously laid open and pried into the merciful bowels of our first mother, who without forcing on man's part yielded her spacious fertile bosom on every hand for the satisfaction, sustenance, and delight of her first sons. Then it was that lovely and unspoiled young shepherdesses . . . went roaming from valley to valley and hillock to hillock with no more garments than were needed to cover decently that which modesty requires. . . .

"Thoughts of love, also, in those days were set forth as simply as the simple hearts that conceived them, without any roundabout and artificial play of words by way of ornament. Fraud, deceit, and malice had not yet come to mingle with truth and plain-speaking. . . .

"It was for the safety of such as these, as time went on and depravity increased, that the order of knights-errant was instituted, for the protection of damsels, the aid of widows and orphans, and the succoring of the needy. It is to this order that I belong my brothers, and I thank you for the welcome and the kindly treatment that you have accorded to me and my squire. By natural law, all living men are obliged to show favor to knights-errant, yet without being aware of this you have received and entertained me; and so it is with all possible good will that I acknowledge your own good will to me."

We find Don Quixote speaking in chapter 13 to a group of shepherds and inquiring if they had not read in the annals and histories of England about the famous exploits of King Arthur (a legendary king and his knights supposed to have flourished in the middle of the first thousand years of our era): "It was, moreover, in the time of that good king that the famous order of the Knights of the Round Table was instituted; and as for the love of Sir Lancelot of the Lake and Queen Guinevere, everything took place exactly as the story has it, their confidante and go-between being the honored matron Quintanona, whence comes that charming ballad that is such a favorite with us Spaniards:

> *Never was there a knight*
> *So served by maid and dame*
> *As the one they call Sir Lancelot*
> *When from Britain he came—*

to carry on the gentle, pleasing course of his loves and noble deeds"—and, we may add, his madness and the final renunciation of knight errantry (he died a saintly man), and this is exactly what is going to happen to Don Quixote.

Note that these speeches of his contain no comic element whatsoever. He *is* a knight-errant. Immediately after speaking of Lancelot, he speaks of another favorite of his: "From that time forth, the order of chivalry was passed on and propagated from one individual to another until it had spread through many and various parts of the world. Among those famed for their exploits was the valiant Amadis of Gaul, with all his sons and grandsons to the fifth generation." Cervantes and his curate reject as poor stuff those sons and grandsons, but keep Amadis; and in this, critical posterity follows them. Don Quixote concludes: "And that, gentlemen, is what it means to be a knight-errant, and what I have been telling you of is the order of chivalry which such a knight professes, an order to which, as I have already informed you, I, although a sinner, have the honor of belonging; for I have made the same profession as have those other knights. That is why it is you find me in these wild and lonely places, riding in quest of adventure, being resolved to offer my arm and my person in the most dangerous undertaking fate may have in store for me, that I may be of aid to the weak and needy."

Now let us draw certain significant parallels between the grotesque in chivalry books* and the grotesque in *Don Quixote*. In Malory's romance, *Le Morte d'Arthur*, book nine, chapter 17, Sir Tristram retired into the

---

* At this point VN said to his class, "You will please acquaint yourself with those mimeographed odds and ends of chivalry romance distributed to you—passages from two books: (1) *Le Morte d'Arthur*, Sir Thomas Malory's book of King Arthur and of his nobles, Knights of the Round Table, such as Sir Tristram and Sir Lancelot, written around 1470. Spanish versions of this, besides old ballads referring to the same cycle of romances, had been imbibed by Don Quixote. (2) *Amadis of Gaul*, by Vasco Lobeira, a Portuguese, second half of the fourteenth century; the English from a Spanish version is by Robert Southey, English poet, first half of the nineteenth century. *Amadis* is, of course, Don Quixote's great favorite. The samples selected from both works are merely to show what kind of thing attracted Don Quixote and was echoed in his own adventures." See Appendix I.

wilderness after he thought his lady, Iseult la Belle, had not been quite faithful to him.* At first he played on the harp; later he went naked and became lean and poor of flesh; and so he fell in the fellowship of herdsmen and shepherds, and daily they would give him some of their meat and drink. And when he did any mad mischievous deed they would beat him with rods, and so they clipped him with shears and made him like a fool. Ladies and gentlemen, there is no real difference between these occurrences and the atmosphere of the episodes in the mountains of Spain—beginning with part one, chapter 24, of Don Quixote's adventures and the story of the ragged wild man Cardenio.

In Malory's romance, *Le Morte d'Arthur*, the end of book eleven, Lancelot by enchantment is made to lie with the fair Elaine, whom he is mystified into mistaking for Queen Guinevere, his only love. Guinevere in the next room is heard clearing her throat: Lancelot recognizes her hemming, learns he is with the wrong lady, and in crazy distress jumps out of the window, a madman. In book twelve, chapter 1, he roams the wildwood in his underwear, living on berries and brook water. He still has his sword, however. During a grotesque battle with a knight he tumbles by chance into the bed of some lady or other, frightens her out of it, and falls asleep there in oafish fashion. This feather bed is placed on a horse litter, and he is carried bound hand and foot to a castle where he is chained as a madman but given good food and well looked after. In *Don Quixote* you will easily discover parallel scenes and the same atmosphere of dazed valor, of cruel ridicule.

If we go back from Malory of the fifteenth century to the thirteenth century we find the earliest text dealing with Lancelot of the Lake and Guinevere, a French prose romance, the *Roman de la Charrete* by Chrétien de Troyes. (The theme under different names had been current in Ireland centuries earlier.) In this thirteenth-century romance a cart passes driven by a dwarf who tells Lancelot that if he climbs into the cart he will be driven to Queen Guinevere. He accepts and braves disgrace. (The disgrace element depends on the fact that carts were used to parade criminals.) Don Quixote submitting to the disgrace of the ox cart because he is told by enchanters that he will be driven to Dulcinea is exactly in the same boat, in the same cart. I am prepared to contend that the only difference between Sir Lancelot or Sir Tristram, or any other knight, and Don Quixote is that

* On a detached sheet VN has the following note: "Note on *The Divine Comedy* by Dante Alighieri: Dante placed Tristram among the carnal sinners in the second circle of Hell (which he visited, guided by the ghost of Virgil, in 1300). And Francesca de Rimini and her lover Paolo (the brother of her husband, lord of Rimini) are also there, as you remember. They had kissed for the first time while reading of the adventures of Lancelot of the Lake. In that romance it was Guinevere, King Arthur's wife, who gave a kiss to Lancelot."

the latter did not find any real knight to fight in an age when gunpowder had replaced magic potions.

I wish to stress the fact that in romances of chivalry all was not Ladies and Roses and Blazons, but that scenes occurred in which shameful and grotesque things happened to those knights and they underwent the same humiliations and enchantments as Don Quixote did—and that, in a word, Don Quixote cannot be considered a distortion of those romances but rather a logical continuation, with the elements of madness and shame and mystification increased.

The canon who in chapter 47 of part one converses with the curate voices the author's views—or at least such views as an author could safely hold in his time. Very reasonable, very demure—this outlook. Indeed, it is quite curious, how with these churchmen and churchbound writers, reason—man-made reason—plays the dominant part, while fancy and intuition are banned: a curious paradox, for where would our gods be if we gave complete priority to pedestrian common sense, or jogging horse sense. "What shall we say of the readiness with which a hereditary queen or empress throws herself into the arms of an unknown knight-errant?," asks the canon. "Could any person, save one with a barbarous and uncultivated mind, find pleasure in reading that a great tower filled with knights goes sailing over the sea like a ship with a favoring wind and is tonight in Lombardy and tomorrow morning in the land of Prester John of the Indies, or in other domains such as Ptolemy never discovered and Marco Polo never laid eyes on?" (Where would science be if we followed the decrees of reason?) Works of fiction, says the canon, "should be so written that the impossible is made to appear possible, things hard to believe being smoothed over and the mind held in suspense in such a manner as to create surprise and astonishment while at the same time they divert and entertain so that admiration and pleasure go hand in hand."

Yet Don Quixote can be eloquent in his description of knight-errantry, as in chapter 50: "Tell me: could there be anything more fascinating than to see before us, right here and now, so to speak, a lake of bubbling pitch, with a host of snakes, serpents, lizards, and all sorts of fierce and terrifying animals swimming about in it, while from the middle of it there comes as mournful a voice as ever was heard, saying, 'Thou, O knight, whoever thou mayst be, who standest gazing upon this dreadful lake, if thou wouldst attain the boon that lieth covered beneath these dark waters, show then thy valor and thy stout heart by leaping into the midst of this black and burning liquid, for if thou dost not, thou shalt not be held worthy of looking upon the mighty marvels locked and contained in the seven castles of the seven fays that are situated beneath its ebony expanse.' And no sooner does the knight hear that awful voice than, without taking any further thought or pausing to consider the peril involved, he plunges into that seething lagoon, burdened with the full weight of his armor and commending his soul to God and Our Lady.

"And then, not knowing where he is or what the outcome is to be, he suddenly finds himself amidst flowering meadows to which the Elysian fields cannot compare. . . .

". . . Having beheld all this, he now descries, trooping out of the castle gate, a goodly number of damsels. . . .

". . . And the one who appears to be the leader of them all now extends her hand to the bold knight who has cast himself into the boiling lake and, without saying a word, conducts him into the splendid palace or castle, where she makes him strip until he is as bare as when his mother bore him, and then bathes him in lukewarm water, after which she anoints him all over with sweet-smelling unguents and clothes him in a shirt of finest sendal, all odorous and perfumed, as another maid tosses a mantle over his shoulders, one which at the very least, so they say, must be worth as much as a city and even more.

"And how pleasing it is when, after all this, we are told how they take him to another chamber, a great hall, where he finds the tables all laid in a manner that fills him with amazement. What must be his feelings as he sees them pouring over his hands water that has been distilled from amber and fragrant flowers? As they seat him upon a chair of marble? . . . And then, when the repast is over and the tables have been cleared, as the knight leans back in his chair, picking his teeth, it may be, as is his custom [a delightful detail], there enters unexpectedly through the doorway of the great hall a damsel far more beautiful than any of the others; and, seating herself at his side, she begins telling him to whom it is that castle belongs and how she is being held in it under a magic spell, along with other things that astonish him and amaze the one who reads his history. What, I ask you again, could be more charming than all this?"*

Don Quixote's eloquence to the contrary, the conversation in chapter 47 between the canon and the curate is a kind of summary of what the curate had expounded in the bookburning chapter 6 in the beginning of *Don*

---

* VN adds: "We shall see in part two the fulfillment of that gentle dream when the ducal pair entertain Don Quixote in precisely this fashion (except that modesty causes him to refuse to be stripped). But what a fulfillment! I can hardly name any other book where detached cruelty is driven to such a diabolically sharp point as in the scenes in the ducal castle of part two, where as one critic called Krutch, who needs one, amazingly says: Don Quixote is entertained by a kindly duchess." The reference is to Krutch, *Five Masters*, p. 97.

Quixote. We are now back at the initial situation. Certain books of chivalry are harmful because they are too fancy and too crude in style. " 'Never,' concluded the canon, 'have I seen any book of chivalry. . . . [which was not] made up of so many disparate members that it would seem the author's intention was to create a chimera or a monster rather than a well-proportioned figure. In addition to all this, they are crude in style, unconvincing in the exploits that they relate, lascivious in the love affairs that they portray, uncouth in their efforts at courtliness, prolix in their descriptions of battles, absurd in their dialogue, nonsensical in their accounts of journeyings, and, finally, destitute of anything that resembles art; for which reason it is they deserve to be banished from the Christian state as not being of public utility.' " However, I repeat, the books were not worth attacking with a novel of a thousand pages. But by the end of part one, shrewd Cervantes has not one but two churchmen on his side.

It would take too long to follow in tedious detail every twist and turn that the chivalry theme—the supple backbone of the book's structure—takes throughout the whole work. When I treat of Don Quixote's victories and defeats the device will become absolutely clear. I shall wind up my account of the chivalry books theme by indicating one of its most charming variations, toward the end of Don Quixote's adventures, namely, in chapter 58 of the second part. The knight and his squire come across a dozen men in a meadow, sitting on their cloaks and taking their dinners. Four large objects in linen covers lie on the grass around them. Don Quixote wants to see what they are and one of the men uncovers the objects, which prove to be images sculptured in relief which they are transporting from one parish to another parish. The first carved image represents a knight, in a blaze of gold, thrusting his lance through the mouth of a dragon. Don Quixote identifies him at once: "This," he says, "was one of the best knights-errant that the heavenly militia ever had. His name was Don St. George and he was, moreover, a protector of damsels." (St. George slew the dragon to protect a king's daughter.)

The next proves to be St. Martin dividing his cloak with a poor man; and again Don Quixote, with a kind of tender dignity, comments: " 'This knight, also,' he said, 'was one of the Christian adventurers, and it is my opinion, Sancho, that he was even more liberal than he was valiant, as you may see from the fact that he is here dividing his cloak and giving the beggar half of it; and it undoubtedly must have been winter at the time or otherwise he would have given him all of it, he was so charitable' "—a rather pathetic deduction on Don Quixote's part. A third carved image is revealed, showing St. James trampling down Moors. " 'Ah!' exclaimed Don

Quixote, 'this is a real knight and one of Christ's own cohorts. He is Don San Diego Matamoros, the Moor-slayer, one of the most valiant saints and men of arms that this world ever had or Heaven has now.' " A fourth shows St. Paul fallen from his horse, with all the detail usual in a picture of his conversion. " 'This man in his day,' said Don Quixote, 'was the greatest enemy that the Church of Our Lord God had to combat, and he became the greatest champion it will ever have, a knight-errant in life, and in death a steadfast saint, a tireless worker in the Lord's vineyard, teacher of the Gentiles with Heaven for a school and Jesus Christ as instructor and schoolmaster.' "

There were no more images, and so Don Quixote bade them be covered again and said—the whole tone of the scene is evangelical—"I take it as a good omen, my brothers, . . . to have seen what I have today; for these saints and knights followed the same profession that I do, which is that of arms. The only difference between them and me is that they, being saints, waged a holy warfare, while I fight after the manner of men. They conquered Heaven by force of arms, for Heaven suffereth violence; but, up to now, I do not know what I have won with all the hardships I have endured. However, if my lady Dulcinea were but free of those that she is suffering, it may be that my fortunes would improve, and with a sounder mind I should be able to tread a better path than the one I follow at present," he mutters, in a dim tremor of insight into the condition of his poor brain. Sancho remarks, as they resume their journey, "Truly, sir, . . . if what happened to us today can be called an adventure, it has been one of the sweetest and pleasantest that we have had in all our wanderings." Indeed, this scene most artistically sums up our gentle knight-errant's case and foreshadows his approaching end.

It is very wonderful how strangely the intonation of Don Quixote in this scene approaches the intonation of another madman created in the same year as he:

> *I am a very foolish fond old man,*
> . . . .
> *And, to deal plainly,*
> *I fear I am not in my perfect mind.*
> *—King Lear, IV. vii*

Cruelty And Mystification

I now plan to tackle the mystification theme, the cruelty theme. This is how I am going to proceed. First of all, I am going to pass in review samples of cheerful physical cruelty in part one of the book. Remember that my complete account of Don Quixote's victories and defeats will come much later: I want you to look forward to that play-by-play account. So for the present all I shall do is to illume a corner of the torture house by means of my little torchlight, and this is the first thing I shall do today—samples of cheerful physical cruelty in part one. Secondly I shall discuss the mental cruelties of part two; and since these mental cruelties are mainly mystification, I shall have to speak of the various enchantments and enchanters. Our first enchanter will be Sancho—and this will introduce the Dulcinea theme. Another interesting case will be Don Quixote in an act of self-enchantment—the Montesinos cave episode. After that I shall be ready to attack the principal enchanters of the second part, the Duchess and her Duke.

I feel that there is something about the ethics of our book that casts a livid laboratory light on the proud flesh of some of its purpler passages. We are going to speak of cruelty.

The author seems to plan it thus: Come with me, ungentle reader, who enjoys seeing a live dog inflated and kicked around like a soccer football; reader, who likes, of a Sunday morning, on his way to or from church, to poke his stick or direct his spittle at a poor rogue in the stocks; come, ungentle reader, with me and consider into what ingenious and cruel hands

51

I shall place my ridiculously vulnerable hero. And I hope you will be amused at what I have to offer.

It is simply not true that as some of our mellow-minded commentators maintain—Aubrey Bell, for instance—that the general character that emerges from the national background of the book is that of sensitive, keen-witted folks, humorous and humane. Humane, indeed! What about the hideous cruelty—with or without the author's intent or sanction—which riddles the whole book and befouls its humor? Let us not drag the national element in. The Spaniards of Don Quixote's day were not more cruel in their behavior toward madmen and animals, subordinates and non-conformers, than any other nation of that brutal and brilliant era. Or, for that matter, of other, later, more brutal and less brilliant eras in which the fact of cruelty remains with its fangs bared. That the rustler in the chain gang which Don Quixote meets on the road had been given the rack is mentioned as a matter of course, for torture was as generously—though more openly—applied in old Spain or old Italy as it is in our time in totalitarian states. In Don Quixote's day Spaniards thought insanity comic but (as Krutch points out) so did the Englishmen of a later date who used to make visits of pleasure to Bedlam.

Both parts of *Don Quixote* form a veritable encyclopedia of cruelty. From that viewpoint it is one of the most bitter and barbarous books ever penned. And its cruelty is artistic. The extraordinary commentators who talk through their academic caps or birettas of the humorous and humane mellowly Christian atmosphere of the book, of a happy world where "all is sweetened by the humanities of love and good fellowship,"* and particularly those who talk of a certain "kindly duchess" who "entertains the Don" in the second Part—these gushing experts have probably been reading some other book or are looking through some rosy gauze at the brutal world of Cervantes's novel. There is a legend that one sunny morning King Philip the Third of Spain (a freak in his own right, who had succeeded in 1598 his father, the gloomy and fish-cold Philip the Second)

* VN cites Bell, *Cervantes*, p. 12. A typical quotation comes from pp. 12-13: "This spaciousness is indeed the characteristic note of Spain, and in this as in other respects Cervantes was a true representative of the Spain of the sixteenth century, of the Spain of all time. Havelock Ellis, in describing Cervantes ('as sweetly humane as Chaucer') added that he was 'the most typical of Spaniards.' In his tolerant moderation, his genial humour, his broad humanity, sensitive pride, and courteous dignity, as in his courage, energy, and endurance, he was a true Spaniard, a true Castilian. In almost every scene and chapter of his works there is a note of merry outspokenness and frank laughter, with, it may be added, plenty of good cheer.... Spaniards of all kinds appear in these pages, a crowd of very vivid figures; but the general character that emerges is that of a sensitive keen-witted nation, humorous and humane." Ed.

VN notes "a Sir Herbert J. C. Grierson, who is a scream, in a trashy article" *Don Quixote: Some War-time Reflections on Its Character and Influence, English Association*, Pamphlet No. 48 (London, 1921), p. 4."

upon looking from the balcony of his palace was struck by the singular behavior of a young student who was sitting on a bench in the shade of a cork oak (*quercus suber*) with a book and frantically clapping his thigh and giving vent to wild shrieks of laughter. The king remarked that the fellow was either crazy or was reading *Don Quixote*. A rapid courtier ran out to find the answer. The fellow, as you have guessed, was reading *Don Quixote*.

What exactly provoked this outburst of wild merriment in the gloomy world of the Philips? I have listed a whole set of jollities for the merry young student to choose from. Remember, I am looking at the book today only from this special viewpoint; there are many other things in our knight's adventures of which I shall talk later. So we start in chapter 3 with the innkeeper who allows a haggard madman to stay at his inn just in order to laugh at him and have his guests laugh at him. We go on with a shriek of hilarity to the half-naked lad flogged with a belt by a hefty farmer (chapter 4). We are convulsed with laughter again in chapter 4 when a mule driver pounds the helpless Don Quixote like wheat in a mill. In chapter 8 another belly laugh is given unto us by the servants of some traveling monks, who pull every hair from Sancho's beard and kick him mercilessly. What a riot, what a panic! Some carriers in chapter 15 beat Rocinante so hard that he drops to the ground half-dead—but never mind, in a minute the puppet master will revive his squeaking dolls.

If Don Quixote is not actually administered an enema of snow water and sand, as one of the characters in a book of chivalry was, he gets very close to it. Attitudes of excruciating pain such as that of Sancho Panza in the same chapter 15* provoke another moan of mirth. By this time Don Quixote has lost half an ear—and nothing can be funnier than losing half an ear except of course losing three-quarters of an ear—and now, please, notice the blows that he received during one day and one night: (1) wallops with packstaves, (2) a punch on the jaw at the inn, (3) sundry blows in the dark,** (4) a bang on the pate with an iron lantern. And the next day

* "Venting himself of thirty 'Ohs' and 'Ahs' and sixty sighs and a hundred-twenty imprecations of various sorts, with curses for the one who had got him into this, [Sancho] arose, pausing halfway like a Turkish bow bent in the middle, without the power to straighten himself. It was with the greatest difficulty that he succeeded in saddling his ass, which, making use of the unwonted freedom it had enjoyed that day, had wandered off some little distance. He then managed to get Rocinante on his feet, and if that animal had possessed the power to complain, you may be sure that he would have been an equal for Sancho and his master." Ed.

** "When [the muleteer] saw that the girl was doing her best to free herself and Don Quixote was trying to hold her, he decided that the joke had gone far enough; raising his fist high above his head, he came down with so fearful a blow on the gaunt jaws of the enamored knight as to fill the poor man's mouth with blood. Not satisfied with this, the mule driver jumped on his ribs and at a pace faster than a trot gave them a thorough going-over is nicely started by his losing most of his teeth when stoned by some shepherds. The fun becomes positively rollicking by chapter 17 when in the famous blanket-tossing scene, some artisans—woolcombers and needlemakers, described as "merry fellows all of them, well intentioned, mischievous, and playful"—amuse themselves at Sancho's expense by tossing him in a blanket as men do with dogs at Shrovetide—a casual allusion to humane and humorous customs. The young student whom King Philip observes is again convulsed as he reads in chapter 18 of Don Quixote and Sancho vomiting over each other. And what fun there is in the scene of the galley slaves in chapter 22—another famous episode. Don Quixote asks one of the men for what sins is he in this evil plight. Another answers for him: " 'This one, sir,' he said, 'is going as a canary—I mean, as a musician and singer.' " What, says Don Quixote, "do musicians and singers go to the galleys too?" The galley slave replied, " 'Yes, sir; and there is nothing worse than singing when you're in trouble.'

" 'On the contrary,' said Don Quixote, 'I have heard it said that he who sings frightens away his sorrows.'

" 'It is just the opposite,' said the prisoner; 'for he who sings once weeps all his life long.'

" 'I do not understand,' said the knight.

"One of the guards then explained. 'Sir Knight, with this *non sancta* tribe, to sing when you're in trouble means to confess under torture. This sinner was put to the torture and confessed his crime, which was that of being a *cuatrero*, or cattle thief, and as a result of his confession he was condemned to six years in the galleys in addition to two hundred lashes which he took on his shoulders; and so it is he is always downcast and moody, for the other thieves, those back where he came from and the ones here, mistreat, snub, ridicule, and despise him for having had confessed and for not having had the courage to deny his guilt. They are in the habit of saying that the word *no* has the same number of letters as the word *si*, and that a culprit is in luck when his life or death depends on his own tongue and not that of witnesses or upon evidence; and, in my opinion, they are

---

from one end to the other. The bed, which was rather weak and not very firm on its foundations, was unable to support the muleteer's added weight and sank to the floor with a loud crash. This awoke the innkeeper. . . .

". . . When [Sancho] saw himself being treated like this by an unknown assailant, he rose the best way he could and grappled with her, and there then began between the two of them the prettiest and most stubbornly fought skirmish that ever you saw.

". . . There was the mule driver pounding Sancho, Sancho and the wench flaying each other, and the landlord drubbing the girl; and they all laid on most vigorously, without allowing themselves a moment's rest. The best part of it was, the lamp went out, leaving them in darkness, whereupon there ensued a general and merciless melee, until there was not a hand's breadth left on any of their bodies that was not sore and aching (chapter 16). Ed.

not very far wrong.' "* This is the humorous and humane world of some of our mellower Cervantesists.

Let us pursue our inquiry into the young student's mirth. Physical cruelty is of course fun, but mental cruelty may be still more amusing. In chapter 30 there is a charming young lady, Dorotea, a great favorite with Cervantesists; and of course she was too quick and intelligent not to understand what delightful possibilities Don Quixote's madness contained, so that seeing that everyone was making fun of him she was anxious not to be left out. Anxious not to be left out. Wise, lovely, winsome Dorotea!

We are back at the enchanted inn, or *venta*, in chapter 43, and there is another scene that is supposed to tickle the readers pink. Don Quixote stands upon the saddle of his horse to reach the barred window at which he imagines a lovelorn damsel is standing—and the servant girl, who impersonates her, ties his hand with the halter of Sancho's donkey in such a way that, when his horse moves, Don Quixote is left suspended, in which position he remains for two hours, despairing, bewildered, and bellowing like a bull, while the maid servant and the innkeeper's daughter, and presumably millions of readers, are doubled up with laughter, as probably were many in the crowd sixteen centuries earlier when the martyred God of those people was given vinegar instead of water.

The episodes at the inn end in Don Quixote being tied up and put into a cage on an ox cart by his friends the curate and the barber, who want to bring him home and cure him of his madness. We come now to a last fight in the first part. This is in chapter 52. While carting Don Quixote home, the curate falls into conversation with a learned and amiable canon, and they sit down for a picnic beside the road and have Don Quixote come out of his cage to join them in order to amuse them, to have sport with him as the saying went. During this picnic Don Quixote gets involved in a quarrel with a passing goatherd, whom he hits in the face with a loaf of bread. The goatherd tries to choke Don Quixote, but Sancho comes to the rescue by throwing the goatherd onto the tablecloth and upsetting or smashing everything upon it. Don Quixote endeavors to get on top of the goatherd, who, with his face all bloody from Sancho's kicks, is groping for a knife on the tablecloth.

Now keep an eye on the good canon, the good curate, and the good barber, remembering that the canon is Cervantes himself in disguise as a member of the clergy and remembering that the curate and the barber are

---

* VN somewhat paraphrased his account of his scene and, possibly for his private amusement, recast the galley slave's speech in Negro dialect.

Don Quixote's closest friends and are anxious to cure him of his madness. The canon and the curate prevent the goatherd from using a knife, but the barber helps the goatherd to get Don Quixote down again where he rains such a shower of blows on him that the knight's face poured blood as freely as the goatherd's. The barber is doing this, I suppose, for fun's sake. Now keep an eye on the others. The canon and the curate are bursting with laughter; the troopers of the highway patrol dance for joy—and everyone cheers the fighters on as men do at a dogfight. It is on this familiar dog note—nothing funnier than a dog being tortured in a sunny street—it is on this note that the first part of *Don Quixote* ends. Our young student is by now limp with laughter, has, in fact, fallen off his bench. We shall leave him lying there, although there is still a second part to read with more screams of merriment.

Let none think, however, that the symphony of mental and physical pain presented in *Don Quixote* is a composition that could be played only on musical instruments of the remote past. Nor should anyone suppose that those strings of pain are twanged nowadays only in remote tyrannies behind iron curtains. Pain is still with us, around us, among us. I am not referring to such trivialities—though they also have their place in the history of pain—as the banged heads and kicked groins and punched noses that are such delectable features of our movies and comics. What I have in mind are more trivial things, under the best of governments. Now and then freakish children in our schools are still tortured by their comrades as thoroughly as Childe Quixote was tortured by his enchanters; and now and then bums, colored and white, are as lustily kicked in the shins by burly policemen as the armored tramp and his squire were on the roads of Spain.

But let us turn to the second part of our humane, humorous book.* Compared to the fun in the first part, the mirth-provoking cruelty of the second part reaches a higher and more diabolical level in regard to the

---

* Following this sentence is a full page that VN marked for omission, possibly because of time limitations. It reads: " 'There was in Seville a certain madman whose madness assumed one of the drollest forms that ever was seen in this world.' (The Cohen translation has 'the oddest,' Putnam has 'the drollest'—I prefer the latter). Thus Cervantes in the prologue to the second part. He was at work on the fifty-ninth chapter around 1612 when he discovered—or made believe he discovered—the so-called spurious continuation of his *Don Quixote* by the mysterious and possibly also spurious Alonso Fernández de Avellaneda, who was begotten in Tordesillas and published his *Second Volume of the Ingenious Gentleman, Don Quixote de la Mancha* at Tarragona. The passage about the certain madman is going to develop into a parable stressing the difficulties of writing a book as good as the true *Don Quixote*—a task that Avellaneda, according to our author, was unfit to perform.

" 'There was in Seville a madman whose madness was one of the drollest ever seen in this world.' Prepare, reader, for an explosion of mirth that will catapult you into the drolleries of the second part. This madman, Cervantes continues, would take a hollow reed sharpened at one end, then would catch a dog in the street or elsewhere; and holding down with his foot one of the animal's hind legs and raising the other with his hand, he would fix the reed in such a way as to blow the dog up round as a ball."

mental forms it takes and sinks to a new low of incredible crudity in its physical aspect. The mystification theme becomes more prominent; enchantments and enchanters swarm. It is under their colors that I intend to wander through the second part. They had of course been present in the first part—Sancho himself had mystified his master when he carried a garbled message to a nonexistent Dulcinea. In fact, the trick was quite subtle since he lied and deceived his master not by saying he had seen Dulcinea the princess, but by saying he had seen the Tobosan girl Aldonza, whom actually he had not bothered to see. We shall thus mark that it is Sancho in the first part who starts the trend of Dulcinea's enchantment, her transformation from princess into a particular or generalized peasant wench.

The second part opens with Sancho trying his hand at a second act of enchantment on the same lines. He manages to persuade his master—by now his victim—that one of three peasant girls they meet (none of whom is Aldonza) is Dulcinea transformed.

At the end of chapter 8 of the second part they reach El Toboso. Don Quixote's purpose is to find Dulcinea there. Both knight and squire are secretly worried about her. The Don because a very vague, very secret doubt is forming cloudlike in the otherwise limpid heavens of his madness; and the squire because he has never seen her but has deceived his master into thinking he transmitted a letter to her, in the first part. In the next chapter there is a stumbling search in the dark for a palace in a back alley. Sancho suggests that Don Quixote hide in a forest while he goes to find Dulcinea. It was a device of genius to keep Dulcinea out of the first part. Will Cervantes produce her now?

As in the first part Don Quixote now sends Sancho with a message to Dulcinea, a message that Sancho again does not deliver. There is in chapter 10 a lovely paragraph: " 'Go, my son,' Don Quixote said to him, 'and do not let yourself be dazed by the light from that sun of beauty that you go to seek. Ah, happy are you above all the squires in the world! Be sure to remember, and do not let it slip your mind, just how she receives you. Note whether she changes color while you are giving her my message and if she is restless and perturbed upon hearing my name. It may be that you will find her seated in sumptuous and royal state, in which case she will perhaps fall back upon a cushion; or if she be standing, see if she rests first upon one foot and then upon the other. Observe if she repeats two or three times the answer she gives you and if her mood varies from mildness to austerity, from the harsh to the amorous. She may raise a hand to her hair to smooth it back, though it be not disordered.' " (A charming detail, this.)

Sancho comes riding back. He sees three peasant girls riding and now decides what to do. Hastening back to Don Quixote he finds the knight sighing and uttering amorous laments.

" 'What is it, Sancho, my friend? Am I to be able to mark this day with a white stone or a black one?'

" 'It would be better,' replied Sancho, 'if your Grace marked it with red ocher like the lists on the professors' chairs [of bachelors qualifying for degrees], so that all could see it very plainly.'

" 'That means, I take it,' said Don Quixote, 'that you bring good news.'

" 'Good news it is,' replied Sancho. 'All your Grace has to do is to put spur to Rocinante and ride out into the open, and there you will see the lady Dulcinea del Toboso in person, who with two of her damsels has come to pay her respects to your Grace.

" ' . . . She and her damsels are all one blaze of gold, pearls, diamonds, rubies, and brocade cloth with more than ten borders. Their hair falling loose over their shoulders are so many sunbeams playing with the wind.' "

Don Quixote hastens out of the wood but at the moment of encounter a curious sadness, a very real sadness, hangs over him as if suddenly, at this crucial moment, an awful doubt arises in him: Does Dulcinea exist? " 'I see nothing,' declared Don Quixote, 'except three farm girls on three jackasses.' " Nevertheless, with Sancho, he falls on his knees before her. "His eyes were fairly starting from their sockets and there was a deeply troubled look in them as he stared up at the one whom Sancho had called queen and lady; all that he could see in her was a village wench, and not a very pretty one at that, for she was round-faced and snub-nosed. He was astounded and perplexed and did not dare open his mouth." But urged by Sancho he comes to believe that this girl, smelling of raw garlic, with dull red hair and a bristly mole at the corner of her lips, is Dulcinea under the spell of a wicked enchanter. He addresses her: "And thou, who art all that could be desired, the sum of human gentleness and sole remedy for this afflicted heart that doth adore thee! The malign enchanter who doth persecute me hath placed clouds and cataracts upon my eyes, and for them and them alone hath transformed thy peerless beauty into the face of a lowly peasant maid; and I can only hope that he has not likewise changed my face into that of some monster by way of rendering it abhorrent in thy sight. But for all of that, hesitate not to gaze upon me tenderly and lovingly, beholding in this act of submission as I kneel before thee a tribute to thy metamorphosed beauty from this humbly worshiping heart of mine."

Thinking she was being made fun of, the wench addressed as Dulcinea prodded her donkey with a spiked stick with the result that she was thrown to the ground by the animal's capers. "When he saw this, Don Quixote hastened to lift her up while Sancho busied himself with tightening the girths and adjusting the packsaddle, which had slipped down under the animal's belly. This having been accomplished, Don Quixote was about to take his enchanted lady in his arms to place her upon the she-ass when the girl saved him the trouble by jumping up from the ground, stepping back a few paces, and taking a run for it. Placing both hands upon the crupper of the ass, she landed more lightly than a falcon upon the packsaddle and remained sitting there astride it like a man.

" 'In the name of Roque!' exclaimed Sancho, 'our lady is like a lanner, only lighter, and can teach the cleverest Cordovan or Mexican how to mount. She cleared the back of the saddle in one jump, and without any spurs she makes her hackney run like a zebra, and her damsels are not far behind, for they all of them go like the wind.' "*

Henceforth throughout the second part Don Quixote will be worrying about how to accomplish the disenchantment of Dulcinea: how to transform the ugly peasant wench back into the beautiful Dulcinea, whom he vaguely remembers as another peasant girl, a handsome one, in El Toboso.

Another type of deception: The curate and the barber agree to the bachelor's suggestion that he, Sansón Carrasco, should take the road as a knight-errant, pick up somewhere a quarrel with Don Quixote and overcome him in battle. Then he would bid him go home—and remain there for one or two years, or more. Unfortunately it so happens that it is the bachelor who is defeated and badly battered.** Don Quixote rides off well satisfied.

---

* Don Quixote looks after the girls as they ride off, "and when they were no longer visible he turned to Sancho and spoke.

" 'Sancho,' he said, 'you can see now, can you not, how the enchanters hate me? . . . I would further call your attention, Sancho, to the fact that, not content with merely transforming my Dulcinea, they must change her into a figure as low and repulsive as that village girl, robbing her at the same time of that which is so characteristic of highborn ladies, namely, their pleasing scent, which comes from always being among amber and flowers. For I would have you know, Sancho, that when Dulcinea leaped upon her hackney as you call it (though I must say, it seemed to me more like a she-ass), the odor that she gave off was one of raw garlic that made my head swim and poisoned my heart. . . .

" '. . . But tell me one thing, Sancho: that thing that looked to me like a packsaddle which you were adjusting, was it a flat saddle or a sidesaddle?'

" 'It was neither one nor the other,' replied Sancho, 'but a *jineta*, with a field-covering so rich that it must have been worth half a kingdom.'

" 'Oh, if I could but have seen all that, Sancho! I tell you again, and I will tell you a thousand times, that I am the most unfortunate of men.' " Ed.

** The bachelor measured off sufficient ground and then turned his horse and bore down on Don Quixote at a mild trot, which was all that his nag could manage. But when he saw Don Quixote was not facing him but had been diverted by helping Sancho up into a cork tree, "he reined in his mount and came to a stop midway in his

From the point of view of the structure, the two deceptions—Sancho deceiving Don Quixote into thinking that Dulcinea is under a spell and the bachelor disguising himself as a knight-errant to meet Don Quixote on his own dream terms—these two deceptions are the two feet on which the whole second part must stand or stumble. From now on, whatever plot is unfolded it will do so against the background of Don Quixote's longing for the ultimate disenchantment of Dulcinea; while, on the other hand, the unfortunate Knight of the Mirrors, the badly battered bachelor, is expected to take the field again as soon as he can sit in a saddle. Thus the reader, while watching the various meanders of the story and the various characters that appear, is supposed to rely upon Dulcinea appearing and the bachelor disguising himself again when the author deems it necessary. The bachelor will fight again and be victor; Dulcinea will be disenchanted—but she will never appear.

We have now reached the episode of Montesinos's cave in part two, which I intend to discuss. I shall then analyze the ducal enchantments, the series of mystifications in the ducal castle. I shall draw your attention, finally, to a couple of great passages in the book—artistically redeeming it.

Montesinos is a character from the literature of chivalry, the protagonist of the so-called "Ballads of Montesinos." (A Welsh enchanter, Merlin, had tampered with some other characters of those ballads.) This curious episode is contained in chapters 22, 23, and the first pages of chapter 24; and various references to it are found in later chapters, with a kind of sequel to the whole affair in chapters 34 and 35 when the Duchess and Duke use the cave adventure, of which Don Quixote has told them, as a foundation for one of the elaborate mystifications of which they make Don Quixote a victim.

The episode of the cave of Montesinos has been called a compromise with reality. As an adventure it is unique in the book since it is a case not

---

course, for which his horse was extremely grateful, being no longer able to stir a single step. To Don Quixote, on the other hand, it seemed as if his enemy was flying, and digging his spurs with all his might into Rocinante's lean flanks he caused that animal to run a bit for the first and only time, according to the history, for on all other occasions a simple trot had represented his utmost speed. And so it was that, with an unheard-of fury, the Knight of the Mournful Countenance came down upon the Knight of the Mirrors as the latter sat there sinking his spurs all the way up to the buttons without being able to persuade his horse to budge a single inch from the spot where he had come to a sudden standstill.

"It was at this fortunate moment, while his adversary was in such a predicament, that Don Quixote fell upon him, quite unmindful of the fact that the other knight was having trouble with his mount and either was unable or did not have time to put his lance at rest. The upshot of it was, he encountered him with such force that, much against his will, the Knight of the Mirrors went rolling over his horse's flanks and tumbled to the ground, where as a result of his terrific fall he lay as if dead, without moving hand or foot." Ed.

only of self-enchantment but of what appears to be deliberate self-enchantment on the part of our striped madman. We are never quite sure whether Don Quixote is or is not aware that he has invented the whole episode,* and the various allusions to his state of mind in this connection are very interesting. Don Quixote decides to investigate a vertical cave, possibly an old mine shaft if we wish to be realistic. The entrance is clogged with brambles and fig trees through which he slashes his way with his sword after having tied a thousand or more feet of rope around his waist. He lets himself down. Sancho and a certain young scholar pay out the rope. They have payed out a couple of hundred feet and then there is silence. Finally Don Quixote is pulled out in a blissful swoon. In chapter 23 he tells of the wonderful adventures that befell him in the cave. Among other marvels, he has seen there Dulcinea, still enchanted, running about with two other peasant girls—apparently a reflected image of the same trio that Sancho had produced in an earlier chapter. She behaves in his dream not like Princess Dulcinea, but as Aldonza the country girl, and indeed Don Quixote is rather flippant about the whole business. In the beginning of chapter 24 the chronicler of his history says that he cannot possibly suppose that Don Quixote had deliberately made up the whole thing and was lying—he who was the most truthful gentleman on earth. The episode adds a bizarre touch to Don Quixote's personality, and commentators have seen in the colored darkness of that cave a series of symbols relating to the very core of the question what is reality, what is truth. However, I am inclined to consider the episode as just another twist that Cervantes gives to the Enchanted Dulcinea theme in order to keep the reader entertained and Don Quixote busy. The problem now is how to disenchant Dulcinea.

* The most overt hint, although even it is ambiguous, comes at the end of chapter 41. Sancho has been elaborating his experiences on the magic horse Clavileño when he peeked under the bandage over his eyes, but when he comes to reaching the Sign of Capricorn and playing with the goats while the horse waited, Don Quixote denies the possibility, for they had not passed through the sphere of fire to reach the heaven of the goats. Sancho indignantly affirms the truth of his story, which amuses the Duke and Duchess, and the chapter ends, "Don Quixote now came up to him, to whisper in his ear. 'Sancho,' he said, 'if you want us to believe what you saw in Heaven, then you must believe me when I tell you what I saw in the Cave of Montesinos. I say no more.' " In chapter 23 Sancho at first flatly declared, on hearing the Don's narrative: "But forgive me, master, if I tell you that God—I was about to say the devil may take me if I believe a word of your Grace's story." However, he stoutly defends his master against lying, by asserting that "Merlin or those enchanters that laid a spell on the whole crew you say you saw and talked with down there have put into your noddle or your memory all this rigmarole that you've been telling us, and all that remains to be told." Don Quixote vigorously denies this, but when he then comes to recognizing Dulcinea and the other two girls among the ladies, "Sancho Panza thought he would lose his mind or die of laughing. Knowing as he did the truth respecting Dulcinea's supposed enchantment, since he himself had been the enchanter and the concoctor of the evidence, he now was convinced beyond a doubt that the knight was out of his senses and wholly mad." Ed.

THE DUCAL ENCHANTMENTS

We now come to the main pair of villainous enchanters in the book, the Duchess and her Duke. The cruelty of the book reaches here atrocious heights. The ducal mystification theme occupies in all twenty-eight chapters and about 200 pages of the second part (chapters 30 to 57), and then an additional couple of chapters (69 and 70) deal with the same theme, after which there are only four chapters or about thirty pages to go to the end of the book. As I shall explain later, it is probable that the break, the gap of eleven chapters between the first set of chapters and the second set, is due to Cervantes having to deal in all haste with an enchanter in his own life, a mysterious writer who published a spurious *Second Volume of Don Quixote* while Cervantes was writing his own second part. The spurious continuation is first mentioned in chapter 59. Then Cervantes throws Don Quixote and Sancho back into the torture house.

So the whole ducal episode takes in all thirty chapters, almost a fourth of the whole work. The ducal theme starts in chapter 30 with Don Quixote and his squire emerging from a wood and seeing in the haze of a sunset a glittering group. Green seems to be the author's favorite color, and the beautiful huntress they now meet is dressed in green and rides a horse caparisoned in green. She has read the first part of the adventures of Don Quixote and she and her husband are anxious to meet its hero and have some good tigerish sport with him. This Diana (a Diabolical Diana, let it be noted at once) and her husband decide that they will humor Don Quixote in every way and that as long as he stays with them they will treat him as a knight-errant, with all the customary ceremonies as described in the books of chivalry; for they have read those books and are very fond of them, in a sleek, chop-licking way.

Don Quixote then rides up with his visor raised, and as he is about to dismount, Sancho comes alongside to hold his stirrup for him; but unfortunately, as he descends from his gray, the squire catches his foot in one of the ropes of his packsaddle in such a manner that he could not get it loose and is left hanging there with his face and chest on the ground—various symbols and parodies of the strappado torture, hoisting and dropping the subject by means of ropes, are liberally scattered through the novel. "Now, Don Quixote was not used to dismounting without his stirrup being held, and, thinking that Sancho was already there to see to it, he threw himself off with a lurch, bringing with him Rocinante's saddle, which must have been poorly fastened, and, as a result, both he and the saddle came tumbling to the earth. Needless to say, he was very much ashamed and could only mutter curses between his teeth at the unfortunate Sancho, who still had his feet in the stocks." Poor Don Quixote ought to have taken this for a warning and an omen; for this is the ominous beginning of a long and cruel series. But "The duke thereupon ordered his huntsmen to assist the knight and squire, and they proceeded to lift Don Quixote, who was greatly shaken by his fall but who nonetheless, limping along as best he could, now came forward to kneel before the noble pair." His hosts are identified by one commentator as real people, the Duke and Duchess of Villahermosa, but this is just an example of the kind of human interest stuff that some Cervantesists delight in. Actually, the Diabolical Diana and her Duke are mere enchanters, invented by the master enchanter, Cervantes, and nothing else.

At the Duke's castle Don Quixote is given a great cloak of sumptuous scarlet cloth. (And I am singularly reminded of Another Martyr who was also given sumptuous clothes and called a King and jeered at by Roman soldiers.) This marvelous welcome greatly astonished Don Quixote; "indeed, it may be said that this was the first time that he really and wholly believed himself to be a true knight-errant and not a fanciful one, for here he was being treated in the very same manner as knights-errant in ages past, according to the storybooks he had read." He discourses at table and the ducal pair, the two smiling tigers, purr and plot.

Now Cervantes starts to weave an interesting pattern. There is going to be a double enchantment, two sets of spells which sometimes meet and mix, and sometimes run different ways. One series of spells are those that are planned in all detail by the ducal pair and more or less faithfully acted out by their servants. But sometimes the servants take the initiative, either to amaze and surprise their masters or because they just cannot fight off the temptation to play with the lean madman and the larded simpleton. At the meeting of the two spells the idiotic Duke and his feral Duchess are sometimes almost as aghast with wonder as if they had not thought up these or similar enchantments themselves. Never forget that the secret flaw in the Devil's might is stupidity. And once or twice the servants go too far and are rebuked and applauded at the same time. And finally the Diabolical Duchess takes an active physical part in the spells as we shall soon see.

The sequence of cruel pranks begins in chapter 32 with a solemn servant maid soaping the docile Don's face. This is the first joke thought up by the servants. Their masters are moved to anger and laughter, not knowing whether to punish the girls' "presumption"* or reward them for the pleasure of seeing Don Quixote in that sorry state, soaped face and all. I suppose our friend, the young student-reader is again convulsed at this point. Then Sancho is tormented by the kitchen boys who try to wash his face in filthy sops, and the Duchess is shown dying with laughter. Thereafter Sancho is mockingly petted by her as a kind of court fool, and the Duke promises him the governorship of an island.

Don Quixote and Sancho had both been wary of spells, but now, without realizing it, they have fallen into the hands of enchanters—the Duke and the Duchess! "Great was the pleasure which the duke and duchess found," says our text, "in the conversation of Don Quixote and Sancho Panza, and being more anxious than ever to play a few jokes upon them that would have all the appearance of adventures," they seized upon the earlier episode in which Don Quixote had explored the deep shaft of a cave and had had a marvelous dream in its depths. The Duchess and Duke now decide to take what the knight had told them concerning this Cave of Montesinos as their starting point in perpetrating a hoax that should be truly out of the ordinary. Notice that whatever spells Sancho had been able to weave are now drowned in the general enchantment; and what tickles the Duchess especially is Sancho's vast simplicity, for he has come to believe that Dulcinea *has* been enchanted though he himself had plotted the whole business, as we know.

And so, a week later, having instructed the servants in everything that was expected of them, they proceed to take Don Quixote on a hunting expedition with as large a retinue of huntsmen and beaters as if he were a king. Sancho comes to grief, but Don Quixote hunts splendidly, attacking a huge boar which he and the others kill. Then comes the next hoax that the Duke and Duchess play on him. There is a kind of haze in the air that is a great help to the Duke and Duchess in carrying out what they have in mind. A little after twilight, just as night is falling, it seems of a sudden as if the entire wood is on fire. (Remember, this is the sunset of Don Quixote's life that illumes everything with a gold-and-green weird glow.) A moment later, here, there, and everywhere, a countless number of trumpets and other martial instruments are heard, as if many troops of cavalry were passing by. Then come innumerable cries of the kind the Moors give when joining battle, mingled with the blare of trumpets and bugles, the roll of drums, creating a furious and continuous din. (I repeat: Note that as often as not the Duke and Duchess are ridiculously aghast at their own

* In a deleted aside, VN remarks, "I like the term 'presumption' in this connection."

inventions either because of improvements by the servants or because they are lunatics in their own right.) In the midst of the general fear, silence falls upon them as a postilion dressed like a demon passes, playing upon a huge hollow horn. When questioned by the Duke, " 'I am the devil,' replied the courier in a horrendous voice. 'I come to see Don Quixote de la Mancha. Those whom you see here are six troops of enchanters who are bringing with them in a triumphal car the peerless Dulcinea del Toboso. She is under a magic spell and is accompanied by the gallant Frenchman, Montesinos. They come to inform Don Quixote as to how she, the said lady, may be disenchanted.' "

Dulcinea shall be restored to Don Quixote if—now comes the rib-splitting joke—if Sancho consents to take 3,000 lashes on his bare behind. Otherwise, says the Duke when he hears of the requirement, you do not get your island. The whole thing is very medieval, coarse, and stupid fun, as all fun that comes from the devil. Authentic humor comes from the angels. "The duke and duchess now returned to their castle with the object of following up the jest which had thus been begun, as there was no serious occupation that gave them greater pleasure than this." This is the gist of all these ducal chapters—chop-licking satisfaction with a joke and the immediate planning of another just as brutal.

I shall not stop at the episode of the Distressed Duenna (chapters 36-41) beyond saying that two lovers, according to her story, were transformed into an ape and a crocodile by an enchanter Malambruno, and "These two rash lovers shall not regain their former shape until the valiant Manchegan shall come to meet me [Malambruno] in singlehanded encounter, since it is for his great valor alone that the fates have reserved this unheard-of adventure." There is the description of the Flying Horse that will carry Don Quixote to the remote kingdom of Candaya where those lovers are. "This steed is guided by means of a peg that he has in his forehead, which serves as a bridle, and he goes through the air at such a speed that it seems as if the very devils themselves must be carrying him.

". . . Malambruno, through his arts, contrived to get possession of him and employs him in the journeys which he is all the time making here and there throughout the world. He is here today and tomorrow in France, and the next day in Potosí and the best of it is, this horse neither eats nor sleeps nor does he have to be shod. Without wings, he ambles through the air so smoothly that his rider can carry a cup full of water in his hand without spilling a single drop. . . ." This is an old theme. Similar flying machines are found in the *Arabian Nights*, also with a guiding peg in the neck.

The Distressed Duenna and her other female servants have also been enchanted and have magically grown beards, and they will be unbearded if Don Quixote is successful in disenchanting the lovers. The theme of the beard plays a curious part in the book (recall the washing of the beards in the beginning of the ducal episode) and it seems to have started from the initial allusions to shaving in part one—all that concern with barbers and with Don Quixote's helmet which was a barber's basin.

The wooden horse Clavileño is brought out, Don Quixote and Sancho (the latter under protest) mount and are blindfolded. "The knight tried the peg, and no sooner had he laid hands upon it than the duennas and all the others there present began calling out to them, 'God guide you, valiant knight! God be with you, intrepid squire! Now, now, you are going through the air, swifter than a dart! Already those below are gazing up at you in astonishment!' " Don Quixote and Sancho converse as they think they fly through the air, although actually their mount stands motionless on the ground. The knight admonishes Sancho: " 'Do not squeeze me so much or you will throw me off. There is really no reason for you to be disturbed or frightened, for I can swear that in all the days of my life I never had an easier-going mount. It is as if we never stirred from one spot. Banish all fear, my friend, for the truth is, everything is going as it should and we have the wind to our poop.'

" 'So we do,' replied Sancho. 'On this side, it's as strong as if they were blowing on me with a thousand pairs of bellows.'

"This was the truth, for a number of large bellows were producing the breeze in question. The whole adventure had been so thoroughly planned by the duke and duchess and their major-domo that not a single essential detail was lacking to make it perfect.

" 'Without any doubt, Sancho,' remarked Don Quixote as he felt the puff, 'we must have reached the second aerial region, where the snow and hail are produced; it is in the third region that the thunder and lightning are engendered, and if we keep on ascending at this rate, we shall soon be in the region of fire. I do not know how to control the peg to keep us from mounting so high that the flames will scorch us.'

"Even as he said this they felt a warmth upon their faces, which came from pieces of tow, easy to ignite and to extinguish, suspended from the end of a reed held at some distance from them. . . .

"The entire conversation of the two brave horsemen was heard by the duke and duchess, who were extremely amused by it; and, wishing to put a finishing touch to this extraordinary and well-planned adventure, they now set fire to Clavileño's tail with some bits of tow, whereupon the horse, which was filled with detonating rockets, at once blew up with a loud noise, hurling Don Quixote and Sancho Panza to the ground half-scorched." It is then announced that merely by undertaking the adventure, Don Quixote has satisfied the requirements, and Malambruno has released the pair of lovers, and the bearded duennas, from his spell on orders from Merlin. Idiotic—the whole affair. In a word, the ducal castle is a kind of laboratory where two poor souls, Don Quixote and Sancho, are vivisected.

In chapter 42 "The duke and duchess were so well pleased with the successful and amusing outcome of the adventure of the Distressed One that they made up their minds to continue with the jest, seeing what a suitable subject they had when it came to accepting the imaginary for the real. Accordingly, having instructed their servants and vassals as to how to behave toward Sancho in the government of his promised island, they informed the squire the next day . . . that he was to make ready to go and assume his gubernatorial duties, as his islanders were waiting for him as for the showers of May." Don Quixote advises Sancho as to how to conduct himself in office. His directions are quite commonplace, and are modeled on similar noble and wise instructions in ancient books; but it is curious to contrast the mercy he speaks of in his advice on how to govern* with the merciless behavior of his tormentors. Sancho enters upon his governorship, a village of about a thousand inhabitants, one of the best in the Duke's domain, with a wall around it. Relying on his good memory, he proves himself to be quite a Solomon in his judgments.

* Don Quixote begins his advice thus: "Sancho, my friend, I thank Heaven with all my heart that good Fortune should have come your way before I have met with her. I had counted upon my luck to enable me to pay you for your services, but here am I at the beginning of my adventures while you, ahead of time and contrary to all reasonable expectation, are seeing your desires fulfilled. . . . You to my mind are beyond any doubt a blockhead, you neither rise with the sun nor keep nightly vigil, you are not industrious, and yet, as a result of the mere breath of knight-errantry that has been breathed upon you, you find yourself without more ado the governor of an island, as if it were nothing at all.

"I say all this, Sancho, in order that you may not attribute to your own merits the favor you have received. Rather, you should give thanks to Heaven for its beneficence, and, after that, to the great profession of knight-errantry for the potentialities inherent in it. Having, then, disposed your heart to believe what I have said to you, be attentive, my son, to this your Cato, who would counsel you and be the guiding star that leads you to a safe harbor as you set forth upon the storm-tossed sea that is now about to engulf you; for office and high trusts are nothing other than a deep abyss of trouble and confusion. . . .

" . . . Never be guided by arbitrary law, which finds favor only with the ignorant who plume themselves on their cleverness. Let the tears of the poor find more compassion in you, but not more justice, than the testimony of the rich. Seek to uncover the truth amid the promises and gifts of the man of wealth as amid the sobs and pleadings of the poverty-stricken. When it is a question of equity, do not bring all the rigor of the law to bear upon the delinquent, for the fame of the stern judge is no greater than that of the merciful one. If the rod of justice is to be bent, let it not be by the weight of a gift but by that of mercy. . . .

"When a guilty man comes under your jurisdiction, remember that he is but a wretched creature, subject to the inclinations of our depraved human nature, and insofar as you may be able to do so without wrong to the other side, show yourself clement and merciful; for while the attributes of God are all equal, that of mercy shines brighter in our eyes than does that of justice." Ed.

I shall divert for a moment the current of my study of the ducal enchantments to direct your attention to a point of great art. I think Cervantes felt that he was taking the line of least resistance—and suddenly the story develops a very special pair of very special wings. Art has a way of transcending the boundaries of reason. I wish to submit the following point: this novel would have died of the laughter its picaresque plot was meant to provoke had it not contained episodes and passages that gently usher or sweep the reader into the dreamworld of permanent and irrational art. So—in part two, around chapter 40 of the book, Sancho at last gets his island. Chapters 42 and 43 treat of the advice that Don Quixote gives Sancho before the latter sets out to govern his island. Well does Don Quixote know how inferior the squire is to him, but his inferior is successful; he, the master, is not only denied his ultimate dream, the disenchantment of Dulcinea, but he has entered upon a strange decline. He knows fear. He knows the gloom of poverty. While plump Sancho is getting his rich island, lean Quixote is still in the same situation as he was when he started on the long and—in retrospect—dreary and inept sequence of his adventures. The main, if not the only, interest of his instructions to Sancho (as a fine Spanish commentator Madariaga has suggested to me) is that these instructions are but a means of raising himself in his own esteem above his successful inferior (p. 153).

Don Quixote, it should be borne in mind, is the maker of his own glory, the only begetter of these marvels; and within his soul he carries the most dread enemy of the visionary: the snake of doubt, the coiled consciousness that his quest is an illusion. There is something in the tone of those instructions of his to Sancho that evokes in one the image of an elderly, seedy, obscure poet, who has never been successful in anything, giving to his sturdy, popular, extravert son a sound bit of advice as to how to be a prosperous plumber or politician. In chapter 44, which is the chapter I had in view when I alluded to the artistic dream element in the book, Sancho has been taken away to be governor and Don Quixote is left alone in that horrible ducal castle, a reality in comparison to his fancy, a castle where every turret conceals a claw, where every crenation is a fang. Reality out-Quixotes Quixote: Sancho is gone, and Don Quixote is strangely alone. There is a sudden lull, a melancholy and deep pause. Oh—I know, Cervantes makes haste to tell the reader, the ruder kind of reader—yes, reader, the funny fat squire, your favorite clown, has gone but "Meanwhile, listen to what happened to his master that same night, and if it does not make you laugh, it will at least cause you to part your lips in an apelike grin; for Don Quixote's adventures are to be greeted either with astonishment or with mirth." As a matter of fact, the anthropoid reader is apt to skip the all-important passage that I am now coming to, and is apt to skip it in order to get quickly to the so-called sidesplitting but in reality atrocious and brutal and fundamentally foolish episode of the cats.*

Sancho has gone and Don Quixote is strangely alone and suddenly feels himself permeated with a strange sense of loneliness and yearning, something more than merely a sense of solitude, a kind of purposeless nostalgic longing. He retires to his room, declines any servant to enter, and having locked the door proceeds to undress by the light of two wax candles. He is alone but the curtains are, as it were, not drawn over the window of the story and we see through the window bars the gleam of the bright green stockings he is slowly shedding and studying—just as in reading another famous story, where the grotesque and the lyrical are somewhat similarly interwoven, Gogol's *Dead Souls*, we shall glimpse in the middle of the night a bright window and the glossy leather of a pair of new boots that a dreaming lodger admires without end.

But Don Quixote's stockings are anything but new. O disaster, the narrator sighs as he contemplates the bursting of several stitches in the left stocking which now has the appearance of a piece of lattice work. The wretched sense of poverty** mingles with his general dejection and he finally goes to bed, moody and heavy-hearted. Is it only Sancho's absence and the burst threads of his stockings that induce this sadness, this Spanish *soledad*, this Portuguese *saudades*, this French *angoisse*, this German *sehnsucht*, this Russian *toska*? We wonder—we wonder if it does not go deeper. Remember that Sancho, his squire, is the crutch of Quixote's madness, the prop of his delusion, and now Don Quixote is strangely alone. He puts out the candles, but it is a very warm night and he cannot sleep. Rising from his bed Don Quixote partly opens the grated window and looks out on a moon-charmed garden and becomes aware of feminine

* VN adds the comment: "It is a great pity that in the abridged translation in the Viking Portable Cervantes, this and other important passages are omitted. I warn you against all abridgements."

** At this point Cervantes interjects a passionate apostrophe by Cid Hamete Benengeli, the supposed narrator of the history: "O poverty! poverty! I know not what could have led that great Cordovan poet to call thee a 'holy, unappreciated gift.' . . . Why dost thou love to dog the steps of gentlemen and the wellborn rather than those of other folk? Why dost thou oblige them to go with patched shoes, while some of the buttons on their doublets are of silk, others of hair, and others still of glass? Why must their ruffs be all wrinkled instead of being properly crimped with an iron? . . .

" . . . Poor wretch, I say, so worried about his honor that he fancies the patch on his shoe can be seen a league away and who is concerned over the sweat stains on his hat, his threadbare cloak, and his empty stomach, imagining that they must all be equally visible!" Don Quixote, Benengeli continues, "was led to reflect on all this as he surveyed the burst threads in his stockings. . . . which he would even have been willing to patch with thread of another color, one of the greatest signs of poverty that a gentleman can exhibit in the course of his long-drawn-out and threadbare existence." Ed.

voices conversing—especially the voice of Altisidora, the Duchess's maid, a young girl, a child, who in the scheme of atrocious cruelty governing this and other scenes, poses as a lovelorn maiden passionately attached to La Mancha's bravest knight.

As he stands at the grated window, there comes the sound of a string instrument gently plucked; whereupon Don Quixote is deeply moved. His yearning, his loneliness, are resolved now in that twang of music, in that twinge of beauty. The inward hint, the veiled suspicion that Dulcinea may not exist at all, is now brought to light by contrast with a real melody, with a real voice; the real voice deceives him, of course, as much as his dream of Dulcinea does—but at least it belongs to a real damsel, and a charming one, and not to Maritornes, the homely whore of part one. He is deeply moved because at that moment all the innumerable adventures of a like sort—barred windows, gardens, music, and lovemaking—all he has read of in those now strangely true books of chivalry—come back to him with a new impact, his dreams mingling with reality, his dreams fertilizing reality. And the voice of the little damsel Altisidora (with the rolling R of Reality) so close at hand, in the garden, becomes for a moment, physically and mentally, more vivid than the vision of Dulcinea del Toboso, with all those limp, lisping l's of lean illusion. But his innate modesty, his purity, the glorious chastity of a true knight-errant, all this proves stronger than his manly senses—and after listening to the song in the garden he bangs the window shut, and now even more gloomy than before—"as if," says Cervantes, "some dire misfortune had befallen him," he goes to bed, leaving the garden to the fireflies and to the moaning girl-music and leaving the rich island to his ruddy squire.

This is an admirable scene—one of those scenes that pander to the imagination and deliver more than they seem to contain: dreamy, longing, gaunt, with those threadbare emerald stockings of his that lie crumpled on the floor, and the grated window, now shut, and the warm Spanish night that henceforth for three centuries is to become the breeding place of romantic prose-and-verse in all languages, and fifty-year-old Quixote fighting one delusion by means of another delusion—melancholy, miserable, tempted, excited by little Altisidora's musical moans.

Back to the torture house. The next night Don Quixote asks for a lute and sings a song he has composed that is intended to discourage Altisidora by his fidelity to Dulcinea "when suddenly from a gallery directly above his window they let down a rope to which were attached more than a hundred bells, and then they emptied a large bag filled with cats that had bells of a smaller size fastened to their tails. And so great was the din of the bells and so loud the squalling of the felines that even though the duke and duchess were the ones who had thought up the joke, they still were startled by it all. As for Don Quixote, he was quaking with fear. As luck would have it, two or three of the cats came in through the window of his room, darting from side to side, and it was as though a legion of devils had been let loose there. As they ran about seeking a means of escape, they put out the candles that were burning in the chamber. . . .

"Getting to his feet, Don Quixote drew his sword and started slashing at the window grating as he shouted, 'Away with you, malign enchanters! Out with you, witching rabble! Know that I am Don Quixote de la Mancha, against whom your evil intentions are of no avail!'

"Turning on the cats that were rushing around the room, [Don Quixote] made many thrusts at them, but they dashed for the window and leaped out—all except one, which, finding itself thus belabored by Don Quixote's sword, sprang at his face and seized his nose with its claws and teeth, causing him to cry out with pain at the top of his voice. When they heard this, the duke and duchess, who suspected what the trouble was, ran to his room and opened the door with their master key, only to behold the poor knight struggling with all the strength that he had to pull the cat away from his face.

" . . . The cat, however, only growled and held on; but the duke finally pulled it off and tossed it out the window. Don Quixote's face was perforated like a sieve and his nose was not in very good shape; yet for all of that, he was very much displeased that they had not permitted him to finish the hard-fought battle with that scoundrelly enchanter." In still another session with his torturers, when Doña Rodríguez seeks his help to redress the wrongs done to her daughter, in the tumult in the darkness that follows he is pinched by the Duchess herself.

Meanwhile, Sancho governs his island wisely until his stage-enemies invade the town, the culminating trick that is going to be played on the unfortunate Sancho. Mark that the Duke and Duchess are not present at the torture, but derive all necessary pleasure from the account that is given them later. The supposed defenders of the town call on Sancho to arm himself and lead them. Frightened as he is, "Arm me, then, for Heaven's sake," said Sancho. Two large shields are tied with rope, one in front of and the other behind him so that he cannot bend or move, and he is told to lead the villagers. Then a battle is staged, which consists of everybody trampling him as he lies helpless on the floor. He faints when they finally unbind him. When he comes to himself, he asks what time it is and is told that it is already daylight, and they have been victorious. Without saying another word, he starts to dress himself amid profound silence as they all watch and wait to see why he should be in such a hurry to put his clothes on. This silence reminds one of young school bullies who have been tormenting a fat weak boy, and now in silence Sancho gets up, wipes his face. Then, too sore to walk fast, he slowly makes his way to the stable, followed by all those present. There he embraced his gray, talked to him tenderly, adjusted the packsaddle, without a word from any of the bystanders. Then with great pain and difficulty he climbed upon the gray's back and spoke to them: "Clear the way, gentlemen, and let me go back to my old freedom. Let me go look for my past life so that I may be resurrected from this present death"—an almost Proustian note. In this one scene Sancho reveals a dignity and a slow sadness comparable to the melancholy emotions of his master.

Chapter 57 begins: "By now Don Quixote had come to feel that it would be well for him to quit a life of idleness such as he was leading in the castle; for he believed he was doing a great wrong in depriving the outside world of his presence, by keeping himself shut up like this, and leisurely enjoying all the innumerable comforts and luxuries with which my lord and lady surrounded him as a knight-errant. It seemed to him that he would have to give an accounting to Heaven for this sloth and seclusion; and so it was that one day he begged permission of the ducal pair to take his leave. They granted his request, at the same time showing how very sorry they were to have him go." Some adventures on the road to Barcelona involve him with the great brigand Roque Guinart, who makes arrangements to pass the Don and Sancho on to friends in Barcelona who can have sport with them. They are met by Roque's friend Don Antonio Moreno; and as they are entering the city with him some small boys, forcing their way through the crowd, lift up the tails of Rocinante and the gray and insert a bunch of furze (a prickly plant). The animals begin leaping and rearing and toss their riders to the ground. Those will laugh at this who just love bucking horses in commercial rodeos—bucking nags fitted with special corrosive belly straps.

In Barcelona, another kindly enchanter takes care of Don Quixote. Don Antonio was "a gentleman of wealth and discernment who was fond of amusing himself in an innocent and kindly way. Having taken the knight into his house, he began casting about for some harmless means of bringing out his mad traits." The first thing he does, accordingly, is to have Don Quixote remove his armor, which leaves him clad only in his tight-fitting chamois doublet, after which he leads him out onto the balcony overlooking the city in order that the people gathered there, including the small boys, may have a look at him. And there Don Quixote stands, an ignoble show, with the boys gaping at his gaunt and melancholy figure—lacking only a crown of thorns. That afternoon they take him out riding in such a heavy greatcoat "which at that season of the year would have made ice itself sweat." On the back of it they sewed a piece of parchment with an inscription in large letters "This is the king—" sorry—"THIS IS DON QUIXOTE DE LA MANCHA." "From the moment they set out, the placard attracted the attention of all those who had come to behold the spectacle, and the knight for his part was astonished to find so many people gazing at him and calling him by name. Turning to Don Antonio, who rode alongside him, he said, 'Great are the prerogatives of knight-errantry, seeing that it makes the one who follows that calling known and famous in all parts of the earth. If you do not believe me, Señor Don Antonio, your Grace has but to observe the lads of this city, who, though they have never seen me, nevertheless recognize me.'"

Afterward, at a party, the clumsy and tired Don Quixote is made to dance by two mischievous ladies, and finally, exhausted and depressed, amid screams of mirth he sits down in the middle of the ballroom floor, and kindly Don Antonio, seeing no further fun can be squeezed out of the martyr, has his servants carry him off to bed.

But the Duke and Duchess are not through with Don Quixote and Sancho. In chapter 68 armed horsemen are sent out to bring them back for some more fun. They discover the dejected pair on a country road, and with threats and imprecations they carry the pair to a castle which the knight recognizes as the Duke's. The horsemen dismount, pick up Don Quixote and Sancho bodily, and carry them into a courtyard. "There nearly a hundred torches, fixed in their sockets, were flaring, while the adjoining galleries were illuminated by more than five hundred lamps. . . . In the middle of the courtyard a funeral mound about two yards high had been reared, completely covered by an enormous black velvet canopy, and on the steps leading up to it more than a hundred white wax tapers in silver candlesticks were shedding their glow. Upon this catafalque lay the lifeless body of a maiden, so lovely as to make even death itself seem beautiful. Her head rested upon a brocade pillow and was crowned with a plaited garland of sweet-smelling flowers of various sorts; her hands were folded over her bosom and between them was a bough of the yellow palm of victory." It is Altisidora, disguised as a dead or sleeping beauty.

After much pageantry, a song, and speeches by characters representing Rhadamanthus and Minos, it is revealed that Altisidora can be released from the enchantment and brought to life only if Sancho's face is slapped and pinched. Despite his protests, six duennas of the household march in, and on Don Quixote's request Sancho allows himself to be smacked in the face by the duennas and various members of the household, "but the thing he could not stand was the pinpricks. When it came to that, he rose from his chair with a show of anger and, seizing a lighted torch that stood near by, began laying about him among the duennas and all his other tormentors, crying, 'Away with you, ministers of Hell! I am not made of brass so that I do not feel such unusual torture as this!'

"Then it was that Altisidora, who must have been tired of lying on her back for so long a time, turned over on her side, beholding which, all the bystanders shouted, with one voice as it were, 'Altisidora is alive! Altisidora lives!' And Rhadamanthus commanded Sancho to forego his wrath, seeing that their purpose had now been achieved." As the knight and Sancho are sleeping that night, Cervantes remarks, behind the silk mask of his Arabic historian Cid Hamete, "it is his personal opinion that the jesters were as crazy as their victims and that the duke and duchess were not two fingers' breadth removed from being fools when they went to so much trouble to make sport of the foolish." The episode just related has for its chapter 69 heading, "Of the strangest and most extraordinary adventure that has befallen Don Quixote in the entire course of this great history." One is under the impression that the author thinks that the more pageantry there is on the stage, the more supers, costumes, lights, kings, queens, et cetera, the greater the adventure will seem to the reader (as to today's moviegoer).

There is one last deception. Sancho by lashing at trees in the dark makes his master believe that he is giving himself the flogging that will disenchant Dulcinea—that in fact the necessary number of lashes has been administered and that somewhere in the mist Dulcinea is now actually being disenchanted. A star, a flushed sky, a growing sense of victory, of achievement. I would like you to note that this flogging of the beech trees is performed by means of the same donkey's halter that was used for two previous enchantments—the spell Sancho cast on Rocinante in the episode in part one, chapter 20, just before the adventure of the fulling mills, and the suspension in chapter 43 of Don Quixote at the inn window by the servant girl Maritornes.

The Chroniclers Theme, Dulcinea, and Death

THE CHRONICLERS THEME

As you remember, I earlier listed ten points or devices in relation to the structure of our book. Some of these devices, such as the use Cervantes makes of quotations from ballads, popular sayings, or his play on words, could only be mentioned in passing since we are unable to palpate the original text through the alien layers of translation—no matter how good. We stopped for a couple of minutes at some other points, such as the excellent art of the dialogue in the book and the pseudo-poetical conventional manner of its descriptions of nature. I drew your attention to the fact that in the evolution of literature the personalization of sensual environment lagged behind the personalization of human talk. In somewhat greater detail I discussed the inset stories and the Arcadian theme, drawing your attention to the multiplication of narrative levels and to some primitive forms of character grouping in a given place. The theme of chivalry books occupied us for some time, and I tried to show that the grotesque element found in *Don Quixote* is not foreign to romances of chivalry that he read.

Next came a rather detailed discussion of the mystification theme, during which I stressed the elements of cruelty in the book. It seemed to me that in our brutal day, when one of the few things that may save our world is Freedom from Pain, the complete and permanent outlawing of any kind of cruelty, it seemed to me that under these circumstances I was justified in drawing your attention to the cruelty of the so-called fun in our book. I pointed out the fact that to consider our bitter and barbarous book as a sample of the humane and the humorous is an attitude and a judgment that are not sound. I have just now attempted to bring out the only thing that really matters in this business of literature—the mysterious thrill of art, the impact of aesthetic bliss. There remains one point of device in our list of structural items that has to be tackled today—this is what I called the chroniclers theme.

In the first eight chapters of the first part Cervantes pretends to be a reviser working on some anonymous chronicle, the work of some "wise magician" as Don Quixote calls him, "whoever you be," the Don continues, "to whom shall fall the task of chronicling this extraordinary history of mine!" At the end of chapter 8 Don Quixote attacks the squire of a lady, a Biscayan whom we see with uplifted sword ready to parry Don Quixote's blow. Unfortunately, says Cervantes, we shall have to leave them in this position because the anonymous text ends here and I have been unable to find anything else concerning the exploits of Don Quixote.

This device of breaking the story off at a crucial moment is of course quite common in romances of chivalry, which Cervantes is imitating. So let us mark that chronicler number one is an anonymous historian.

In chapter 9 Cervantes plays the part of a bothered compiler who must now undertake his own research. "It appeared impossible and contrary to all good precedent," he says, "that so worthy a knight should not have had some scribe to take upon himself the task of writing an account of these unheard-of exploits; for that was something that had happened to none of the knights-errant who, as the saying has it, had gone forth in quest of adventures, seeing that each of them had one or two chroniclers, as if ready at hand, who not only had set down their deeds, but had depicted their most trivial thoughts and amiable weaknesses, however well concealed they might be. The good knight of La Mancha surely could not have been so unfortunate as to have lacked what Platir and others like him had in abundance . . . and . . . even though it might not have been written down, it must remain in the memory of the good folk of his village and the surrounding ones. This thought left me somewhat confused and more than ever desirous of knowing the real and true story, the whole story, of the life and wondrous deeds of our famous Spaniard, Don Quixote, light and mirror of the chivalry of La Mancha, the first in our age and in these calamitous times to devote himself to the hardships and exercises of knight-errantry and to go about righting wrongs, succoring widows, and protecting damsels. . . .

" If I speak of these things, it is for the reason that in this and in all other respects our gallant Quixote is deserving of constant memory and praise, and even I am not to be denied my share of it for my diligence and the labor to which I put myself in searching out the conclusion of this agreeable narrative."

Cervantes pretends that chance helped him and that in the marketplace of Toledo he came across an Arabic manuscript in several books or bundles. The author is a Morisco, a Spanish Moor, whom Cervantes invents from toe to turban, Cid Hamete Benengeli, Arab Historian as he describes himself on the title page. Through this silk mask Cervantes will speak. A Spanish-speaking Moor, he says, translated the whole manuscript for him into Castilian in little more than a month and a half. This again is a common device—the discovered manuscript—which will stay with writers well into the nineteenth century. There is, says Cervantes, a picture in the beginning of the manuscript illustrating the battle between Don Quixote and the Biscayan—depicting them precisely as described at the end of chapter 8, their swords upraised, et cetera. Mark how neatly the description of the attitudes in which they froze at the breaking point is now made into a picture. Whereupon the story is picked up again, the picture becomes alive, the fight goes on—like those movies of football games stopping and then again coming into motion.

This carefree playing with slick devices must have been little in keeping with Cervantes's actual mood in 1603 or 1604. He was working furiously, without rereading or planning. Poverty prodded the writing of the first part. Poverty and exasperation engendered the second part produced ten years later, for during the writing of this second part Cervantes had to cope with an enchanter in real life as cruel as any he had invented to torment his invented hero and more alive than the grave, eloquent, and meticulous historian he invented to record the exploits of his invented hero; but let us not anticipate. So in part one we have, not counting Cervantes himself, two historians, the anonymous one of the first eight chapters and Cid Hamete Benengeli of the rest of the book.

Cervantes also protects himself, as later authors were to do, by appeals to the authority of the history that he had had translated and to the fact that its Moorish author was a guarantee against hyperbole applied to a Spanish hero: "If there is any objection to be raised against the veracity of the present [story], it can be only that the author was an Arab, and that nation is known for its lying propensities; but even though they be our enemies, it may readily be understood that they would more likely have detracted from, rather than added to, the chronicle. So it seems to me, at any rate; for whenever he might and should deploy the resources of his pen in praise of so worthy a knight, the author appears to take pains to pass over the matter in silence; all of which in my opinion is ill done and ill conceived, for it should be the duty of historians to be exact, truthful, and dispassionate, and neither interest nor fear nor rancor nor affection should swerve them from the path of truth, whose mother is history, rival of time, depository of deeds, witness of the past, exemplar and adviser to the present, and the future's counselor. In this work, I am sure, will be found all that could be desired in the way of pleasant reading; and if it is lacking in any way, I maintain that this is the fault of that hound of an author rather than of the subject."

In the second part yet another device is introduced. A new character, Sansón Carrasco, a Bachelor of Arts, informs Don Quixote that although only a month has elapsed since his return from his wanderings (Cervantes never bothers about such discrepancies, explaining them away by alluding to magic), the story of Don Quixote's adventures, that is, our first part, set down by Benengeli and revised by Cervantes, has been published and is widely read. Very amusing is the discussion of various faults that, according to Carrasco, readers find with the book. I have no time to go into this but remark only that Cervantes does his best to deal with the inexplicable problem of whether Sancho did or did not have his ass stolen in the Sierra Morena. Don Quixote's reactions to all this should be carefully noted.

Now, very early in part two, in chapter 14, Carrasco disguised as the Knight of the Mirrors (reflections, and reflections of reflections, shimmer through the book)—sly disguised Carrasco declares in the presence of our Don Quixote: "Finally, she [his lady, Casildea de Vandalia] commanded me to ride through all the provinces of Spain and compel all the knights-errant whom I met with to confess that she is the most beautiful woman now living and that I am the most enamored man of arms that is to be found anywhere in the world. In fulfillment of this behest I have already traveled over the greater part of these realms and have vanquished many knights who have dared to contradict me. But the one whom I am proudest to have overcome in single combat is that famous gentleman, Don Quixote de la Mancha; for I made him confess that my Casildea is more beautiful than his Dulcinea, and by achieving such a conquest I reckon that I have conquered all the others on the face of the earth, seeing that this same Don Quixote had himself routed them. Accordingly, when I vanquished him, his fame, glory, and honor passed over and were transferred to my person. . . . Thus, the innumerable exploits of the said Don Quixote are now set down to my account and are indeed my own." In fact, he might have added, since a knight's glory is his identity, I *am* Don Quixote. Thus the fight that our real Don Quixote has with this reflected Don Quixote is, in a way, a fight with his own shadow; and in this first fight with Carrasco, our man wins.

Now a very curious thing is going to happen. While Cervantes is inventing enchanters who supposedly have written his book and while Don Quixote within the book is clashing with enchanters stemming from romances of chivalry, Cervantes—the real author—is suddenly confronted by an enchanter on the level of so-called real life. And he will use this circumstance as a special device to amuse the reader.

Cervantes invented his Arabic historian. So-called "real life" produced an arrogant Aragonese who stole our knight-errant. While Cervantes was still working at the second part of Don Quixote's adventures, which were to be published (after some delay) in 1615, a spurious "Second Part" was printed at Tarragona in northern Spain and was put on the market probably at the moment when the ten-year copyright that Cervantes had on his first part had expired, that is, on the 26th of September 1614. The author of this spurious continuation signed it with the name "Alonso Fernandez de Avellaneda," almost certainly a pseudonym, and the problem of his identity remains unsolved. What Cervantes says of him in the preface to his own second part and elsewhere in it, and also internal evidence, tends to show that the person was a middle-aged Aragonese (born at Tordesillas), a professional writer, with a more intimate knowledge of church matters (especially pertaining to the Dominican order) than Cervantes had, as well as being a fervent and jealous admirer of playwright Lope de Vega (who had disapproved of *Don Quixote* before it had been officially published), at whom Cervantes had taken one or two vicious digs in his first part. A number of names have been suggested. I shall not discuss them. It remains anybody's guess. Generations of Cervantesists have tried to find Avellaneda's real name anagrammatically or acrostically hidden in the first lines of the spurious *Don Quixote*. Let me drop the dark hint that a great-grandmother of Cervantes was called Juana Avellaneda, and that some have contended that the fake *Don Quixote* was composed by Cervantes himself for the express purpose of having at hand a new device in the second part that he signed—his own people meeting people belonging to the Avellaneda book. I repeat, nobody knows who Avellaneda really was, and his style is different from that of Cervantes, being less ample, more pointed, with briefer descriptions.

In Avellaneda's continuation, Don Quixote—a cheap, cardboard Don Quixote, lacking completely the dreamy charm and the pathos of the original gentleman—sets out for Saragossa to participate in an armored tourney there. He is accompanied by a rather good Sancho. It should be recalled that at the end of part one, the real Don Quixote is said to have gone to Saragossa after the adventures depicted in the book. And Cervantes in his second part has his hero set out north for Saragossa and travel along that road until he hears some people at an inn discussing the spurious Don Quixote and his adventures at Saragossa, upon hearing which Don Quixote contemptuously decides to go to Barcelona instead so as not to coincide with the phantom crook. Another detail: In the spurious continuation, Don Quixote falls out of love with Dulcinea and transfers his platonic adoration to the monstrous Queen Zenobia. She was a tripe-woman, sold sausages, had a cookshop—Bárbara Villalobos, a huge female, blear-eyed, blubber-lipped, with a scar on her cheek, aged fifty.

The ducal theme of the real second part is curiously echoed in Avellaneda's continuation—I suppose that kind of coincidence depends on a literary convention—but we do have in Avellaneda's book a similar grandee Don Álvaro, who, like the Duke and Duchess, uses Don Quixote to have sport with him. But on the whole Avellaneda's attitude is kinder, more humane, than that of Cervantes. It is not true that—as the more ardent lovers of Cervantes say—Avellaneda's book is absolutely without value. On the contrary it has a brisk racy way about it and there are a number of passages in no way inferior to some of the slapstick scenes in our book.*

How will Cervantes end the series of Don Quixote's adventures? There is one encounter that is sure to come, one man that our man is sure to meet. In drama this is called *la scène à faire*, the scene that must come.

Throughout the authentic second part the reader is uneasily aware that the bachelor Carrasco, somewhere behind the scenes, is steadily recovering from the bad cropper he came in his first encounter with Don Quixote and is anxious to meet him again. Whatever happens to Don Quixote, on the road, in the magic cave, in the ducal castle, or at Barcelona, Don Quixote is, so to speak—I am going to use an ugly word—on probation. It is but a respite, and at any moment Carrasco, in some brilliant, tinkling, and flashing disguise may bar Don Quixote's road and clout and clown him to his doom. And this is exactly what happens. In chapter 64 Don Quixote is challenged again by Carrasco, the former Knight of the Mirrors, now in a new disguise and calling himself the Knight of the White Moon. He is moved by two conflicting forces: one evil, the thirst for revenge; the other

* On the other hand, on an early trial page, later marked for omission, VN noted Sancho's desertion of his master for a rich lord who pays and feeds him well, while Don Quixote is tricked by Don Álvaro in quest of enemies to conquer into ending his knight-errantry in a Toledo lunatic asylum: "He was kept there, was cured, left the asylum, soon was mad again, and traveled all over Old Castile finding many fantastic adventures. Instead of Sancho he took a pregnant woman disguised as a man for his squire. He was very much surprised when a child was born to her. After leaving her at an inn in good hands, he set off on new adventures, taking the name of Knight of the Tribulations (Caballero de los Trabajos). This is the last page of Avellaneda's book—and no wonder Cervantes put his foot down and decided to kill his hero rather than to have him running all over Spain under false colors with pregnant squires. Avellaneda is responsible, in a way, for our man's death."

good, his initial intention to force Don Quixote to quit, to go home like a good boy and not meddle with knight-errantry for at least a year or until he is cured of his madness.

Now follow me closely. Let us give free rein to our own fancy, driven to a pleasant frenzy by reading too much of Don Quixote's adventures. It seems to me, then, that Cervantes when he arrives at the scene of that final duel misses the point that he has almost made. It seems to me that here he had before him, prepared and set up by his own efforts, a climax that would have been in keeping with the mirrory quality of the disguised Carrasco, Knight of the moonlike Mirrors.* Let me remind you that Carrasco in the beginning of the second part, in chapter 14, at his first hostile meeting with Don Quixote had alluded to his having become Don Quixote by conquering another Don Quixote. What other Don Quixote? Carrasco seems to identify himself with a spurious Don Quixote. It seems to me that the chance Cervantes missed was to have followed up the hint he had dropped himself and to have made Don Quixote meet in battle, in a final scene, not Carrasco but the fake Don Quixote of Avellaneda. All along we have been meeting people who were personally acquainted with the false Don Quixote. We are as ready for the appearance of the false Don Quixote as we are for that of Dulcinea. We are eager for Avellaneda to produce his man. How splendid it would have been if instead of that hasty and vague last encounter with the disguised Carrasco, who tumbles our knight in a jiffy, the real Don Quixote had fought his crucial battle with the false Don Quixote! In that imagined battle who would have been victor—the fantastic, lovable madman of genius, or the fraud, the symbol of robust mediocrity? My money is on Avellaneda's man, because the beauty of it is that, in life, mediocrity is more fortunate than genius. In life it is the fraud that unhorses true valor. And since I am daydreaming, let me add that I bear a grudge to the fate of books; writing under another name a pretended, a spurious, continuation in order to intrigue the reader of the authentic one would have been a little moonburst of artistic technique. Avellaneda himself should have turned out to be, in a disguise of mirrors, Cervantes.

DULCINEA

At this point let us sum up what we know of Dulcinea del Toboso. We

* In the phrase "Knight of the moonlike Mirrors" (as in VN's manuscript) "moonlike" is a later addition, and the sentence originally ran, "Knight of the Mirrors and now Knight of the Polished Moon, a magician's mirror if you know what I mean."

know that the name is Don Quixote's romantic invention; but we also know from him and his squire that at the village of El Toboso, a few miles from his own village, there did exist the prototype of his princess. We are told that her name was, in the reality of the book, Aldonza Lorenzo—and that she was a handsome farmgirl, a wonderful hand at salting pork and winnowing wheat. That is all. The emerald-green eyes, which Don Quixote with his and his creator's love of green, gives to the lady are probably a romantic invention like her fancy name. What else do we know? Sancho's account of her is of course to be rejected since he makes up the story of delivering his master's message to her. He knew her well, however—a brawny girl, tall and sturdy, with a strong voice and a mocking laugh. Sancho in chapter 25 about to take the message to her, describes her to his master: "and I may tell you that she can toss a bar as well as the lustiest lad in all the village. Long live the Giver of all good things, but she's a sturdy wench, fit as a fiddle and right in the middle of everything that's doing. She can take care of any knight-errant or about to err that has her for a mistress! Son of a whore, what strength she has and what a voice! . . . And the best of it is, there's nothing prudish about her; she's very friendly with everybody and always laughing and joking."

We are informed at the end of chapter 1 that Don Quixote had been in love with Aldonza Lorenzo at one time—platonic love to be sure, but the implication seems to be that whenever he chanced to pass through El Toboso in former years, he admired that good-looking peasant girl. Thus "it seemed to him that she was the one upon whom he should bestow the title of mistress of his thoughts. For her he wished a name that should not be incongruous with his own and that would convey the suggestion of a princess or a great lady; and, accordingly, he resolved to call her 'Dulcinea del Toboso,' she being a native of that place. A musical name to his ears, out of the ordinary and significant, like the others he had chosen for himself and his appurtenances." In chapter 25 we are told that in all the twelve years he has loved her (he is now about fifty), in all these twelve years he has seen her only three or four times and he never spoke to her; nor indeed did she notice that he was looking at her.

In the same chapter he lectures Sancho: "Similarly, Sancho, as regards my need of Dulcinea del Toboso, she is worth as much to me as any highborn princess on this earth. Not all the poets who praised their ladies under names of their own choosing actually had such mistresses. Do you think that the Amarillises, the Phyllises, the Sylvias, the Dianas, the Galateas, the Filidas, and all the others of whom the books, ballads, barbershops, and theaters are full were in reality flesh-and-blood women who belonged to those that hymned their praises? Certainly not; most of the writers merely invented these creatures to provide them with a subject for their verses in order that they might be taken for lovelorn swains and respected as individuals capable of an amorous passion. And so it is enough for me to think and believe that the good Aldonza Lorenzo is beautiful and modest. So far as her lineage is concerned, that is a matter of small importance; no one is going to look into it by way of conferring on her any robes of nobility, and, as for me, she is the most highborn princess in the world." And Don Quixote concludes: "For you should know, Sancho, if you do not know already, that the two things that more than any others incite to love are great beauty and a good name, and these two things are to be found to a consummate degree in Dulcinea; for in beauty none can vie with her, and in good name few can come up to her. But to bring all this to a conclusion I am content to imagine that what I say is so and that she is neither more nor less than I picture her and would have her be, in comeliness and in high estate. Neither Helen nor Lucretia nor any of the other women of bygone ages, Greek, Latin, or barbarian, can hold a candle to her. And let anyone say what he likes; if for this I am reprehended by the ignorant, I shall not be blamed by men of discernment."*

In the course of the knight's mad adventures something happens to his recollection of Aldonza Lorenzo and the background of the particular fades, Aldonza is swallowed up by the romantic generalization represented by Dulcinea so that in chapter 9 of part two when they have arrived in Toboso in search of his lady Don Quixote can state rather testily to Sancho: "Look, you heretic, have I not told you any number of times that I have never in all the days of my life laid eyes upon the peerless Dulcinea, that I have never crossed the threshold of her palace but am enamoured of her only by hearsay, as she is famous far and wide for her beauty and her wit?" This image permeates the whole book, but she will never be seen at El Toboso as the reader expects.

---

* When in chapter 64 of part two he has been unhorsed and threatened with death by the Knight of the White Moon, the Don is indomitable in defending the ideal of his inspiration. "Stunned and battered, Don Quixote did not so much as raise his visor but in a faint, wan voice, as if speaking from the grave, he said, 'Dulcinea del Toboso is the most beautiful woman in the world and I the most unhappy knight upon the face of this earth. It is not right that my weakness should serve to defraud the truth. Drive home your lance, O knight, and take my life since you already have deprived me of my honor.' " For Carrasco the question of beauty had been no more than the pretext for their combat; hence he responds: "Let the fame of my lady Dulcinea del Toboso's beauty live on undiminished. As for me, I shall be content if the great Don Quixote will retire to his village for a year or until such time as I may specify, as agreed upon between us before joining battle." Ed.

DEATH

Sansón Carrasco, masquerading as the Knight of the White Moon, easily defeats Don Quixote in Barcelona and exacts from him a promise to return to his own village for a year. After describing to Don Antonio Moreno his plan, now successful after its first disaster, Carrasco adds the assurance: "Since he is the soul of honor when it comes to observing the ordinances of knight-errantry, there is not the slightest doubt that he will keep the promise he has given me and fulfill his obligations. . . . I beg you not to disclose my secret or reveal my identity to Don Quixote, in order that my well-intentioned scheme may be carried out and a man of excellent judgment be brought back to his senses—for a sensible man he would be, once rid of the follies of chivalry."*

As Don Quixote and Sancho Panza leave Barcelona for their village, the Don is excited and upset. He wears no armor and is dressed for the road while Sancho goes along on foot, the armor being piled on the donkey's back. "But I can tell you one thing: that there is no such thing as luck in this world," he says to Sancho, "and whatever happens, whether it be good or bad, does not occur by chance but through a special providence of Heaven; hence the saying that each man is the architect of his own fortune. I was the architect of mine, but I did not observe the necessary prudence, and as a result my presumptuousness has brought me to a sorry end. I should have reflected that Rocinante, weak as he is, could not withstand the Knight of the White Moon's powerful steed. In short, I was too daring; I did my best but I was overthrown. However, although I sacrificed my honor, I cannot be accused of failing to keep my word. When I was a knight-errant, valiant and bold, my deeds and the might of my arm supported my reputation, and now that I am an ordinary squire I will back up my word by keeping the promise I have given. Proceed, then, friend Sancho, and let us go to fulfill the year of our novitiate in our native province, for during that period of retirement we shall obtain fresh strength, which will enable us to return to the profession of arms, one that I never can forget."

Is Dulcinea never to appear?

On his way home, in chapter 72, Don Quixote meets—not the spurious Don Quixote as we might hope, but one of the characters in the spurious continuation, namely, the Don Álvaro Tarfe who more or less plays in Avellaneda's book the part that the Duke or Don Antonio plays in the

* Don Antonio's reply, though self-serving, may strike a note of response in the reader: "My dear sir, . . . may God forgive you for the wrong you have done the world by seeking to deprive it of its most charming madman!" Ed.

original. Avellaneda's Don Quixote was a very good friend of mine, says Don Alvaro to the real Don Quixote. "It was I who took him away from his native heath, or, at least, I induced him to come and attend a tournament that was being held in Saragossa, whither I was bound. The truth of the matter is, I did him many favors and kept him from a flogging at the hands of the executioner as a result of his rash conduct." Don Quixote decides to stop all this and has a notary draw up a document stating that the real Don Quixote and Sancho Panza are not the ones referred to in Avellaneda's book.

"They traveled all that day and night with nothing occurring worthy of note save for the fact that Sancho completed his task, which made Don Quixote so exceedingly happy that he could scarcely wait for daylight to see if he would meet with his by now disenchanted lady along the highway; and each time that he encountered a woman he would go up to her in the hope of recognizing Dulcinea del Toboso, for he believed that Merlin could not lie and that his promises were infallible. Occupied with such thoughts and anxieties as these, they mounted a slope from the top of which they had a view of their village, at the sight of which Sancho fell on his knees."

Vague omens on their arrival disturb Don Quixote, a dispute between two boys about a cricket cage, and then a hunted hare that takes refuge under Sancho's donkey and which he catches and presents to his master. " '*Malum signum, malum signum*,' the knight was muttering to himself. 'A hare flees, the hounds pursue it, Dulcinea appears not.' " They meet the curate, the barber, and the bachelor Carrasco and all the others at his house: "the knight at once drew his guests to one side and in a few words informed them of how he had been overcome in battle and had given his promise not to leave his village for a year. . . . He accordingly meant to spend that year as a shepherd, he said, amid the solitude of the fields, where he might give free rein to his amorous fancies as he practiced the virtues of the pastoral life; and he further begged them, if they were not too greatly occupied and more urgent matters did not prevent their doing so, to consent to be his companions."

Again I am reminded of a certain intonation in *King Lear* when he comforts Cordelia (V.iii):

> " . . . . *So we'll live,*
> *And pray, and sing, and tell old tales and laugh*
> *At gilded butterflies. . . .*"

Don Quixote's end came when he was least expecting it. "Whether it was owing to melancholy occasioned by the defeat he had suffered, or was, simply, the will of Heaven which had so ordained it, he was taken with a fever that kept him in bed for a week, during which time his friends, the curate, the bachelor, and the barber, visited him frequently, while Sancho Panza, his faithful squire, never left his bedside.

". . . In any case, the physician told them, they should attend to the health of his soul as that of his body was in grave danger.

". . . The knight then requested them to leave him alone as he wished to sleep a little, and they complied. He slept for more than six hours at a stretch, as the saying is, and so soundly that the housekeeper and niece thought he would never wake."

Upon awaking he cried out in a loud voice, thanking God for His mercy. "The mercy that I speak of," he added, "is that which God is showing me at this moment—in spite of my sins, as I have said. My mind is now clear, unencumbered by those misty shadows of ignorance that were cast over it by my bitter and continual reading of those hateful books of chivalry. I see through all the nonsense and fraud contained in them, and my only regret is that my disillusionment has come so late, leaving me no time to make any sort of amends by reading those that are the light of the soul. I find myself, niece, at the point of death, and I would die in such a way as not to leave the impression of a life so bad that I shall be remembered as a madman; for even though I have been one, I do not wish to confirm it on my deathbed."

He becomes again, as he tells his friends, "no longer Don Quixote de la Mancha but Alonso Quijano, whose mode of life won for him the name of 'Good.' " This is a touching scene, especially as it continues.

" 'Ah, master,' cried Sancho through his tears, 'don't die, your Grace, but take my advice and go on living for many years to come; for the greatest madness that a man can be guilty of in this life is to die without good reason, without anyone's killing him, slain only by the hands of melancholy. Look you, don't be lazy but get up from this bed and let us go out into the fields clad as shepherds as we agreed to do [and laugh at gilded butterflies]. Who knows but behind some bush we may come upon the lady Dulcinea, as disenchanted as you could wish. If it is because of worry over your defeat that you are dying, put the blame on me by saying that the reason for your being overthrown was that I had not properly fastened Rocinante's girth.' " Dulcinea *is* disenchanted. She is death.

Don Quixote makes his will, then "stretching himself at length in the bed, fainted away. They all were alarmed at this and hastened to aid him. The same thing happened very frequently in the course of the three days of

VLADIMIR NABOKOV

Кроме ссылок на перевод"
все, конечно, переведены
на мой счет.

A quiet country gentleman, Señor Quijana, turned knight-errant.

p.25 Close on to fifty, of a robust constitution but with little flesh on his bones and a face that was lean and gaunt.

p.32 When he raises his pasteboard visor, he reveals a "withered, dust-covered face".

His voice is gentle and courteous.

p.34 His improvised helmet is tied on with green ribbons the knots of which could not be undone.

p.35 His suit-of-armor was black and moldy

p.39 His composure, his beautiful calm manner and self-control, so oddly in contrast with his mad fits of belligerent rage. Also Chapter VII.

He is a gallant gentleman, a man of infinite courage, a hero in the truest sense of the word. This very important point should be kept in mind all the time, in reading about all his encounters.

p.88 He is a purist. He cannot hear a village lad mispronounce words or use the wrong one.

p.92 He chose "toil, anxiety and arms" "" sweat, tears and _as another much fatter gentleman his part._ blood.

The people he meets are farmers and friars, carters, mule drivers, goatherds and shepherds, but very few horsemen.

p.112 Samples of his metapractical wisdom are numerous: "I must remind you, brother Panza, that there is no memory to which time does not put an end and no pain that death does not abolish."

p.183 Rocinante is a lean horse, but moreover slow-paced and phlegmatic.

life that remained to him after he had made his will. The household was in a state of excitement, but with it all the niece continued to eat her meals, the housekeeper had her drink, and Sancho Panza was in good spirits; for this business of inheriting property effaces or mitigates the sorrow which the heir ought to feel and causes him to forget."

The last cruel sting, well in keeping with the irresponsible, infantile, barbed and barbarous world of the book.

VLADIMIR NABOKOV

Victories And Defeats

One commentator in a well-known essay on Cervantes remarks that during his long series of battles "Never by any chance does [Don Quixote] win."* Of course, one has to read a book in order to to write about it. We have, and are in a position to refute our commentator's incomprehensible assertion.

I am not only going to refute it. I am going to prove, by means of a play-by-play account of the forty episodes in which Don Quixote acts as a knight-errant that these episodes reveal several amazing points of artistic structure; a certain balance and a certain unity; impressions which could not have been produced had all his encounters ended for him in defeat.

In his forty encounters he has to do with a great variety of creatures and contraptions:

Animals: Lions, a wild boar, bulls, sheep, cats.
Horsemen and herdsmen: Mule-drivers, bull-drivers, goatherds, and shepherds.

---

* The reference, as given by VN, is to Krutch, *Five Masters*, p. 78. The full quotation goes: "The fertility of Cervantes' invention has been many times praised but the real marvel is not so much that he could devise endless adventures for his Knight and Squire but that in every one of them each character should be, as in the brief adventure just referred to [the fulling mill], both right and wrong. Never by any chance does the knight win; and yet never, in another sense does he lose. At the beginning of each new incident we see why he is going to fail but we never feel that he ought to do so. In derision he is dubbed 'The Knight of the Rueful Countenance' but, like many who have adopted proudly an epithet first hurled at them in mockery, he wears it with pride instead of shame. It is not his business to be successful or to be gay—the Sanchos can be that—but rather to be consistent. Chivalry is the noblest ideal which he knows and he will not ask if it pays." Ed.

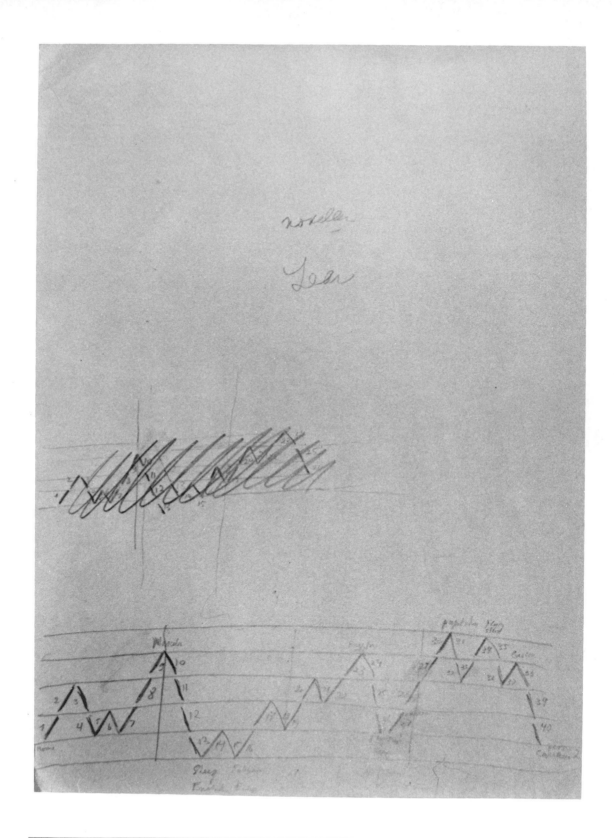

Nabokov's chart of Don Quixote's victories and defeats

Wayfarers: Such as priests, students, criminals, vagabonds, and various damsels.
Machines: Windmills, fulling mills, water mills, and a flying steed.

Now in the capacity of knight-errant he is several things:

In two encounters Don Quixote acts as *a protector of lovers in distress*:

Episode Thirty: part two, chapters 25-27, "The Puppet Show."
Episode Thirty-Four: part two, chapter 41, "The Flying Steed."*

In two encounters Don Quixote acts as *a conqueror of kings and kingdoms*:

Episode Five: part one, chapter 7, "The Acquiring of a Squire."
Episode Sixteen: part one, chapter 21, "Mambrino's Helmet."

In two encounters he acts as *a slayer of monsters*:

Episode Twenty-Eight: part two, chapter 17, "The Lions."
Episode Thirty-Three: part two, chapter 34, "The Wild Boar."

In four encounters he acts as *the upholder of his honor*:

Episode One: part one, chapter 3, "The Watch of the Armor."
Episode Eight: part one, chapter 8, "The Biscayan Knight."
Episode Ten: part one, chapter 15, "The Carters."
Episode Twenty-Seven: part two, chapters 14-15, "The First Fight with Carrasco."

In five encounters he acts as *a peacemaker*:

Episode Twenty: part one, chapters 37-38, "The Supper."
Episode Twenty-Two: part one, chapter 44, "The Dishonest Guests."
Episode Twenty-Three: part one, chapter 45, "The Free-for-All in the Inn Yard."
Episode Twenty-Nine: part two, chapter 21, "The Feud at the Wedding."**
Episode Thirty-One: part two, chapters 25-27, "The Braying Villages."

In five encounters he acts as *a defender of damsels in distress*:

Episode Seven: part one, chapter 8, "The Rout of the Friars."

---

* VN discusses forty encounters in detail, but in this particular survey of Don Quixote in different capacities he lists fifty-three episodes owing to some duplication. Episodes Thirty and Thirty-Four are repeated under his eighth category of Don Quixote as a *redresser of wrongs*.

** Episodes Twenty-Two, Twenty-Three, and Twenty-Nine are repeated under the eighth category of Don Quixote as a *redresser of wrongs*. Ed.

Episode Nine: part one, chapter 14, "Marcela."
Episode Nineteen: part one, chapters 35 and 37, "The Second Dream Battle."
Episode Twenty-Six: part one, chapter 52, "The Procession Praying for Rain."
Episode Thirty-Seven: part two, chapters 54-56, "The Gascon Lackey."*

In six encounters Don Quixote acts as *a champion of Dulcinea and other princesses*:

Episode Three: part one, chapter 4, "The Encounter with Merchants."
Episode Eighteen: part one, chapter 24, "The Ragged Knight."
Episode Twenty-Four: part one, chapter 46, "The Caging of Don Quixote."**
Episode Thirty-Eight: part two, chapter 58, "The Bulls."
Episode Thirty-Nine: part two, chapter 60, "The Fight with Sancho."
Episode Forty: part two, chapters 64-65, "The Second Fight with Carrasco."

In nine encounters Don Quixote acts as *a redresser of wrongs*:

Episode Two: part one, chapter 4, "The Flogged Farmboy."
Episode Fourteen: part one, chapter 19, "The Rout of the Mourners."
Episode Seventeen: part one, chapter 22, "The Liberation of the Galley Slaves."
Episode Twenty-Two: part one, chapter 44, "The Dishonest Guests."
Episode Twenty-Three: part one, chapter 45: "The Free-for-All in the Inn Yard."
Episode Twenty-Nine: part two, chapter 21, "The Feud at the Wedding."
Episode Thirty: part two, chapters 25-26, "The Puppet Show."
Episode Thirty-Four: part two, chapter 41, "The Flying Steed."
Episode Thirty-Seven: part two, chapters 54-56, "The Gascon Lackey."†

---

* Episode Seven is repeated under the ninth category of Don Quixote as *an enemy of enchanters*; Episode Thirty-Seven is repeated there and in the eighth category of the knight as *a redresser of wrongs*. Ed.
** Episode Twenty-four is repeated under the ninth category of Don Quixote as *an enemy of enchanters*. Ed.
† Episode Fourteen is repeated in the ninth category of Don Quixote as *an enemy of enchanters*. Episode Thirty is repeated in the ninth category and had already been listed under the first, *the protector of lovers in distress*. Episode Thirty-Four is repeated in the ninth category and had already been listed under the first and also the sixth, *the defender of damsels in distress*. Episode Thirty-Seven is repeated in the ninth category and had already been listed in the sixth. Ed.

In eighteen encounters Don Quixote acts as *an enemy of enchanters*, almost one-half of the whole number, forty:*

Episode Four: part one, chapter 7, "The First Dream Battle."
Episode Six: part one, chapter 8, "The Windmills."
Episode Seven: part one, chapter 8, "The Rout of the Friars."
Episode Eleven: part one, chapters 16-17, "The Jealous Carter."
Episode Twelve: part one, chapter 17, "The Trooper."
Episode Thirteen: part one, chapter 18, "The Sheep."
Episode Fourteen: part one, chapter 19, "The Rout of the Mourners."
Episode Fifteen: part one, chapter 20, "The Fulling Mills."
Episode Twenty-One: part one, chapter 43, "The Strappado."
Episode Twenty-Four: part one, chapter 46, "The Caging of Don Quixote."
Episode Twenty-Five: part one, chapter 52, "The Fight with the Goatherd."
Episode Twenty-Seven: part two, chapters 14-15, "The First Fight with Carrasco."
Episode Thirty: part two, Chapters 25-27, "The Puppet Show."
Episode Thirty-Two: part two, chapter 29, "The Watermills."
Episode Thirty-Four: part two, chapter 41, "The Flying Steed."
Episode Thirty-Five: part two, chapter 46, "The Cats."
Episode Thirty-Six: part two, chapters 48, 50, "The Pinchers."
Episode Thirty-Seven: part two, chapters 54-56, "The Gascon Lackey."

This is the first point we shall remember: his main enemies are enchanters.

Let us now follow him through his forty encounters. In most of them there is a delusion. The delusion ends in either victory or defeat, and the victory is often a moral one. Behind the delusion stands the actual event. We shall count as we go, the winning and losing points. The match starts. Let us see who wins: Don Quixote or his enemies.

The forty episodes that make up the book occur in the course of 175 days, counting a pause of one month in between, in all, from the beginning of July to the middle of December, according to a Spanish calculator.

---

* This is not quite accurate because of the extensive duplication in this category with earlier ones. In fact, only eleven of the listed encounters have not been mentioned before: these are Four, Six, Eleven, Twelve, Thirteen, Fifteen, Twenty-One, Twenty-Five, Thirty-Two, Thirty-Five, and Thirty-Six. Ed.

PART ONE

EPISODE ONE: THE WATCH OF THE ARMOR (CH. 3)

Delusion: Upholder of his honor. Don Quixote, at the inn which he takes for a castle, is ready to destroy anyone who interferes with his ceremonial vigil.

Result: His First Victory—on the very threshold of knighthood.

Actual Event: As he paces the geometrical moonlight in the inn yard, two carriers, in order to water their mules, disturb his armor in getting at the trough where it lies. Don Quixote repels and severely wounds them.

One love (1 - 0)

EPISODE TWO: THE FLOGGED FARMBOY (CH. 4)

Delusion: Redresser of wrongs. Don Quixote mistakes for a knight the farmer who flogs the boy.

Result: His Second Victory, an incomplete moral one.

Actual Event: By threats and spear-shaking he stops a farmer who is belting his young servant Andrés. Later, in chapter 31 Andrés turns up again and rebukes the abashed Don for having caused the farmer to give him an even more severe beating after the redresser of wrongs had cheerfully ambled away. A pious commentator (Bell, *Cervantes*, p. 209) remarks that "Don Quixote was punished for . . . concerning himself with a multitude of affairs which did not concern him"—as if, let me say, justice and mercy did not concern everybody.

The score is 2 love (2 - 0)

EPISODE THREE: THE ENCOUNTER WITH THE MERCHANTS (CH. 4)

Delusion: Champion of princesses. Don Quixote attacks thirteen brigands who refused to confess that Dulcinea is the fairest maiden in the whole world.

Result: His First Defeat.

Actual Event: The persons he attacks are six merchants with four servants and three muleteers, one of whom pounds the Don, when he falls off his horse, with bits of his own lance. The belabored knight howls threats with the utmost courage. (He later, in chapter 7, transforms the so-called "brigand" into Orlando the Furious, a character in Ariosto's book *Orlando Furioso*.) This is the end of his first sally.

The score is 2 - 1

94   VLADIMIR NABOKOV

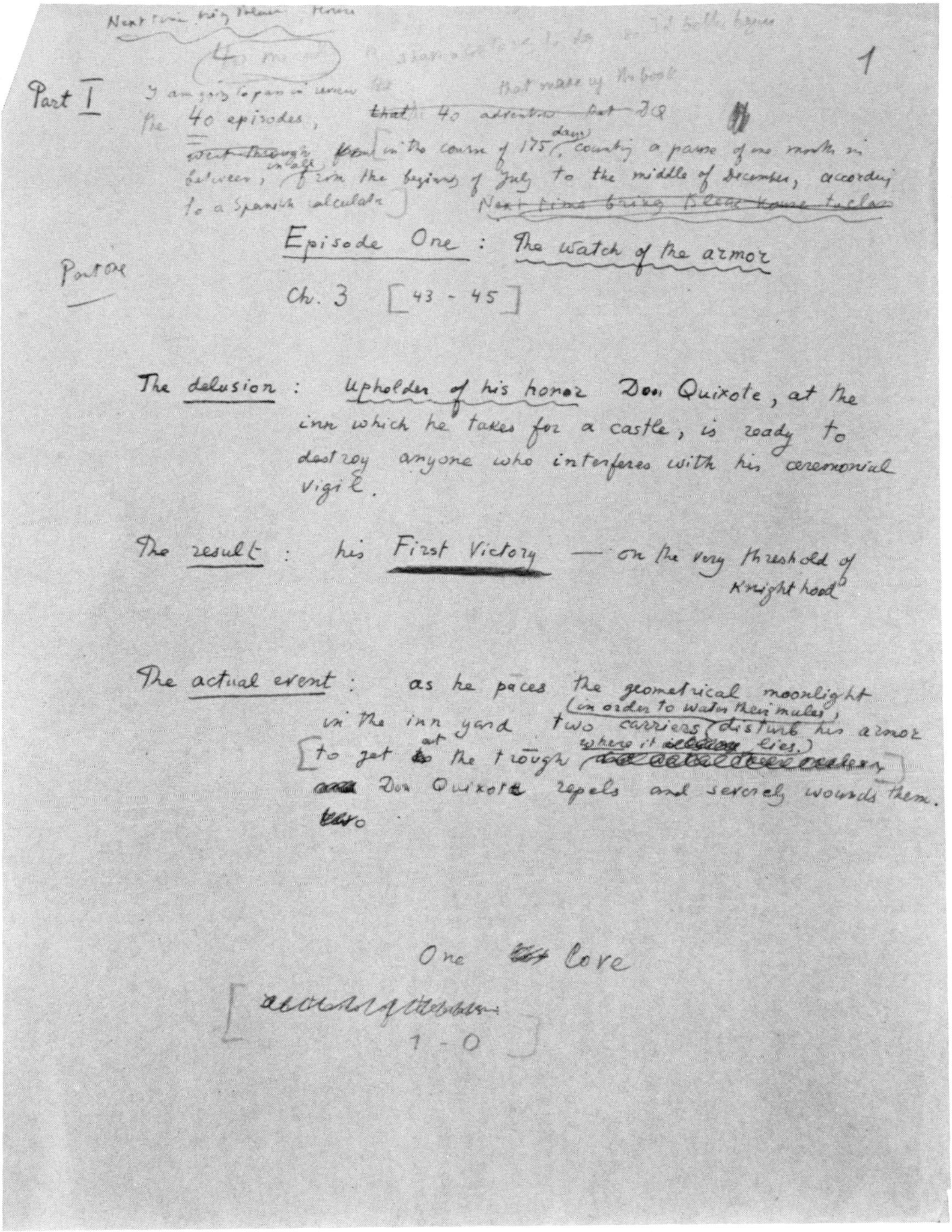

1

Next time bring Bleak House

Part I

I am going to pass in review the 40 episodes, ~~that~~ 40 adventures that make up the book DQ

~~went through~~ in all ~~from~~ [in the course of 175 days, counting a pause of one month in between, from the beginning of July to the middle of December, according to a Spanish calculator] ~~Next time bring Bleak House to class~~

Part one

Episode One : The watch of the armor

Ch. 3 [43 - 45]

The delusion : Upholder of his honor Don Quixote, at the inn which he takes for a castle, is ready to destroy anyone who interferes with his ceremonial vigil.

The result : his First Victory — on the very threshold of knighthood

The actual event : as he paces the geometrical moonlight in the inn yard two carriers (in order to water their mules) disturb his armor [to get at the trough where it lies.)] Don Quixote repels and severely wounds them.

One ~~tie~~ love

[~~[illegible]~~
1 - 0]

Nabokov's explanation of Don Quixote's first victory

EPISODE FOUR: THE FIRST DREAM BATTLE (CH. 7)

Delusion: *Enemy of enchanters*. He fights Orlando's supporters in a dream.

Result: His Second Defeat (not final, however, since the battle is interrupted).

Actual Event: He leaps out of bed, slashing the air with his sword, and is tucked back by the priest and the barber. They have removed his books to the yard (where the housekeeper burns them) and walled up the room where the books had been. Don Quixote accuses the enchanter Frestón of having caused the room to vanish.

The score is 2 - 2

EPISODE FIVE: ACQUIRING A SQUIRE (CH. 7)

Delusion: *Conqueror of kingdoms*. He does all he can to persuade a laborer that he may wind up as the governor of a rich island if he becomes his squire.

Result: His Third Victory, a moral one.

Actual Event: Sancho Panza, after much persuasion, consents to leave his family and follow the Don. Later, in chapter 10, his master tells him that if no island is available he will give him the kingdom of Denmark (which, however, has just been annexed [1601] by another Spear-Shaker). This is the beginning of the second sally.

The score is 3 - 2

EPISODE SIX: THE WINDMILLS (CH. 8)

Delusion: *Enemy of enchanters*. He battles with thirty-five gesticulating giants whom the magician Frestón transforms into windmills to thwart him.

Result: His Third Defeat.

Actual Event: As the windmills, a new-fangled contraption, loom before Don Quixote, a little wind comes up and starts turning the vanes, one of which badly injures the charging knight.

The score is 3 - 3

After which three fine victories come in a row:

EPISODE SEVEN: THE ROUT OF THE FRIARS (CH. 8)

Delusion: *Enemy of enchanters* and *defender of damsels in distress*. He attacks two black-clad, begoggled, sunshaded magicians on dromedaries, who have captured a coach with a princess.

Result: His Fourth Victory.

The Actual Event: Two Benedictines, wearing travelers' spectacles and riding on big fat mules, happen to be going the same way as a lady who is driving to Seville, accompanied by five horsemen and a couple of muleteeters who thrash Sancho while his master routs the good friars.

The score is 4 - 3

EPISODE EIGHT: THE BISCAYAN KNIGHT (CH. 8-9)

Delusion: *Upholder of his honor*. Don Quixote attacks a knight from Biscay who has insulted him.

Result: His Fifth Victory.

Actual Event: Unmuled by the Don, this Biscayan (a squire of the lady that appeared in the preceding episode) falls, with blood spouting out of his nostrils, mouth, and ears. (Cervantes likes to have no orifice unaccounted for.)

After this most satisfactory encounter, Don Quixote enters on a brief period of comparative lucidity.

The score is 5 - 3

EPISODE NINE: MARCELA (CH. 14)

Delusion: None.

Result: His Sixth Victory, a moral one.

Actual Event: *Defender of damsels in distress*. Don Quixote with strong words forces some vindictive mourners at the grave of the lovelorn youth Grisóstomo, who had courted Marcela, to leave Marcela alone, and no one stirs from the spot.

(In connection with the terminology I use for keeping the score, I want to remind you that the ancient game of court tennis, which after all was the ancestor of our game, is often mentioned by writers of that time and in *Don Quixote* is played—according to Altisidora—by devils in hell who use for balls books full of wind and wool.)

The score is 6 - 3, and Don Quixote has won the first set in his match with Evil. (*The whole match is supposedly a best out of five affair, but only four sets will be played.*)

Now Don Quixote is going to lose four games in a row:

EPISODE TEN: THE CARTERS (CH. 15)

Delusion: None.
Result: His Fourth Defeat. The perfectly lucid Don reproaches himself for having put hand to sword against churls. To fight only with social equals was a rule of chivalry which is reflected in the modern duelling code of Europe and Latin America.*
Actual Event: Upholder of his honor. Don Quixote attacks more than twenty carters who have badly beaten his horse and who now proceed to cudgel him with their packstaves.

The score is 6 - 4 (0 - 1 in the second set)

EPISODE ELEVEN: THE JEALOUS CARTER (CH. 16-17)

Delusion: Enemy of enchanters. Don Quixote is attacked by a giant, a Moorish magician.
Result: His Fifth Defeat.
Actual Event: He is terribly beaten by a carter at an inn, who thinks our pure gaunt Don is making love to the wench Maritornes, the carter's repulsive girl friend.

The score is 6 - 5 (0 - 2 in the second set)

EPISODE TWELVE: THE TROOPER (CH. 17)

Delusion: Enemy of enchanters. Don Quixote is attacked by an apparition—the Moorish magician in another form (according to Sancho).
Result: His Sixth Defeat.
Actual Event: A trooper, with whom the Don quarrels, hits him on the head with an iron lamp. (This scene leads to the mixture of a magic cure-all potion—rosemary, oil, salt, and wine—of which Don Quixote and Sancho drink a quart, with medieval results.)

---

* In his discarded section of notes from which he drew the final form of "Victories and Defeats," VN added, "although I think only Spain, Italy, France, Hungary and Poland were those European countries where duels were still fought before the last war." Ed.

The score is 6 - 6 (0 - 3 in the second set)

EPISODE THIRTEEN: THE SHEEP (CH. 18)

Delusion: *Enemy of enchanters*. Don Quixote fights an army of giants and knights.

Result: His Seventh Defeat.

Actual Event: He attacks a herd of sheep in a cloud of dust and is knocked down by the herdsman. (Compare the real shepherds with the Arcadian ones, incidentally.) Mark the theme of reality and transformation in this scene. According to the Don, the army is transformed into sheep by enchantment, just as the giants had become windmills. (Cervantes, the enchanter, will transform the flower of chivalry, Don Quixote himself, into a commonsensical, penitent bourgeois in the last, deathbed, chapter of the work.)

The score is 6 - 7 (0 - 4 in the second set)

EPISODE FOURTEEN: THE ROUT OF THE MOURNERS (CH. 19)

Delusion: *Enemy of enchanters* and *redresser of wrongs*. Don Quixote fights twenty-six demons carrying away a dead or wounded knight.

Result: His Seventh Victory.

Actual Event: He attacks a funeral procession—twenty horsemen in white with blazing torches, and six mourners in black. These timid people start running across the fields still bearing their torches, which makes them look like moving stars in the darkness or masked figures at some festival. Mark the calm with which Don Quixote accepts the explanation of the innocent people whom he has been knocking about, incidentally breaking the leg of a Master of Arts, a sour, pedantic, and rather likeable young priest. Don Quixote admits his mistake but as usual lays the blame on enchanters. "I did not realize that I was insulting priests or sacred things of the Church, which I respect and revere as the good Catholic and loyal Christian that I am; I thought, rather, that it was phantoms and monsters from the other world that I was attacking." (After this victory his squire dubs him Knight of the Mournful Countenance in allusion to the appearance of his sunken cheeks due to the loss of teeth in previous defeats.)

The score is 7 - 7 (1 - 4 in the second set)

Delusion: *Enemy of enchanters*. Don Quixote finds a spell cast on his motionless mount when he wishes to ride toward the din in the dark made by half a dozen giants.

Result: His Eighth Defeat.

Actual Event: The enchanter here is Sancho who, yearning for a night's rest and fearing a new adventure, shackles Rocinante with the halter of his donkey. The giants prove next day to be fulling hammers.

The score is 7 - 8 (1 - 5 in the second set)

EPISODE SIXTEEN: MAMBRINO'S HELMET (CH. 21)

Delusion: *Conqueror of kingdoms*. Don Quixote recognizes in the golden gleam on the head of a man riding in the rain and the sun the helmet of Mambrino, a Moorish king (from *Orlando Innamorato* by Boiardo, fifteenth-century Italian poet). He attacks.

Result: His Eighth Victory.

Actual Event: The man is a barber (barber no. 2 of the book) who had put the brass basin of his profession on his head as protection from the rain.

The score is 8 - 8 (2 - 5 in the second set)

EPISODE SEVENTEEN: THE LIBERATION OF THE GALLEY SLAVES (CH. 22)

Delusion: *Redresser of wrongs*. Don Quixote cannot understand why human beings should be chained and sent to the galleys—forced by the king to row (cheap human motor power of the day).

Result: His Ninth Victory, with an aftersting of defeat.

Actual Event: He liberates from the hands of four armed guards four thieves, and two others, a venerable pimp and a student who played too many pranks. The liberated six stone him. Mark that his halo, the brass helmet, glows through the chapter. The whole scene has curious mystic implications. Indeed, Don Quixote here is less a parody of a knight-errant than a brother of Jesus, and this little theme will be dimly followed up in two or three later scenes.

The score is 9 - 8 (3 - 5 in the second set)

* VN appends a note, "for cleaning cloth (or grooving iron)."

Delusion: None.

Result: His Ninth Defeat.

Actual Event: *Champion of princesses*. Don Quixote quarrels with a lovelorn vagabond Cardenio, whom he meets in the mountains. They quarrel over the chastity of a feminine character in *Amadis of Gaul*. Cardenio knocks down Don Quixote with a stone.

The score is 9 - 9

In the second set the score is now 3 - 6, and Don Quixote has lost the second set after winning the first one 6 - 3. Mark that it is here that the web of novellas begins to be spun, with all the characters, in increasing numbers, meeting at the inn. Don Quixote's activities tend to be lost in this tangle.

EPISODE NINETEEN: THE SECOND DREAM BATTLE (CH. 35 AND 37)

Delusion: *Defender of damsels in distress*. Don Quixote decapitates a giant.

Result: His Tenth Victory.

Actual Event: While fighting in his sleep he slashes at skins full of red wine. We are back at the starting point of his sally, which he began by fighting with enchanters in a dream.

The score is 10 - 9 (1 - 0 in the third set)

Mark the following point. The well-meaning priest and the initial barber have tricked Don Quixote into leaving the mountains where on top of his basic madness he has deliberately evolved a secondary pretended madness in honor of his Dulcinea as penitent knights do in books. He is now made to believe with the assistance of a vagabond damsel called Dorotea that she needs his help against a giant who has invaded the kingdom of which she says she is the princess. This story that Dorotea makes up is not more fantastic than her real troubles. At the very moment that Don Quixote dreams of beheading the giant of her invention, Dorotea, at the inn, is actually reunited with her lover, a person as unreal as any giant. The dream fight on one level of unreality (chivalry romance) seems to influence and direct events on another level of unreality (the Italian novella theme).

Delusion: None.

Result: I should classify this episode as Don Quixote's Eleventh and Greatest Triumph.

Actual Event: Don Quixote, the peacemaker, is given the place of honor at the head of the table. The company, consisting of twelve people, has developed by now a kind of tenderness and respect for him. He is the link; he is the peacemaker. In a solemn speech he talks of writers and of warriors, a theme close to the heart of Cervantes, who was both. Don Quixote considers the profession of letters less lofty in its purpose than the profession of arms. The former has for goal human knowledge which leads to the formulation of just laws, but the profession of arms, he says, has for purpose peace, which is the greatest blessing that man can wish in this life. This scene is the melancholy and significant climax of the first part. The grotesque nonsense of the novel retreats in the candlelight. The whole tone of the scene, with the gentle Don presiding at a supper of twelve guests, almost disciples at this last hour (he is soon to be tortured and caged) reminds one vaguely of some picture of the Last Supper described in the New Testament. We forget that none of the guests is very kind ethically, or very convincing esthetically, and all we hear is the sad quiet voice speaking of peace: "For the first good news that mankind and the world received was that which the angels brought on the night that was our day: 'Glory to God in the highest, and on earth peace, good will toward men.' And the salutation which the great Master of Heaven and earth taught his chosen disciples to use when they entered any dwelling was, 'Peace be to this house.' "

The score is 11 - 9 (2 - 0 in the third set)

Delusion: *Enemy of enchanters.* Don Quixote is made, by one of them, to hang by the wrist at the window of a brokenhearted damsel.

Result: His Tenth Defeat.

Actual Event: Prankish Maritornes, the servant girl at the inn, uses the halter of Sancho's ass to attach Don Quixote from the inside of the window in such a manner that when the horse he has been standing upon moves away he is left dangling for two hours in appalling pain, like a man enduring the torture called "strappado"—or like a crucified man.

The score is 11 - 10 (2 - 1 in the third set)

EPISODE TWENTY-TWO: THE DISHONEST GUESTS (CH. 44)

Delusion: None.
Result: His Twelfth Victory, a moral victory.
Actual Event: Two anonymous guests try to leave the inn without paying and start to beat the innkeeper when he demands his money. Don Quixote, the peacemaker and *redresser of wrongs*, comes to the rescue. His mild and persuasive reasoning prevails and the two rascals pay their full reckoning.

The score is 12 - 10 (3 - 1 in the third set)

EPISODE TWENTY-THREE: THE FREE-FOR-ALL IN THE INN YARD (CH. 45)

Delusion: None.
Result: His Thirteenth Victory, again a moral one.
Actual Event: During the confused fight in the inn yard among a number of people who hardly remember how and why it all started, Don Quixote, peacemaker and *redresser of wrongs*, cries in a voice of thunder, "Hold, all of you!" And he is obeyed.

The score is 13 - 10 (4 - 1 in the third set)

Now come three defeats in a row.

EPISODE TWENTY-FOUR: THE CAGING OF DON QUIXOTE (CH. 46)

Delusion: *Enemy of enchanters* and *champion of princesses*. He is carried by masked phantoms into a cage, which stands on an ox cart, and is told in a magic chant that he must undergo this spell in order to be eventually united in marriage to his Dulcinea.
Result: His Eleventh Defeat.
Actual Event: The priest and the initial barber, with the help of the other people at the inn, all in various disguises, use this device to trick and truck him home. You have marked the utter cruelty of the whole business—the melancholy, quiet, enchanted man, meditating there in his wooden cage while the two priests (the curate and a canon they meet on the way) discuss subtle literary matters—the art of writing elegant and useful books.

The score is 13 - 11 (4 - 2 in the third set)

Delusion: *Upholder of his honor* and *enemy of enchanters*. He fights a demon who has insulted him.

Result: His Twelfth Defeat (not absolute, since the fight is interrupted).

Actual Event: The demon is a goatherd. I have discussed the scene in another connection (above, p. 55).

The score is 13 - 12 (4 - 3 in the third set)

EPISODE TWENTY-SIX:
THE PROCESSION PRAYING FOR RAIN (CH. 52)

Delusion: *Defender of damsels in distress*. Don Quixote (who has been let out of his cage for a little while to amuse his enchanters) attacks a band of brigands who are carrying away a highborn lady.

Result: His Thirteenth Defeat.

Actual Event: The lady is an image of the Virgin which the penitents praying for rain are carrying. One of the bearers of this holy image almost kills Don Quixote by means of the pole that props it. Don Quixote is brought home in a daze and remains resting there for a month.

This is the end of the first part of the book. The score is even—thirteen victories against thirteen defeats (or in terms of tennis 6 - 3, 3 - 6, 4 - 4, interrupted by rain).

The second part of the book will begin with four victories in a row.

PART TWO

EPISODE TWENTY-SEVEN:
THE FIRST FIGHT WITH CARRASCO (CH. 14-15)

Delusion: *Upholder of his honor* and *enemy of enchanters*. Don Quixote fights with the Knight of the Mirrors, who maintains that he has met and conquered Don Quixote before. The Knight of the Mirrors is changed by enchantment into the likeness of Sansón Carrasco after the fight.

Result: Don Quixote's Fourteenth Victory.

Actual Event: Well-meaning Carrasco's frustrated plan had been to conquer, in the disguise of a knight, mad Don Quixote and order him to go home. The whole second part of the book will be unfolded between

Carrasco's defeat and his second victorious encounter with Don Quixote in Episode Forty—the last battle. The duration of Don Quixote's adventures, in the second part, will consequently depend on the length of fuming but still well-meaning Carrasco's convalescence.

The score is 14 - 13 (5 - 4 in the third set)

EPISODE TWENTY-EIGHT: THE LIONS (CH. 17)

Delusion: None, except for a vague allusion to enchanters.
Result: His Fifteenth Victory, a great moral one.
Actual Event: Two caged lions, fierce hungry beasts, are being sent by the Governor of Oran to the King of Spain as a present. Their keeper explains this to Don Quixote, slayer of monsters, who has barred their passage on the highway. Lions against *me*? says Don Quixote with a slight smile, and slitting his eyes, "Lion whelps against me? And at such an hour? Then, by God, those gentlemen who sent them shall see whether I am the man to be frightened by lions. Get down, my good fellow, and since you are the lionkeeper, open the cages and turn those beasts out for me; and in the middle of this plain I will teach them who Don Quixote de la Mancha is, notwithstanding and in spite of the enchanters who are responsible for their being here." One of the cages is opened. The lion, beautifully described, a lazy formidable animal stretching and yawning and licking the dust out of his eyes. Don Quixote confronts him, waiting for him to descend from the cart, but finally permits the door to be closed again. There is nothing fancy about this scene—it is a real man facing a real lion.

The score is 15 - 13 (with this Don Quixote wins the third set 6 - 4; two sets against one: this is getting quite exciting).

EPISODE TWENTY-NINE: FEUD AT THE WEDDING (CH. 21)

Delusion: None.
Result: His Sixteenth Victory.
Actual Event: *Redresser of wrongs* and *peacemaker*. Don Quixote with forcible words and spear-shaking breaks up a fight between two sets of supporters of two different bridegrooms at a wedding, and everybody esteems him for what he is, a man of worth and value.

The score is 16 - 13 (1 love in the fourth set)

EPISODE THIRTY: THE PUPPET SHOW (CH. 25-26)

Delusion: *Redresser of wrongs, enemy of enchanters, protector of lovers in distress* (in this case, Don Gaiferos, King of Bordeaux, one of Charlemagne's chieftains, and beautiful Melisendra). Don Quixote mangles a multitude of Moors, whom enchanters transform afterward into broken puppets.

Result: His Seventeenth Victory.

Actual Event: Ginés de Pasamonte, one of the galley slaves Don Quixote had freed, now disguised by means of a patch of green silk on one eye, gives a performance of marionettes for the destruction of which Don Quixote coolly pays, still contending that he has rescued the lovers, by now safe in France.

The score is 17 - 13 (leading 2 to nothing in the fourth set after taking two: he should win the match!)

EPISODE THIRTY-ONE: THE BRAYING VILLAGES (CH. 27-28)

Delusion: None.

Result: His Fourteenth Defeat (psychologically a very bad and ominous one).

Actual Event: A "braying" competition (who can imitate an ass better) between two villages ends in a fight which Don Quixote, in the lucid role of peacemaker, almost manages to break up by explaining in what cases nature, honor, patriotism, and the Catholic Faith permit battle; but Sancho interrupts his master's speech with an unfortunate quip and for the first time in his life Don Quixote, under a shower of stones, at all haste retreats.

The score is 17 - 14 (2 - 1 in the fourth set)

EPISODE THIRTY-TWO: THE WATERMILLS (CH.33)

Delusion: *Enemy of enchanters.* Don Quixote leaps into an empty bark that invites him to sail to the rescue of some knight or princess, but enchanters prevent him from reaching the castle that looms before him.

Result: His Fifteenth Defeat.

Actual Event: The wheels of big watermills moored in midriver begin to suck in the boat. Don Quixote and his squire are saved by some millers.

The score is 17 - 15 (2 - 2 in the fourth set)

EPISODE THIRTY-THREE: THE WILD BOAR (CH. 34)

Delusion: None, except that with sword in hand and braced shield he behaves like the slayer of dragons he is rather than like the country sportsman he had been.

Result: His Eighteenth Victory, a very minor one.

Actual Event: At a hunting party with the ducal pair he participates in the kill of a huge wild boar.

The score is 18 - 15 (3 - 2 in the fourth set)

EPISODE THIRTY-FOUR: THE FLYING STEED (CH. 41)

Delusion: *Redresser of wrongs, enemy of enchanters, protector of lovers in distress.* He sets out on a flying horse for a remote kingdom and finds when his machine explodes that by the mere attempting of the valorous deed he has accomplished it.

Result: His Nineteenth Victory.

Actual Event: A tedious and complicated prank of the ducal series which I have mentioned before (above, p. 66).

The score is 19 - 15 (leading 4 - 2 in the fourth set)

EPISODE THIRTY-FIVE: THE CATS (CH. 46)

Delusion: *Enemy of enchanters.* He is attacked by a demon

Result: His Sixteenth Defeat (not absolute since Don Quixote wants to go on when the fight is broken up).

Actual Event: One of the bell-maddened cats that have been let loose in a bag into Don Quixote's room at the ducal castle dreadfully injures his face with its teeth and claws.

The score is 19 - 16 (4 - 3 in the fourth set)

EPISODE THIRTY-SIX: THE PINCHERS (CH. 48)

Delusion: *Enemy of enchanters.* He is tortured by them in darkness and silence.

Result: His Seventeenth Defeat.

Actual Event: The Duchess, furious at having Don Quixote learn from a gossip that she has boils on her shapely legs (one of those inevitable secret flaws in a demon's beauty!) attacks him in the dark and with the assistance of charming little Altisidora, her maid, keeps pinching his sparse flesh for half an hour.

The score is 19 - 17 (4 all in the fourth set)

EPISODE THIRTY-SEVEN: THE GASCON LACKEY (CH. 54-56)

Delusion: Redresser of wrongs, defender of damsels in distress, enemy of enchanters. Don Quixote is about to battle with one of the Duke's vassals who has abandoned his bride, but who, just before Don Quixote charges, is transformed by enchanters into lackey Tosilos. Tosilos, who has fallen in love with the maiden, surrenders to Don Quixote and, blandly backed by him, offers to marry the abandoned bride there and then.

Result: Don Quixote's Twentieth Victory.

Actual Event: The Duke and Duchess in arranging the duel had substituted a lackey for their vassal who had fled to Flanders; now deprived of their cruel fun, they are amazed and angry at being outwitted.

The score is 20 - 17 (he can't lose now, but will he win?)

The Don leads 5 - 4 in the fourth set; if he wins the next game he will have won the set and the match.

EPISODE THIRTY-EIGHT: THE BULLS (CH. 58)

Delusion: Champion of princesses. Don Quixote, in sheer honor of some friendly damsels dressed up as shepherdesses, lightheartedly and recklessly posts himself in the middle of the highway to challenge the first person that may appear. Comes a herd of bulls with herdsmen.

Result: His Eighteenth Defeat.

Actual Event: Mark please the shepherdess theme is a reversion to the Arcadian atmosphere in Episode Nine; and after his second battle with Carrasco, in Episode Forty, Don Quixote himself will plan to dress up as a shepherd and live in Arcadian surroundings. Also mark that real sheep and real herdsmen are in brutal contrast with the artificial beribboned world of Arcadian fancies. In Episode Thirteen when attacking the sheep which he mistook for armies, real shepherds knocked him down. Now in Episode Thirty-eight he is overthrown and trampled by bulls and herdsmen and is left battered and stunned; but pathetically he attempts to pursue them on foot, shouting, hurrying, stumbling, falling—and at last, weary and crying with rage, he sits down in the middle of the dusty implacable road. This scene is the beginning of his final downfall.

The score is 20 - 18 (5 - 5 in the fourth set)

EPISODE THIRTY-NINE: THE FIGHT WITH SANCHO (CH. 60)

Delusion: Champion of princesses. Don Quixote believes what the ducal pair had hypnotized him into thinking—namely, that a certain number of lashes applied by Sancho to his (Sancho's) bare buttocks will be instrumental in disenchanting Dulcinea.

Result: His Nineteenth Defeat.

Actual Event: That autumn morning on the road to Barcelona Don Quixote seems to feel that his days are numbered and that Dulcinea must be disenchanted at all cost. He decides to administer those three thousand lashes to Sancho himself and crawls up to his sleeping squire. We see him struggling to undo Sancho's clothes, but Sancho grapples with his master, brings him down flat on his back, and puts his knee on Don Quixote's chest so that Don Quixote can neither stir nor breathe. He makes Don Quixote promise that he will leave him to his own devices—and cheats his master into thinking that he is flogging himself by smacking smooth beech trunks with his donkey's halter, the same halter with which he had tied Rocinante's legs in Episode Fifteen, and the same halter with which Maritornes strapped Don Quixote's wrist at the window. Of all defeats, this tumble with his squire is the most grotesque, ignoble, and atrocious one. In a daze of sadness, and unarmed, Don Quixote lets himself be captured by some goodnatured Robin Hoods, which is part of the same defeat.

The score is 20 - 19 (5 - 6 in the fourth set)

EPISODE FORTY:
THE SECOND AND LAST FIGHT WITH CARRASCO (CH. 64-65)

(The last chance to win the match.)

Delusion: *Champion of princesses.* Don Quixote accepts the challenge of the Knight of the White Moon, who meets him one day on the strand of Barcelona.

Result: His Twentieth Defeat, a decisive one.

Actual Event: Disguised Carrasco, having neatly unhorsed the poor knight, makes him swear to return to his village. This is the end of Don Quixote as knight-errant. While he and Sancho jog listlessly home, some additional agonies are thrown in: a herd of swine tramples them, and later the ducal pair have them dragged back into the torture house, but these are misadventures, not defeats, since Don Quixote is no more a knight.

So the final score is 20 - 20, or in terms of tennis 6 - 3, 3 - 6, 6 - 4, 5 - 7. But the fifth set will never be played; Death cancels the match. In terms of encounters the score is even: twenty victories against twenty defeats. Moreover, in each of the two parts of the book the score is also even: 13 to 13 and 7 to 7, respectively. This perfect balance of victory and defeat is very amazing in what seems such a disjointed haphazard book. It is due to a secret sense of writing, the harmonizing intuition of the artist.

CONCLUSION

In the course of my discussion of the book *Don Quixote*, I have tried to form certain impressions in your open minds. If some minds were only ajar, even then I hope to have managed to impart a bit of information. I repeat what I said at the start of our tour: you are the energetic and excited sightseer; I am only a word-happy and footsore guide. So what were those impressions? Well—I have discussed such matters as the when and where of the book; the connection between so-called "real life" and fiction; the physical and moral features of Don Quixote and his squire; various points of structure such as the chivalry theme, the Arcadian theme, the inset story, the chroniclers, the cruel mystifications that all three—Don Quixote, Sancho, and Cervantes himself—undergo at the hands of enchanters. I have spoken of his Dulcinea and of his death. I have given you samples of the art and poetry of the book, and I have objected to iewing the book as a humane and humorous one.

A Spanish commentator, Diego Clemencín,* remarks that Cervantes "wrote his fable with a carelessness that seems impossible to explain: without any planning, whatever his fancy, his abundant and robust fancy, dictated. He had moreover an unconquerable distaste for revising what he had written—hence the formidable crop of blunders, forgotten or misplaced incidents, incongruous details, names and events, undergoing all kinds of irritating transformations in retrospect or in repetition, and various other flaws pock-marking the book." It has also been said with

---

* "Prologo a la edicion del *Quijote*," in the first of the six volumes of his edition of the book, Madrid, 1833-39. VN seems to have drawn his quotation from some secondary source.

even more ferocity that apart from the account of Don Quixote and Sancho's fascinating conversations and the magnificent illusions which make up Don Quixote's main adventures, the novel is a farrago of prefabricated events, secondhand intrigues, mediocre pieces of verse, trite interpolations, impossible disguises, and incredible coincidences; but somehow the genius of Cervantes, the intuition of the artist he was, manages to hold these disjointed members together, and uses them to give impetus and unity to his novel about a noble madman and his vulgar squire.

That in former times a reader of *Don Quixote* could get a belly-laugh from every chapter of the work seems incredible to the modern reader, who finds the implication of its humor brutal and grim. The fun often sinks to the low level of the medieval farce with all its conventional laughing-stocks. It is sad when an author assumes that certain things are funny in themselves—donkeys, gluttons, tormented animals, bloody noses, et cetera—the stock in trade of ready-made fun. If Cervantes gets away with it in the long run it is only because the artist in him took over. As a thinker, Cervantes shared lightheartedly most of the errors and prejudices of his time—he put up with the Inquisition, solemnly approved of his country's brutal attitude toward Moors and other heretics, believed that all noblemen were God-made and all monks God inspired.*

But he had the eye and thumb of an artist, and his art transcended his prejudices when he created his pathetic hero. The art of a book is not necessarily affected by its ethics. As a thinker Cervantes's mind is both directed and shackled by the classical and academic ideas of his age. As a creator, he enjoys the freedom of genius.**

What, then, is our final judgment?

Don Quixote is one of those books that are, perhaps, more important in eccentric diffusion than in their own intrinsic value. It is significant that the work was immediately translated abroad; in fact, an English translation of the first part appeared as early as 1612 before the second part appeared in Spanish, and so did the first French translation, though in 1614, to be followed by more than fifty different translations into French alone from that date to our day. (It is amusing to think that Molière, the most famous French playwright and actor, took the part of Don Quixote in a French stage adaptation in 1660.) After England and France had given the cue, the following sequence of translations took place: Italian in 1622, Dutch in 1657, Danish in 1676, German in 1794, and Russian still later. I am listing

---

* In the margin VN notes this sentence as a paraphrase of Groussac. The second half, beginning with "he put up with the Inquisition" has a deleting slant line drawn across it.

** VN noted in the margin that this sentence (much revised) is a paraphrase of Madariaga.

complete translations from the original, not excerpts or adaptations from the French, as for instance appeared in Germany in 1621 and 1682 respectively.

There is not much to say for Sancho. He exists only insofar as his master does. Any actor of the roly-poly school can impersonate him easily and improve on the comedy. But with Don Quixote things are different. His image is a complicated and elusive one.

From the very first, in the original itself, the figure of Don Quixote undergoes a shadowy multiplication. (1) There is the initial Señor Quijana, a humdrum country gentleman; (2) there is the final Quijano the Good, a kind of synthesis that takes into account the antithetic Don Quixote and the thetic country gentleman; (3) there is the presupposed "original," "historical" Don Quixote whom Cervantes slyly places somewhere behind the book in order to give it a "true story" flavor; (4) there is the Don Quixote of the imagined Arabic chronicler, Cid Hamete Benengeli, who perhaps, it is amusingly assumed, underplays the valor of the Spanish knight; (5) there is the Don Quixote of the second part, the Knight of the Lions, in juxtaposition to the first part Knight of the Mournful Countenance; (6) there is Carrasco's Don Quixote; (7) there is the coarse Don Quixote of the Avellaneda spurious continuation lurking in the background of the genuine second part. So we have at least seven colors of the Don Quixote specter in one book, merging and splitting and merging again.* And beyond the horizon of the book there is the army of Don Quixotes engendered in the cesspools or hothouses of dishonest or conscientious translations. No wonder the good knight thrived and bred through the world, and at last was equally at home everywhere: as a carnival figure at a festival in Bolivia and as the abstract symbol of noble but spineless political aspirations in old Russia.

We are confronted by an interesting phenomenon: a literary hero losing gradually contact with the book that bore him; leaving his fatherland, leaving his creator's desk and roaming space after roaming Spain. In result, Don Quixote is greater today than he was in Cervantes's womb. He has ridden for three hundred and fifty years through the jungles and tundras of human thought—and he has gained in vitality and stature. We do not laugh at him any longer. His blazon is pity, his banner is beauty. He stands for everything that is gentle, forlorn, pure, unselfish, and gallant. The parody has become a paragon.

* VN originally continued the sentence but then deleted "as the shadow of something on the wall illumed by several moving lights from various angles."

Narrative and Commentary
Part One (1605)

Acountry gentleman read so many books of chivalry that their fantastic adventures seemed to him to be true and worthy of emulation. "At last, when his wits were gone beyond repair, he came to conceive the strangest idea that ever occurred to any madman in this world. It now appeared to him fitting and necessary, in order to win a greater amount of honor for himself and serve his country at the same time, to become a knight-errant and roam the world on horseback, in a suit of armor; he would go in quest of adventures, by way of putting into practice all that he had read in his books; he would right every manner of wrong, placing himself in situations of the greatest peril such as would redound to the eternal glory of his name. As a reward for his valor and the might of his arm, the poor fellow could already see himself crowned Emperor of Trebizond at the very least; and so, carried away by the strange pleasure that he found in such thoughts as these, he at once set about putting his plan into effect." He burnished up some old pieces of armor left him by his great-grandfather, and seeking a name of renown for his nag, he called it Rocinante, and himself—plain Alonso Quijada, Quesada, or Quijana— after the example of Amadis who had added to his name that of his kingdom, "our good knight chose to add his place of origin and become 'Don Quixote de la Mancha'; for by this means, as he saw it, he was making very plain his lineage and was conferring honor upon his country by taking its name as his own." But then "he naturally found but one thing lacking still: he must seek out a lady of whom he could become enamored; for a knight-errant without a lady-love was like a tree without leaves or fruit, a body without a soul." He then thought of a good-looking farm-girl with whom he had once been smitten although she had never noticed him, and "For her he wished a name that should not be incongruous with his own and that would convey the suggestion of a princess or a great lady; and, accordingly, he resolved to call her 'Dulcinea del Toboso,' she being a native of that place."

CHAPTER 2.

"Having, then, made all these preparations, he did not wish to lose any time in putting his plan into effect, for he could not but blame himself for what the world was losing by his delay, so many were the wrongs that were to be righted, the grievances to be redressed, the abuses to be done away with, and the duties to be performed. Accordingly, without informing anyone of his intention and without letting anyone see him, he set out one morning before daybreak on one of those very hot days in July." The skit on chivalry books continues when he speaks of himself in the manner of the books he has been reading. " 'O happy age and happy century,' he went on, 'in which my famous exploits shall be published, exploits worthy of being engraved in bronze, sculptured in marble, and depicted in paintings for the benefit of posterity. O wise magician, whoever you be, to whom shall fall the task of chronicling this extraordinary history of mine! I beg of you not to forget my good Rocinante, eternal companion of my wayfarings and my wanderings.' Then, as though he really had been in love: 'O Princess Dulcinea, lady of this captive heart! Much wrong have you done me in thus sending me forth with your reproaches and sternly commanding me not to appear in your beauteous presence. O lady, deign to be mindful of this your subject who endures so many woes for the love of you.'

"And so he went on, stringing together absurdities, all of a kind that his books had taught him, imitating insofar as he was able the language of their authors. He rode slowly, and the sun came up so swiftly and with so much heat that it would have been sufficient to melt his brains if he had had any." Realizing he has not been dubbed a knight, he determines to ask the favor of the first person he meets. He arrives at an inn, which he mistakes for a castle and the landlord for its castellan.

CHAPTER 3.

After a vile meal which he conceives to be of delicacies, he falls on his knees before the bewildered landlord. "I may tell you that the boon I asked and which you have so generously conceded me is that tomorrow morning you dub me a knight. Until that time, in the chapel of this your castle, I will watch over my armor, and when morning comes, as I have said, that which I so desire shall then be done, in order that I may lawfully go to the four corners of the earth in quest of adventures and to succor the needy, which is the chivalrous duty of all knights-errant such as I who long to engage in deeds of high emprise." Don Quixote's dream comes true only because the innkeeper is a rogue and a sport with a sense of brutal humor. The parody of chivalry literature is continued by Cervantes in a new way. Here it is the roguish innkeeper who plays up to Quixote the dreamer, and reminds him, as it were, of some fine points: knights, no matter how gallant they are— and indeed in assistance to their gallantry—should carry "well-stuffed purses, that they might be prepared for any emergency; and they also carried shirts and a little box of ointment for healing the wounds that they received." The vigil takes place, interrupted by a fight with some mule drivers who disturb his armor in the watering-trough where it lay. Finally the innkeeper dubs him knight in a mock ceremony and Don Quixote sallies forth in search of adventures after thanking the innkeeper for the honor of knighthood. "The innkeeper, who was only too glad to be rid of him, answered with a speech that was no less flowery, though somewhat shorter, and he did not so much as ask him for the price of a lodging, so glad was he to see him go."

CHAPTER 4.

After releasing, as he thinks, a young servant being flogged by a brutish farmer, who redoubles the punishment the moment the knight rides off well content with his redress of a wrong, Quixote rides on his way back to his village to find a squire. He encounters six travelers with their servants. Eager for an adventure, he bars their way and after a haughty gesture, " 'Let everyone,' he cried, 'stand where he is, unless everyone will confess that there is not in all the world a more beauteous damsel than the Empress of La Mancha, the peerless Dulcinea del Toboso.' " One of the merchants, seeing that they were dealing with a madman, demands to be shown the damsel before they are willing to commit themselves. " 'If I were to show her to you,' replied Don Quixote, 'what merit would there be in your confessing a truth so self-evident? The important thing is for you, without seeing her, to believe, confess, affirm, swear, and defend that truth. Otherwise, monstrous and arrogant creatures that you are, you shall do battle with me.' " After further quibbling by the merchant the enraged Don levels his lance and attacks him, but unfortunately Rocinante stumbles in mid-course and the knight is thrown on the ground, where he is well beaten by a muleteer and left lying in the road unable to move.

CHAPTER 5.

A farmer neighbor finds him and escorts him home. " 'Wait, all of you,' said Don Quixote, 'for I am sorely wounded through fault of my steed. Bear me to my couch and summon, if it be possible, the wise Urganda to treat and care for my wounds.'

" 'There!' exclaimed the housekeeper. 'Plague take it! Did not my heart tell me right as to which foot my master limped on? To bed with your Grace at once, and we will take care of you without sending for that Urganda of yours. A curse, I say, and a hundred other curses, on those books of chivalry that have brought your Grace to this.'

"And so they carried him off to bed, but when they went to look for his wounds, they found none at all. He told them it was all the result of a great fall he had taken with Rocinante, his horse, while engaged in combating ten giants, the hugest and most insolent that were ever heard of in all the world."

CHAPTER 6.

The curate and the barber, friends of Don Quixote, inspect his library. His housekeeper and his niece propose even more drastic measures than the priest does, who thinks that some of the books might be pardoned and spared the bonfire that is already prepared in the courtyard, and the barber is still more lenient. (This is a wonderful scene to be read aloud.) Cervantes's own *Galatea* is mentioned among the titles that the two men pore over before consigning them to the flames or putting them aside for preservation. The likes and dislikes of the curate are not very clear; but it is evident that he prefers prose and verse to be polished. There is something curiously Shakespearean in the dialogue here in chapter 6. The literary allusions were no doubt much funnier and more subtle than they seem to us now.

" 'And this,' said the barber, taking up yet another, 'is *The Mirror of Chivalry.*'

" 'Ah, your Grace, I know you,' said the curate. 'Here we have Sir Rinaldo of Montalbán with his friends and companions, bigger thieves than Cacus, all of them, and the Twelve Peers along with the veracious historian

VLADIMIR NABOKOV

Turpin. To tell you the truth, I am inclined to sentence them to no more than perpetual banishment, seeing that they have about them something of the inventiveness of Matteo Boiardo, and it was out of them, also, that the Christian poet Ludovico Ariosto wove his tapestry—and by the way, if I find him here speaking any language other than his own, I will show him no respect, but if I meet with him in his own tongue, I will place him upon my head' [as a token of respect].

" 'Yes,' said the barber, 'I have him at home in Italian, but I can't understand him.'

" 'It is just as well that you cannot,' said the curate. 'And for this reason we might pardon the Captain if he had not brought him to Spain and made him over into a Castilian, depriving him thereby of much of his native strength, as happens with all those who would render books of verse into another language; for however much care they may take, and however much cleverness they may display, they can never equal the original. I say, in short, that this work, and all those on French themes ought to be thrown into, or deposited in, some dry well until we make up our minds just what should be done with them. . . .' " These are charming remarks on translation, generally.

CHAPTER 7.

In this chapter, when despite the curate's easygoing leniency, the housekeeper, a living symbol of ignorance, crass common sense, and old-woman stupidity, burns all the books in the house, one feels still more clearly that the skit on chivalry romance is diluted and drowned in the interest that the author has for his "strange madman." It is important to note the shifting of tone at this point in the story, in these chapters 6 and 7. Another thing: the walling up of the room where the books had been, surely a costly and complicated operation carried out by the curate and the barber, is quite as fantastic and crazy as the enchantments that Don Quixote sees around him. The point is that, though it may be argued that his friends were merely playing up to his madness, you must have a streak of madness yourself to devise and carry out such a stratagem; and the same refers to the various enchantments practiced by a dreadful ducal pair on our knight and his squire in the second part. When Don Quixote inquires where his study and books have vanished to, his housekeeper "had been well instructed in what to answer him. 'Whatever study is your Grace talking about?' she said. 'There is no study, and no books, in this house; the devil took them all away.'

" 'No,' said the niece, 'it was not the devil but an enchanter who came upon a cloud one night the day after your Grace left here; dismounting from a serpent that he rode, he entered your study, and I don't know what all he did there, but after a bit he went flying off through the roof, leaving the house full of smoke; and when we went to see what he had done, there was no study and not a book in sight. There is one thing, though, that the housekeeper and I remember very well: at the time that wicked old fellow left, he cried out in a loud voice that it was all on account of a secret enmity that he bore the owner of those books and that study, and that was why he had done the mischief in this house which we would discover. He also said that he was called Muñatón the Magician.'

" 'Frestón, he should have said,' remarked Don Quixote.

" 'I can't say as to that,' replied the housekeeper, 'whether he was called Frestón or Fritón; all I know is that his name ended in a *tón*.'

" 'So it does,' said Don Quixote. 'He is a wise enchanter, a great enemy of mine, who has a grudge against me because he knows by his arts and learning that in the course of time I am to fight in single combat with a knight whom he favors, and that I am to be the victor and he can do nothing to prevent it. For this reason he seeks to cause me all the trouble that he can, but I am warning him that it will be hard to gainsay or shun that which Heaven has ordained.' "

The composure and artistic nature of this intonation "Frestón, he should have said" is a peach to be palpated and piously savored.

The third farmer who appears in the book is Sancho Panza, whom Don Quixote persuades to become his squire. Sancho Panza is in a way a coarser edition of Don Quixote. Note that he leaves his wife and children for the sake of a *dream*: the governorship of an island, which, no doubt, Don Quixote described to him with inspired eloquence that seduced the poor oaf. Sancho Panza is introduced as a witless fellow. He will change. Already at the end of the chapter his talk is not that of a fool.

CHAPTER 8.

Now comes the famous chapter of the windmills. After a new series of preparations (new buckler, squire, the squire's mount—a gray ass) Don Quixote sets out again in quest of new adventures. The author's intention was to start this new sortie with some stunning feat that would put into shade all his previous adventures. Note how *alive* the windmills are in Cervantes's description. As Don Quixote attacks them "a little wind came up and the big wings began turning"—just at the right moment. The shock of being hit by a vane sobers Don Quixote into assuming that the gesticulating giants he had perceived through the shimmer of his fancy have now transformed themselves into what Sancho said they were all along—windmills. They have taken their cue from the rustic squire. The magician Frestón is at work again.

Very curiously, Don Quixote is shown roaring with laughter at one of Sancho's Panza's remarks: " 'God knows, it would suit me better if your Grace did complain when something hurts him. I can assure you that I mean to do so, over the least little thing that ails me—that is, unless the same rule [as for knights-errant] applies to squires as well.'

"Don Quixote laughed long and heartily over Sancho's simplicity, telling him that he might complain as much as he liked and where and when he liked, whether he had good cause or not; for he had read nothing to the contrary in the ordinances of chivalry."

Note the lovely description with which the next exploit begins—the dromedaries, the goggles, the allusion to the Indies, everything is first-rate from an artistic point of view: "there appeared in the road in front of them two friars of the Order of St. Benedict, mounted upon dromedaries—for the she-mules they rode were certainly no smaller than that. The friars wore travelers' spectacles and carried sunshades, and behind them came a coach accompanied by four or five men on horseback and a couple of muleteers on foot. In the coach, as was afterwards learned, was a lady of Biscay, on her way to Seville to bid farewell to her husband, who had been appointed to some high post in the Indies. The religious were not of her company although they were going by the same road.

"The instant Don Quixote laid eyes upon them he turned to his squire. 'Either I am mistaken or this is going to be the most famous adventure that ever was seen; for those black-clad figures that you behold must be, and without any doubt are, certain enchanters who are bearing with them a captive princess in that coach, and I must do all I can to right this wrong.' "

The author intends to balance the brutal scene of the windmills with a romantic one. Note that all night Don Quixote had kept night-dreaming about his imagined lady love. Now comes a natural sequel. Again muleteers take a hand in the encounter but now they fall upon Sancho Panza while Don Quixote routs the good friars. Indeed, the whole encounter is a great success, even when one of the lady's squires, a Biscayan, attacks him. After receiving a heavy blow, Don Quixote approaches the frightened Biscayan determinedly, raising his sword on high for the fatal blow, as the lady in the coach and her maids are praying to God to save them all. "At this very point the author of the history breaks off and leaves the battle pending, excusing himself upon the ground that he has been unable to find anything else in writing concerning the exploits of Don Quixote beyond those already set forth. It is true, on the other hand, that the second author of this work [Cervantes himself] could not bring himself to believe that so unusual a chronicle would have been consigned to oblivion, nor that the learned ones of La Mancha were possessed of so little curiosity as not to be able to discover in their archives or registry offices certain papers that have to do with this famous knight. Being convinced of this, he did not despair of coming upon the end of this pleasing story, and Heaven favoring him, he did find it. . . ."

CHAPTER 9.

In Toledo Cervantes finds an Arabic manuscript by Cid Hamete Benengeli, Arabic Historian, which he got translated and which includes an illustration of the battle with the Biscayan, the Don with raised sword, that is full of details of the appearance of the Don and Sancho and Rocinante. Cervantes then slips in another device (the interrupted chronicle being a cliche of the chivalry romances): "no story is bad so long as it is true," he writes, and then goes on: "If there is any objection to be raised against the veracity of the present one, it can be only that the author was an Arab," and he remarks that when Benengeli should be praising Don Quixote he "appears to take pains to pass over the matter in silence," which Cervantes asserts, is "ill done" of a historian who should be "exact, truthful, and dispassionate." At any rate, after the picture Benengeli's narrative concludes the fight with a splendid victory by Don Quixote, who spares the Biscayan only at the entreaties of the ladies and their promise that the squire will present himself to Dulcinea del Toboso, so that she may do with him as she pleases. "Trembling and disconsolate, the ladies did not pause to discuss Don Quixote's request, but without so much as inquiring who Dulcinea might be they promised him that the squire would fulfill that which was commanded of him." So, as we shall see, Don Quixote does not come out quite as badly in the pretended translation of the pretended Arabian account as the pretended discoverer of this account suggests.

CHAPTER 10.

After this most satisfying encounter (even though he had lost half an ear in it) Don Quixote resumes his ride "at a good clip." The knight boasts to Sancho that no history contains an account of a greater combat than that he has just performed. " 'The truth is,' said Sancho, 'I have never read history whatsoever, for I do not know how to read or write; but what I would wager is that in all the days of my life I have never served a more courageous master than your Grace; I only hope your courage is not paid for in the place that I have mentioned [prison]. What I would suggest is that your Grace allow me to do something for that ear, for there is much blood coming from it, and I have here in my saddlebags some lint and a little white ointment.' " This is no fool talking, but a man endowed with friendly perception and practical acumen. Don Quixote *is* courageous, and the ointment and lint *are* what he needs at the moment.

A new slant in the parody of chivalry romance is Don Quixote's allusion to a magical potion: "It is a balm the receipt for which I know by heart; with it one need have no fear of death nor think of dying from any wound. I shall make some of it and give it to you; and thereafter, whenever in any battle you see my body cut in two—as very often happens—all that is necessary is for you to take the part that lies on the ground, before the blood has congealed, and fit it very neatly and with great nicety upon the other part that remains in the saddle, taking care to adjust it evenly and exactly. Then you will give me but a couple of swallows of the balm of which I have told you, and you will see me sounder than an apple in no time at all."

Further on, Cervantes keeps up the play of allusions to romances of chivalry on Don Quixote's part. Note the lunch that Don Quixote has to be content with: " 'I have here an onion, a little cheese, and a few crusts of bread,' said Sancho, 'but they are not victuals fit for a valiant knight like your Grace.'

" 'How little you know about it!' replied Don Quixote. 'I would inform you, Sancho, that it is a point of honor with knights-errant to go for a month at a time without eating, and when they do eat, it is whatever may be at hand. You would certainly know that if you had read the histories as I have.' " A humble repast, indeed. A feast of vitamins. Note the beautiful end of the chapter:

"They then mounted and made what haste they could that they might arrive at a shelter before nightfall; but the sun failed them, and with it went their hope of attaining their wish. As the day ended they found themselves beside some goatherds' huts, and they accordingly decided to spend the night there. Sancho was as much disappointed at their not having reached a town as his master was content with sleeping under the open sky; for it seemed to Don Quixote that every time this happened it merely provided him with yet another opportunity to establish his claim to the title of knight-errant."

CHAPTER 11.

The goatherds furnish a hearty supper which is capped by cheese and acorns, at which Don Quixote is moved to extol at some length the beauties of the Golden Age and the virtues of Arcadian life. "This long harangue on the part of our knight—it might very well have been dispensed with—was all due to the acorns they had given him, which had brought back to memory the age of gold; whereupon the whim had seized him to indulge in this futile harangue with the goatherds as his auditors. They listened in open-mouthed wonderment, saying not a word, and Sancho himself kept quiet and went on munching acorns, taking occasion very frequently to pay a visit to the second wine bag, which they had suspended from a cork tree to keep it cool.

"It took Don Quixote much longer to finish his speech than it did to put away his supper; and when he was through, one of the goatherds addressed him.

" 'In order that your Grace may say with more truth that we have received you with readiness and good will, we desire to give you solace and contentment by having one of our comrades, who will be here soon, sing for you. He is a very bright young fellow and deeply in love, and what is more, you could not ask for anything better than to hear him play the three-stringed lute.' " The young man, Antonio, appears and sings a love ballad. When Don Quixote complains of the pain in his ear, the magic balm is replaced by one of the goatherds with a salve made of rosemary, saliva, and salt, which takes away all pain. Don Quixote is quietly drunk: we feel it all through the end of the chapter, without the author's stressing the point.

CHAPTER 12.

Another lad comes up. His story of the love and death of Grisóstomo for Marcela coincidentally echoes Don Quixote's musings about shepherd-esses, and there is also a cork tree which gives its name to the spring where Grisóstomo's grave has been dug. The country lad, Pedro, speaks at first slovenly but, though Cervantes tries to keep up dramatic propriety by making him blunder, in the end he puts into Pedro's mouth language as fine and words as long as Don Quixote's. These two chapters 11 and 12 are moments of dreamy respite in the novel. By the way, here is the best bit of the lad's lyrical story, unsurpassed by the description of similar situations by young romanticists three hundred years later:

"Not far from here is a place where there are a couple of dozen tall beeches, and there is not a one of them on whose smooth bark Marcela's name has not been engraved; and above some of these inscriptions you will find a crown, as if by this her lover meant to indicate that she deserved to wear the garland of beauty above all the women on the earth. Here a shepherd sighs and there another voices his lament. Now are to be heard amorous ballads, and again despairing ditties. One will spend all the hours of the night seated at the foot of some oak or rock without once closing his tearful eyes, and the morning sun will find him there, stupefied and lost in thought. Another, without giving truce or respite to his sighs, will lie stretched upon the burning sands in the full heat of the most exhausting summer noontide, sending up his complaint to merciful Heaven."

CHAPTERS 13 and 14.

By the time of these chapters, when in a conversation with some amused traveling companions who take him for a quaint madman, Don Quixote discusses his profession, the parody—if parody there was—is felt to be at last completely lost in the pathetic. Don Quixote has already won his case with the reader; any person endowed with a sense of pity and beauty—which make up the true artistic sense—is now on Don Quixote's side. Mark the passage in which the knight compares his profession with that of the clergy, specifically the monks: "The religious, in all peace and tranquility, pray to Heaven for earth's good, but we soldiers and knights put their prayers into execution by defending with the might of our good right arms and at the edge of the sword those things for which they pray; and we do this not under cover of a roof but under the open sky, beneath the insufferable rays of the summer sun and the biting cold of winter. Thus we become the ministers of God on earth, and our arms the means by which He executes His decrees. And just as war and all the things that have to do with it are impossible without toil, sweat, and anxiety, it follows that those who have taken upon themselves such a profession must unquestionably labor harder than do those who in peace and tranquility and at their ease pray God to favor the ones who can do little in their own behalf.

"I do not mean to say—I should not think of saying [people had to be careful what they said in those pious days]—that the state of knight-errant is as holy as that of the cloistered monk; I merely would imply, from what I myself endure, that ours is beyond a doubt the more laborious and arduous calling, more beset by hunger and thirst, more wretched, ragged, and ridden with lice. It is an absolute certainty that the knights-errant of old experienced much misfortune in the course of their lives; and if some by their might and valor came to be emperors, you may take my word for it, it cost them dearly in blood and sweat, and if those who rose to such a rank had lacked enchanters and magicians to aid them, they surely would have been cheated of their desires, deceived in their hopes and expectations."

This and the following chapter 14 are a kind of intermezzo. The case of the student shepherd and his shepherdess, a real event, seems far more fantastic than Don Quixote's hallucinations. The whole story of Grisóstomo smacks of the pastoral, artificial, and sentimental; but it is necessary in a way to stress Don Quixote's fire and pluck, and the richness of his visions. Another section of the book ends quietly with this chapter 14. Marcela, the shepherdess, appears at the grave of the man who had hopelessly courted her and very reasonably states her side of the matter. Don Quixote's only part in the Grisóstomo-Marcela affair comes at the end when "thinking to himself that here was an opportunity to display his chivalry by succoring a damsel in distress, [he] laid his hand upon the hilt of his sword and cried out, loudly and distinctly, 'Let no person of whatever state or condition he may be dare to follow the beauteous Marcela under pain of incurring my furious wrath. She has shown with clear and sufficient reasons that little or no blame for Grisóstomo's death is to be attached to her; she has likewise shown how far she is from acceding to the desires of any of her suitors, and it is accordingly only just that in place of being hounded and persecuted she should be honored and esteemed by all good people in this world as the only woman in it who lives with such modesty and good intentions.' " And no one stirred from the spot until Grisóstomo's burial was over.

CHAPTER 15.

Casting around for some new way to introduce a new adventure, Cervantes remembers his hero's hack and has Rocinante suffer a severe beating at the hands of some carters (Yanguesans from northern Castile) who leave the horse "badly battered on the ground." When Don Quixote attacks them he is beaten with their packstaves and so shares defeat with his mount, left in a position fatal for an ordinary horse; but in a sense Rocinante is an enchanted animal, as its owner has an enchanted body, seeing that they survive the terrific beatings they get. However, as Don Quixote notes himself, Amadis of Gaul received once two hundred lashes with a horse's reins, while another knight endured a clyster of sand and snow water. Incidentally, we notice that Sancho Panza is not precisely a coward since he joins in a fray which he knows to be hopeless: " 'What the devil kind of vengeance are we going to take,' asked Sancho, 'seeing there are more than twenty of them and not more than two of us, or maybe one and a half?' "

Note that Don Quixote is not hallucinated in this chapter into taking the carters and their cudgels for knights with lances. On the contrary, he is quite lucid and reproaches himself afterward for having put hand to sword against men who had not been dubbed knights and so were not his equals.

CHAPTER 16.

There are a few kindhearted, humane people in the novel: the neighbor who took Don Quixote back to his village in the beginning was one, and now we meet with three others—an innkeeper's wife, her daughter, and her servant, all three of charitable disposition. "This gentle creature" is the epithet applied to the very ugly servant called Maritornes, the crooked Mary. But note that she will crucify and torture the knight for two hours in the later chapter 63. Up to here Cervantes has kept his story clean, but in this chapter there is a lewd passage when Maritornes, groping her way in her nightgown to the pallet of the muleteer who shared a bedroom with Don Quixote and Sancho, is seized by the knight under the delusion that she is a princess drawn to his bed, only to be rescued by the muleteer who beats the knight, while Maritornes, cast on Sancho, beats and is beaten by him. This scene with the wench and the brawl is well in keeping with the literary claptrap of the author's time. Yet observe, please, that quite apart from the labor of imagination involved in composing chapter after chapter, there is also a shrewd, keen, and sometimes a little desperate concentration on keeping up the reader's interest by means of varying the devices. Observe, too, the delightful plea Cervantes makes for more colorful and precise details in fiction. Here again is a precursor of the true romanticists rather than of the insipid and generalized novels, with their purely moral landscapes, of the eighteenth century:

"Cid Hamete Benengeli [the pretended chronicler] was a historian who was at great pains to ascertain the truth and very accurate in everything, as is evident from the fact that he did not see fit to pass over in silence those details that have been mentioned [the order of the beds in the 'starry stable' where the knight, the squire and the mule driver lay], however trifling and insignificant they may appear to be.

"All of which might serve as an example to those grave chroniclers who give us such brief and succinct accounts that we barely get a taste, the gist of the matter being left in their inkwells out of carelessness, malice, or ignorance. Blessings on the author [anonymous] of the *Tablante de Ricamonte* [1531] and the one [actually, various authors] who wrote that other work in which are related the deeds of Count Tomillas [1498]—with what exactitude they describe everything!"

By the way, the attitude toward these romances of chivalry has considerably improved. Just as for Molière there were "good" Précieuses and "bad" (i.e. "ridiculous") Précieuses, so apparently for Cervantes, as for the pretended chronicler Benengeli—and for the curate of the early pages—there are "good" novels of chivalry and "bad" ones. Since Don Quixote, in his "strange madness" was influenced by the whole lot, good and bad—with a slight tendency toward the good ones, however, because he was an experienced, artistic-minded, and discriminating reader—the parody of the genre is now in a bad way; in other words, the parody theme which had assumed at least six different aspects is on the point of either dying out or evolving some new twist.

CHAPTER 17.

When Don Quixote gets into a quarrel with the trooper of the Holy Brotherhood (highway police) he is hit on the head with an iron lamp. To cure his bruises he makes up the magic balm of Fierabrás, which he had committed to memory, consisting of rosemary (which is a kind of mint), oil, salt, and wine. It would be fine to try it. The description of the effect of half a quart on two different constitutions, Don Quixote and Sancho Panza, one vomiting, then sleeping and waking up much refreshed, the other suffering acute pains in the stomach, then vomiting and going into spasms and convulsions, without any sleep—this description is an excellent clinical observation. The oil, of course, was the chief mischief-maker.

The whole chapter, with the blanket-tossing of Sancho and the ugly and lewd servant girl's beautiful gesture at the end,* is superb.

CHAPTER 18.

Don Quixote undergoes another attack of "strange madness" when he

* Sancho, suffering from his beatings but even more from the effects of the magic potion, "started to take a drink; but perceiving at the first swallow that it was only water, he stopped and asked Maritornes to bring him some wine instead. She complied right willingly, paying for it out of her own money; for it is said of her that, although she occupied so lowly a station in life, there was something about her that remotely resembled a Christian woman. When he had drunk his fill, Sancho dug his heels into his ass's flanks, and the gate of the inn having been thrown wide open for him, he rode away quite well satisfied with himself because he had not had to pay anything, even though it had been at the expense of those usual bondsmen, his shoulders." Ed.

mistakes two flocks of sheep and the clouds of dust they raise for two mighty armies. Sancho protests:

" 'Sir,' he said, 'may I go to the devil if I see a single man, giant, or knight of all those that your grace is talking about. Who knows? Maybe it is another spell, like last night.'

" 'How can you say that?' replied Don Quixote. 'Can you not hear the neighing of the horses, the sound of trumpets, the roll of drums?'

" 'I hear nothing,' said Sancho, 'except the bleating of sheep.' "

A device, whose use is very convenient to end the description of Don Quixote's battles, is to have the mule-drivers or carters or herdsmen, immediately leave the scene, as here, when they see they have downed the madman by stoning him and knocking out some of his teeth, and perhaps have killed him. Another point of interest in this chapter is the theme of reality and transformation. Don Quixote even suggests a scientific experiment that would be conclusive evidence of the enchantment process.

" 'Didn't I tell you, Señor Don Quixote,' Sancho said, 'that you should come back, that those were not armies you were charging but flocks of sheep?'

" 'This,' said Don Quixote, 'is the work of that thieving magician, my enemy, who thus counterfeits things and causes them to disappear. You must know, Sancho, that it is very easy for them to make us assume any appearance that they choose; and so it is that malign one who persecutes me, envious of the glory he saw me about to achieve in this battle, changed the squadrons of the foe into flocks of sheep. If you do not believe me, I beseech you on my life to do one thing for me, that you may be undeceived and discover for yourself that what I say is true. Mount your ass and follow them quietly, and when you have gone a short way from here, you will see them become their former selves once more; they will no longer be sheep but men exactly as I described them to you in the first place.' " But then he hastily draws back and continues: " 'do not go now, for I need your kind assistance; come over here and have a look and tell me how many grinders are missing, for it feels as if I did not have a single one left.' "

The vomiting that takes place shortly in this scene when Don Quixote once again resorts to the magic potion is a little too much of the good thing, especially after the slapstick in the preceding chapter. Knight and squire are now at a very low point.

CHAPTER 19.

Don Quixote routs the mourners in a funeral procession under the delusion that they are devils carrying away the body of a dead or wounded knight.

"All these shirt-wearers were timid folk, without arms, and so, naturally enough, they speedily quit the fray and started running across the fields, still bearing their lighted torches in their hands, which gave them the appearance of masked figures darting here and there on some night when a fiesta or other celebration is being held. Those who wore the mourning, on the other hand, wrapped and swathed in their skirts and gowns, were unable to move, and, accordingly, with no risk to himself, Don Quixote smote them all and drove them off against their will. . . ."

All this is first-rate descriptive prose. We have to rely on the translator: It is a pity we cannot admire this in Spanish and thus enter into closer contact with the pure Castilian style.

"Sancho watched it all, greatly admiring his master's ardor. 'No doubt about it,' he told himself, 'he is as brave and powerful as he says he is.' "

CHAPTER 20.

The sly art with which Cervantes alternates the adventures of his hero is above praise. It was absolutely necessary for the sake of artistic balance to have the knight gain a graceful and easy victory in chapter 19. That procession had no business to go clad in Ku Klux Klan garb with torches and got what it deserved. This is the gist of Don Quixote's observation to the young clergyman whose leg he broke. The reader is perfectly indifferent to the plight of the white-shirted mourners, and is pleased not only with Don Quixote's abstract victory but also with the knowledge that Sancho Panza stole the rich provisions of the masked priests.

Chapter 20 begins with an excellent scientific observation coming from Sancho Panza: " 'It is not possible, sir,' said Sancho, 'that this grass should not betoken the presence near by of some spring or brook that provides it with moisture; and so it would be a good thing if we were to go a little farther, for I am sure we should be able to find someplace where we might quench this terrible thirst that is consuming us and that, undoubtedly, is more painful to bear than hunger.' " Both squire and knight have considerably gained in intelligence since we first met them. In this chapter we also have a specimen of Sancho's story-telling capacity; the passage about the goats being rowed across the stream is excellent for its wit.

A goatherd was going with his flock where his eyes would never more behold the girl who had been unfaithful to him. He came to the bank of the flood-swollen Guadiana River, which he could not cross. " 'As he was looking about, he saw a fisherman alongside a boat so small that it would hold only one person and a goat, but, nevertheless, he spoke to the man, who agreed to take the shepherd and his flock of three hundred to the opposite bank. The fisherman would climb into the boat and row one of the animals across and then return for another, and he kept this up, rowing across with a goat and coming back, rowing across and coming back—Your Grace must be sure to keep count of the goats that the fisherman rowed across the stream, for if a single one of them escapes your memory, the story is ended and it will not be possible to tell another word of it.'

" 'I will go on then, and tell you that the landing place on the other side was full of mud and slippery, and it took the fisherman a good while to make the trip each time; but in spite of that, he came back for another goat, and another, and another—'

" 'Just say he rowed them all across,' said Don Quixote, 'you need not be coming and going in that manner, or it will take you a year to get them all on the other side.'

" 'How many have gone across up to now?' Sancho demanded.

" 'How the devil should I know?' replied Don Quixote.

" 'There, what did I tell you? You should have kept better count. Well, then, by God the story's ended, for there is no going on with it.'

" 'How can that be?' said the knight. 'Is it so essential to know the exact number of goats that if I lose count of one of them you cannot tell the rest of the tale?'

" 'No, sir, I cannot by any means,' said Sancho; 'for when I asked your Grace to tell me how many goats had been rowed across and you replied that you did not know, at that very instant everything that I was about to say slipped my memory; and you may take my word for it, it was very good and you would have liked it.'

" 'So,' said Don Quixote, 'the story is ended, is it?' "

It was. The story that Sancho undertakes to tell is an old gag, however, probably of oriental origin. After this, there is again a scene in the coarse tradition of the day involving Sancho's incontinence of the bowels, followed by the adventure, or rather the non-adventure, of the six fulling hammers (for grooving and spreading iron), which is rather lame.

CHAPTER 21.

They see in the distance, on the highway, a man riding with something gleaming in the rain and the sun. Don Quixote demands, " 'Tell me, do you not see that knight coming toward us, mounted on a dappled gray steed and with a golden helmet on his head?'

" 'What I see and perceive,' said Sancho, 'is a man upon an ass, a gray ass like mine, with something or other on his head that shines.'

" 'Well,' said Don Quixote, 'that is Mambrino's helmet. Go off to one side and let me meet him singlehanded; and you shall see me end this adventure without wasting a word in parley, and when it is ended, the helmet which I have so greatly desired shall be mine.' "

The helmet that Don Quixote secures from overthrowing this barber, barber number two, was a barber's basin which the man had put on his head for protection against the weather. The chapter ends with a lengthy exposition by Don Quixote of a knight-errant's reception in a castle, in which Cervantes gives an admirable summary, without any extravagant caricature, of a typical romance of chivalry. "For every incident," says John Ormsby, the nineteenth-century translator of *Don Quixote* quoted by Putnam, "there is ample authority in the romances." It is a very lyrical and pathetic chapter, which should be studied closely.

CHAPTER 22.

Don Quixote sees "coming toward them down the road which they were following a dozen or so men on foot, strung together by their necks like beads on an iron chain and all of them wearing handcuffs. They were accompanied by two men on horseback and two on foot, the former carrying wheel-lock muskets while the other two were armed with swords and javelins." It was a chain of galley-slaves—people on their way to the galleys where they were forced to row: (1) A young man who had been caught stealing a basket of linen (*a lover* of linen); (2) a melancholy fellow who had "sung"—confessed under torture—that he was a cattle thief (*a singer* on the rack); (3) one condemned for a debt of five ducats (around twelve dollars); (4) a venerable man, a "body broker" (a pimp) who had been paraded in *a robe of state, on horseback*; (5) a student who had played too many pranks (*a Latin scholar*); (6) a mysterious thief, a jailed genius who had written the story of his life in prison, Ginés de Pasamonte, who will provide the sting in Don Quixote's victory by stealing Sancho Panza's ass later on.

Don Quixote addresses them as "my dearest brothers." He is there to "aid those who are oppressed by the powerful." However, the victory he achieves when he attacks the guards turns into defeat at the hands of those he has freed. That the liberated prisoners stone him is as logical a result of his madness (he demands of them that they present themselves before Dulcinea) as their liberation was.

CHAPTER 23.

In the Sierra Morena Don Quixote meets Cardenio, the Ragged One of the Sickly Countenance. (The theft of Sancho's mount is an interpolation by Cervantes himself, but he did not correct later passages where Sancho Panza still has his donkey.) Now begins the adventure of the memorandum book belonging to the rejected lover, Cardenio, which they find. The manuscript is within the manuscript, for let us not forget that from a certain point (beginning with chapter 9 to be exact) the whole account is supposed to come from the pen of an Arabian chronicler.

"Leafing nearly all the way through the little book, [Don Quixote] came upon other verses and letters, some of which he was able to read while others he could not. They were filled, all of them, with complaints, laments, misgivings, expressions of joy and sadness, talk of favors granted and a suit rejected. Some were exalted in tone, others mournful. While Don Quixote was going through the book, Sancho was doing the same with the valise; there was not a corner of it, or of the saddle pad, that he did not search, scrutinize, and pry into, not a seam that he did not rip out, not a tuft of wool that he did not unravel, being determined to let nothing escape him from want of care and proper pains, so great was the covetousness that had been awakened in him by the crowns he had discovered, a hundred or more of them all told. And although he found nothing more, he still felt that the tossings in the blanket, the potion that he had drunk, the benediction of the stakes, the mule driver's punches, the loss of his saddlebags, the theft of his greatcoat, and all the hunger, thirst, and weariness that he had known in his good master's service, had been amply repaid by the finding of this treasure."

Important observation: we know that Don Quixote is ready to turn any reality "no matter how drab" into a plumed and painted illusion. By now, however, reality itself is taking on the colors of the romance he has imbued it with. The story of the forlorn lover in this chapter has all the trappings of those very romances. Don Quixote, on this mountain pass, has reached a crag where illusion and reality merge. There can be no question of any parody of knight-errantry here.

"As the youth [Cardenio] came up, he greeted them in a hoarse, discordant voice, but very courteously. Don Quixote returned his salutation no less politely, and, dismounting from Rocinante, he gently and gracefully went over and embraced the young man, holding him tightly in his arms for some little while, as if he had known him for a long time. The Ragged One of the Sickly Countenance, as we may call him—just as Don Quixote is the Knight of the Mournful Countenance—after permitting himself to be embraced, fell back a step or two and laid his hands upon Don Quixote's shoulders as if to see whether or not he knew him, for it may be that he was no less astonished at beholding the knight's face, figure, and suit of armor than the knight was at seeing him. To make a long story short, the first to speak was the Ragged One, and what he had to say will be set forth in the following pages."

CHAPTER 24.

The story of the Ragged One of the Sickly Countenance is told in this chapter and Don Quixote listens with professional interest. The youth is also called the "Knight of the Mountain" or "of the Wood." Both are now firmly planted in reality, which has completely fused with their knight-errantry.

" 'My own desire,' said Don Quixote, 'is to be of service to you. . . . I would beg you, sir, by all in this life that you love or have loved, to tell me who you are and what it is that has brought you to live and die like a brute beast amid these solitudes, for your person and your bearing show that the life you now lead is one that is alien to you. And I further swear, by the order of knighthood which I, though unworthy and a sinner, have received, and by my profession of knight-errant, that if you accede to my request, I will serve you in accordance with those obligations I have assumed, either by helping you if there is any help to be had, or by weeping with you as I have promised.' " Note that Don Quixote has all his wits about him: when Cardenio begs him not to interrupt his mournful tale, "This remark reminded Don Quixote of the story his squire had told him, when the knight had been unable to remember the number of goats that had crossed the river and the tale had been left hanging in the air."

Cardenio raves about his love: "Ah, good Heaven, how many letters I wrote her! How many charmingly modest answers did I receive! How many love verses did I compose in which my heart declared and translated its feelings, painted its kindled desires, feasted on its memories, and re-created its passion," etc., etc. " 'And then it came about that Luscinda asked me for a book of chivalry to read, one of which she was very fond, the *Amadis of Gaul*—'

"No sooner did he hear a book of chivalry mentioned than Don Quixote spoke up. 'Had your Grace told me,' he said, 'at the beginning of your story that Señora Luscinda was fond of books of that sort, it would not have been necessary for you to add anything more in order to give me an idea of her superior qualities of mind,' " and he proceeded at some length with titles he would especially recommend.

"As Don Quixote was saying all this, Cardenio's head had sunk to his bosom and he gave evidence of being deeply lost in thought. [In fact, his madness had come back upon him.] Although the knight twice requested him to go on with his story, he did not raise his head nor utter a word in reply. Finally, however, after a good while, he did so.

" 'I cannot rid myself of the thought,' he said, 'nor will anyone in the world ever be able to rid me of it or make me believe anything else— indeed, he would be a blockhead who believed the contrary—no, I am convinced that great villain of an Elisabat was living in adultery with the Queen Madásima—'

" 'That,' replied Don Quixote in high dudgeon, 'is not true, I swear it is not!' And he turned upon him angrily as he always did in such cases. 'That is pure malice, or, better, a most villainous assertion. The Queen Madásima was an illustrious lady, and it is not to be presumed that a princess of her high birth would commit adultery with a quack. Whoever says that she would lies like a villain himself, and I will give him so to understand, mounted or on foot, armed or unarmed, day or night, as he may prefer—'

"Cardenio was now staring attentively at the knight, for his madness had come upon him again and he was in no condition to go on with his story, nor was Don Quixote capable of listening to it, so disgusted was he with what he had just heard regarding Queen Madásima. A strange thing! but he felt impelled to defend her as if she had been his own lady, to such a pass had those unholy books of his brought him. Cardenio, then, being mad as I have said, upon hearing himself called a liar and a villain, along with other epithets of the same sort, and not fancying the jest, picked up a stone that was lying near him and let Don Quixote have such a blow in the chest with it as to lay him flat on his back."

This is a masterly stroke on the part of the author! After fusing the illusion of chivalry romances with the reality of rugged mountains and ragged misery, he shifts gears to madness caused not by the emotions of characters in tales of chivalry (and both Don Quixote and Cardenio are such characters at this point), but to madness caused by the reading of such tales. Cardenio's Luscinda, that tender abstraction, is replaced by a still more abstract abstraction, the Queen Madásima of old romances. The whole story of Don Quixote's adventures has come back to its premise: pulp literature softens the brain. At the end of the chapter Sancho rushes to defend his master but is felled by Cardenio's fist, and the goatherd suffers the same fate when he attempts to rescue Sancho. Sancho and the goatherd then maul each other while Cardenio escapes.

CHAPTER 25.

As the knight and his squire ride toward the higher mountains the Madásima and Elisabat case is further discussed. Amadis is shown to be Don Quixote's favorite knight, "one of the most perfect of knights-errant. . . . he was the sole and only one, the very first, the lord of all those in the world in his time." Homer's Ulysses and Vergil's Aeneas "are not depicted or revealed to us as they were but as they ought to have been, that they may remain as an example of those qualities for future generations. In the same way, Amadis was the north star, the morning star, the sun of all valiant and enamored knights, and all those of us who fight beneath the banner of love and chivalry should imitate him."

Don Quixote means to imitate Amadis, as well, by playing the part of a desperate and raving madman.

" 'It strikes me,' said Sancho, 'that those knights who did all that had provocation and some cause for such foolish penances, but what reason has your Grace for going mad, what damsel has rejected you, or what signs have you found that lead you to think the lady Dulcinea del Toboso has been up to some foolishness with a Moor or Christian?'

" 'That,' said Don Quixote, 'is the point of the thing; that is the beautiful part of it. What thanks does a knight-errant deserve for going mad when he has good cause? The thing is to go out of my head without any occasion for it, thus letting my lady see, if I do this for her in the dry, what I would do in the wet.' "

The meeting with the lovelorn knight prompts Don Quixote to send a letter to Dulcinea. Sancho Panza finds out who she is in reality and here is her description:

" 'Aha!' said Sancho, 'so the lady Dulcinea del Toboso is Lorenzo Corchuelo's daughter, otherwise known as Aldonza Lorenzo?'

" 'That is the one,' said Don Quixote, 'and she deserves to be mistress of the entire universe.'

" 'I know her well,' Sancho went on, 'and I may tell you that she can toss a bar as well as the lustiest lad in all the village. Long live the Giver of all good things, but she's a sturdy wench, fit as a fiddle and right in the middle of everything that's doing. She can take care of any knight-errant or about to err that has her for a mistress! Son of a whore, what strength she has and what a voice! They tell me that one day she went up into the village belfry to call some lads who were out in the field that belongs to her father, and although they were more than half a league away, they heard her as plainly as if they had been standing at the foot of the tower. And the best of it is, there's nothing prudish about her; she's very friendly with everybody and always laughing and joking. . . . I'd like to be on my way just to have a look at her again, for it's been a long time since I saw her, and the sun and air do a lot to the complexion of a woman who's all the time working in the field.' "

And this is Don Quixote's wonderful and noble and absolutely logical answer: "For you should know, Sancho, if you do not know already, that the two things that more than any others incite to love are great beauty and a good name, and these two things are to be found to a consummate degree in Dulcinea; for in beauty none can vie with her, and in good name few can come up to her. But to bring all this to a conclusion: I am content to imagine that what I say is so and that she is neither more nor less than I picture her and would have her be, in comeliness and in high estate. Neither Helen nor Lucretia nor any of the other women of bygone ages, Greek, Latin, or barbarian, can hold a candle to her. And let anyone say what he likes; if for this I am reprehended by the ignorant, I shall not be blamed by men of discernment."

Don Quixote writes the letter in Cardenio's memorandum book and Sancho departs on Rocinante (his own gray having been stolen by Ginés de Pasamonte).

CHAPTER 26.

The plot has gradually gathered its coils and develops something more than episodic interest. We are very eager to follow Sancho Panza to El Toboso. On the way he meets the village curate and barber and tells them, " 'My master is up there in the middle of those mountains doing penance and enjoying himself very much,' " which exactly sums up the case. "And then, all in one breath and without stopping, he proceeded to tell them of the state that Don Quixote was in, the adventures that had happened to him, and how he, Sancho, was at present carrying a letter to the lady Dulcinea del Toboso. . . . But when Sancho put his hand in his bosom to search for the book he could not find it, and he would not have been able to find it if he had searched until now, for the reason that Don Quixote still had it, the squire having forgotten to ask him for it." Sancho forgetting the book and the letter is a charming stroke of genius. He delivers mangled parts of the letter and expounds on the riches that await him, Sancho Panza. "He said all this with so much composure and so little show of judgment, wiping his nose from time to time, that his friends could not but marvel once more as they reflected how very infectious Don Quixote's madness must be to have turned the head of this poor man in such a fashion."

In order to persuade Don Quixote to leave the mountain, the curate proposes to disguise himself as a woman, the barber as her squire, and to beg the Don to accompany them to repair the wrong done her by a wicked knight.

CHAPTER 27.

The plot now develops in two directions: we are anxious to have Sancho Panza and Dulcinea brought together, and we are also interested in the masquerade the curate and the barber undertake in order to get Don Quixote home. Sancho Panza, however, turns back and rides with the two.

The curate is a good sport, and what bothers him is not that Don Quixote is doing penance in a rather unchristian and fantastic way, but that he is mad and should be helped and cured. As already observed in connection with the walling up of Don Quixote's study, the priest's actions (disguised as a woman, etc.) show that the good man had a merry streak of madness too.

Don Quixote had not heard the end of Cardenio's story, but now the two friends meet him on their way up the mountain and he tells of his loss of Luscinda to his friend Don Fernando. It is very curious the way a really romantic and dramatic sequence of events develops behind the backs of Don Quixote's books, so to speak. The villain Don Fernando is a suitable match for our hero, who at the moment, however, is thinking of other things. Note how prettily the color and light scheme is worked in when Cardenio describes Luscinda at the wedding: "She was made up and adorned as befitted her rank and beauty, as for a festive or ceremonial occasion. I had neither the time nor the presence of mind to note the details of her costume, but was conscious only of the colors that she wore, crimson and white, and of the glitter of the gems and jewels on her headdress and all over her robe, which, however, could not vie with the striking beauty of her blond hair, which was such as far to outshine the precious stones and the light from the four torches that flared in the room."

CHAPTER 28.

The author realizes that his plot is like a ball of bright yarn being wound—he refers at the beginning of this chapter to the "hackled [roughly cut, combed?], twisting, winding thread" of his work.

A second romantically mad creature, Dorotea, disguised as a boy, is discovered. With Don Quixote, this makes three guys raving in the heart of the Sierra Morena.* Dorotea provides a sample of preciosity and long-windedness—the girl's preamble can be boiled down to five simple statements. Note further the fancy coincidence, a feature of romantic tales, that Dorotea's seducer is Fernando, the enemy of our friend Cardenio. Note Cardenio's behavior when his Luscinda is mentioned: he "did no more than shrug his shoulders, bite his lips, and arch his brows as a double stream of tears poured from his eyes."

Dorotea goes on with her tale to what sounds uncommonly like the strain of the "Beautiful Tennessee Waltz." Cardenio has a pleasant surprise when Dorotea describes Luscinda's wedding: "It seemed that, after the cermony had been performed and Luscinda had given him [Fernando] her promise to be his bride, she had been seized with a violent fainting fit, and when he had opened her bodice to give her air he had found there a letter in her handwriting in which she stated and declared that she could not be his bride for the reason that she belonged to Cardenio—the name, so the man assured me, of a leading gentleman of that same city—adding that if she had said yes to Fernando, it was to avoid having to disobey her parents." Note how the Cardenio-Luscinda adventure is neatly spread over sixty pages (up to here) with interruptions leaving, first, the reader wondering what Fernando had done to Cardenio, and, second, what were the contents of the letter Fernando found on his bride. The only artistic and structural importance of these trivial interpolations is their effect on Don Quixote and upon the general development of the novel. I have already spoken of their connection with the books Don Quixote had read. Actually, there is not much to choose between Dorotea and the young lady you know so well, the one in tattered shorts with the pear-shaped tear and the below-sea-level neckline, Daisy Mae. But Dorotea and her like came first, four hundred years ago, in the infancy of European literature,

* To *Sierra Morena* VN appends the note: "mountain range in the south-western part of Spain; the highest peak is about 8,000 feet, and the parallel is between that of Philadelphia and San Francisco, if that means anything to you who have never been taught geography and have no sense of world figuration whatsoever. What land do you get to if you go straight north along the meridian of Rio de Janeiro? The tip of Greenland; you miss this continent of North America completely."

and it is something of a pity that we have to view them against our will through the foolscap of today's trite commercial concoctions.

CHAPTER 29.

A continuation of the Cardenio-Luscinda-Fernando-Dorotea business. Cardenio says to Dorotea: "I swear to you by the faith of a gentleman and a Christian not to desert you until I see you possessed of Don Fernando. If words will not bring him to recognize his obligations to you, then I will make use of that privilege which my rank as a gentleman gives me and will justly challenge him, calling upon him to give an account of the wrong he has done you, without taking thought of those that I have suffered at his hands and which I shall leave to Heaven to avenge while I here on earth see to righting yours." This is exactly what Don Quixote would have said. The parody of a gallant romance is completely lost here in a gallant romance itself, silly as it is. Life plays up to Don Quixote and his books, but while the windmills and innkeepers of the novel seem to us reasonably real, that is, true to the average reader's conception of windmills and innkeepers, the lovelorn lad and lass we have here seem to us a product of the very thing— sentimental literature—that drove Don Quixote mad. I urge you to grasp this point.

We now have Don Quixote on our hands. Very neatly Dorotea remarks that "she could play the part of the damsel in distress better than the barber; and what was more, she had with her the garments that would enable her to give a most lifelike semblance to the role. All they needed to do was to leave it all to her and she would see to everything that was necessary to the carrying out of their plan, for she had read many books of chivalry and was familiar with the mode of speech that was employed by afflicted maidens when they sought a boon of knights-errant."

We do not appreciate the subtle difference between her real plight and the plight of a damsel in distress in books of chivalry. It seems all one to us, and Don Quixote consequently becomes a real knight-errant, a real helper and avenger, since Dorotea is really a damsel in distress. For readers of the author's day, beginning of the seventeenth century, the difference may have been more accented, since the main fact looming above all others was, to them, (1) the absence of ironclad knights-errant in the Spanish countryside, and (2) the presence of Fernando and Dorotea, and their love affair, in contemporaneous novels. Note how the curate performs the subtle switch from Dorotea's own plight to a story that might appeal to the Don Quixote-Sancho Panza team. She, he says to Sancho, "is heiress in the direct male line to the great kingdom of Micomicón, and she comes here in search of your master to ask a favor of him, which is that he right the injury or wrong which a wicked giant has done her. By reason of the fame as a worthy knight which your master enjoys throughout the known world, this princess has journeyed all the way from Guinea to seek him out."

Note that Sancho Panza is in the plot to bring Don Quixote home in that he believes what the curate invents. The substitution of the giant-killing fantasy for the Fernando affair, with the victim of the latter acting as the victim of the former, is very amusing from the structural point of view. Don Quixote, we presume, might as willingly come to her assistance in her real predicament as related by her. The usurped kingdom she refers to is, after all, a plausible euphemism for her purloined virginity. The chivalry-book theme used to deceive Don Quixote is but a peg higher in the scale of absurdity, as we see the thing now. But the reaction to these absurd matters on the part of Don Quixote who, owing to the artistic and moral genius of his creator, is an artistic reality to the reader of any age—this reaction of his is human and divine and absolutely delightful and pathetic as all his gestures are, and this redeems the interpolations. " 'No matter who she may be,' said Don Quixote, 'I shall do my duty and follow the dictates of my conscience in accordance with the calling that I profess.' And, turning to the damsel, he added, 'Rise, most beautiful one; I grant you the boon you seek.' " At this interview between the knight and Dorotea "The barber was still on his knees, doing his best to keep from laughing and to prevent his [false] beard from falling off, for if that had happened they would not have been able to carry out their clever scheme." But the scheme is not clever, and the matter is nothing to laugh at. What we suddenly glimpse is: a damsel in real distress and a real knight.

The fanciful thoughts of Sancho Panza with respect to the Negroes, his fanciful vassals, are also not so fanciful as that. Mourning the loss of his ass, Sancho trudges along on foot as they leave the mountain, "although he bore it all very cheerfully, being convinced that his master was on the road to becoming an emperor very soon; for there was no doubt that he would marry this princess and become at the very least king of Micomicón. The only thing that troubled Sancho was that the kingdom in question was in the land of the blacks, and his vassals accordingly would be Negroes. But for this he at once thought of a good remedy.

" 'Does it make any difference to me if they are black?' he said to himself. 'What more do I have to do than take a boatload of them to Spain and sell them for ready cash, and with the money buy some title or office and live at ease all the rest of my life? That is to say, unless I'm asleep and am not clever or shrewd enough to make the most of things and sell thirty or ten thousand vassals in the twinkling of an eye! By God, but I'd make them fly, the little with the big, or do the best I could at it; I'd turn the blacks into white or yellow men! But come, I'm making a fool of myself!'

"Occupied with these thoughts, he went along so contentedly that he forgot all about his annoyance at having to travel on foot."

Many fortunes have been made exactly according to Sancho's receipt, both in Holland and in the Southern States, and elsewhere, in the old days, by very commonsensical men. Sancho Panza is the grandpa of all tycoons.

CHAPTER 30.

A structural return to a former incident—the freeing of the galley-slaves by Don Quixote—is performed at the end of the preceding chapter and the beginning of this one, clinching the unity of events. The freed criminals are said (falsely) by the curate to have robbed him. Don Quixote blushes at first, but then makes a strong and noble remark, in keeping with his character: "It is not the business of knights-errant to stop and ascertain as to whether the afflicted and oppressed whom they encounter going along the road in chains like that are in such straits by reason of their crimes or as a result of misfortunes that they have suffered. The only thing that does concern them is to aid those individuals as persons in distress, with an eye to their sufferings and not to their villainies."

Another twist: It seems at first blush not very plausible that young Dorotea should join in the fun and invent fanciful stories about herself when she is in such emotional difficulties. The story she makes up is less fantastic than her real one.

" 'Fate has been kind to me and I have found Señor Don Quixote. As a consequence, I already account and look upon myself as the queen and liege lady of all my realm, since he out of his courtesy and splendid bounty has promised to grant me the boon of going with me wherever I may take him, and that will be nowhere else than to the place where he may confront Pandafilando of the Frowning Look, in order that he may slay him and restore to me those domains that the giant has so unjustly usurped. And all this is bound to come about, for my good father, Tinacrio the Wise, has prophesied it; and he also said, and put down in writing, in Chaldean or Greek characters which I am unable to read, that if this knight, after having beheaded the giant, wished to marry me, I was to give myself at once, with not the slightest demurring, to be his legitimate bride, and I was to yield him possession of my kingdom along with that of my person.'

" 'What do you think of that, friend Sancho?' said Don Quixote at this point. 'Do you hear what is happening? What did I tell you? Just look, we already have a kingdom to rule over and a queen to wed.' "

Two things are bothering the author: (1) the absence of Sancho Panza's mount (a very unnecessary deprivation in the first place), and (2) the fact that owing to the complicated Dorotea affair and her joining in the curate's plot to get Don Quixote home, the author has not had a chance to have Don Quixote and Sancho Panza talk about Dulcinea—a subject which logically should have been at the top of the mess in Don Quixote's brain (though it may be argued that he is more interested in discovering Dulcinea as a fair vision in the mirror of chivalry than as a real person to whom one can send a message). By the end of the chapter the gray is back (due to a second-edition interpolation) and Don Quixote asks about Dulcinea and Sancho Panza's errand.

CHAPTER 31.

" 'What was my beauteous queen engaged in doing when you arrived? Surely you must have found her stringing pearls or embroidering some device in gold thread for this her captive knight.'

" 'No,' replied Sancho [making up the whole thing], 'I did not. I found her winnowing two fanegas [three bushels] of wheat in the stable yard of her house.'

" 'If that is so,' said Don Quixote, 'then you may be sure that those grains of wheat were so many pearls when her fingers touched them. And did you observe, my friend, if the wheat was fine and white or of the ordinary spring-sown variety?'

" 'It was neither,' Sancho informed him; 'it was the reddish kind.'

" 'Then I assure you,' the knight insisted, 'that without a doubt, when winnowed by her hands, it made the finest of white bread. But go on. When you gave her my letter, did she kiss it? Did she place it on her head or accord it any ceremony such as it deserved? If not, what was it that she did?'

" 'When I went to give it to her,' said Sancho, 'she was busy swinging the sieve, with a good part of the wheat in it, from side to side. "Lay it on that sack," she said to me, "I'll not have time to read it until I have finished sifting all that is here."

" 'Discreet lady!' said Don Quixote. 'That was in order that she might take her time in reading it and revel in it.' "

An important note of structure: Cervantes for the sake of keeping the novel together (it threatens to sprawl at this point), has the characters either recall past events or has characters from former chapters appear again. Thus on his errand to Dulcinea, Sancho passes through the village where he had been blanket-tossed. Thus the galley-slaves are mentioned by the priest; thus the robber who stole Sancho's ass appears again in a gypsy's garb; thus the lad whom Don Quixote had attempted to save from the brutal farmer clasps the good knight's knees again. The continuation of these episodes along the main current of the story (which after all began with the bubbles of parody and then flowed on as an account of a pathetic and noble creature's mad fancies)—the continuation and development of these episodes along the main current do give the story the kind of sweeping unity that in our minds is associated with the form of the novel.

CHAPTER 32.

At the inn at which the very mixed company stops there takes place an admirable discussion of books of chivalry—this is yet another subject that Cervantes with much skill brings to the fore to promote and preserve the structural unity of the book. What the servant girl Maritornes, a none-too-happy and none-too-handsome wench, has to say on this subject is worth quoting:

" 'I give you my word, I also like to hear about those things, for they are very pretty, especially when they tell about some lady or other being embraced by her knight under the orange trees while a duenna keeps watch over them, and she herself is dying of envy and fright. I say that all that is better than honey.' [Note the orange trees and the envious chaperone.]

" 'And what do you think, young lady?' said the curate, addressing the innkeeper's daughter.

" 'I really cannot tell you, sir,' she replied. 'Although I do not understand them, I get a great deal of pleasure out of listening to them. The only thing is, I do not like those blows that my father speaks of; I prefer the laments which the knights utter when absent from their lady loves and which sometimes make me weep from sympathy.'

" 'Well, young lady,' said Dorotea, 'would you console them if it was for you that they wept?'

" 'I do not know what I should do,' the girl answered. 'All I know is that some of those ladies are so cruel that they call their knights tigers and lions and a thousand other nasty things like that. Good Lord! I don't know what kind of creatures they can be, without soul or conscience, if they cannot give a decent man so much as a glance but leave him to die or go mad. I don't see how they can be such prudes. If it is their honor they are thinking about, let them marry, for that is all the poor knights desire.' "

The whole conversation is very amusing. The original book burning episode is referred to again when the curate tries to burn certain chivalry books that have been left with the innkeeper. The curate seems to prefer a semblance of reality or history in them.

CHAPTERS 33-35.

An interpolation. A story in manuscript that was in the innkeeper's small but choice library. The curate proposes to read it were the time not better spent in sleeping, but in the nick of time Cervantes remembers that Dorotea may not be in the right mood for sleeping: " 'I shall have my fill of rest,' said Dorotea, 'in passing the time away by listening to some story; for my mind is not as yet sufficiently calm to permit me to sleep when I ought to do so.' " Thus encouraged, in chapter 33 the curate starts to read the "Story of the One Who Was Too Curious for His Own Good" (often known as "The Curious Impertinent"). This triangle of the two friends Anselmo and Lotario and Anselmo's wife Camila whom he seeks to test, with unfortunate results, is in the tradition of the Renaissance. These tales of intrigue were lapped up by contemporaneous readers. I want you to note the sustained metaphor of the mine: "If, then, the mine of her honor, beauty, modesty, and reserve yields you without any labor on your part all the wealth that it holds and that you could want, why do you wish to go deeper into the earth and seek out new veins of new and unheard-of treasure at the risk of bringing everything down, since when all is said it is supported only on the weak props of her frail nature? Bear in mind that when a man seeks the impossible, it is only just that the possible be denied him." We shall call it the Prospector Simile.

The intrigue follows its tricky trail. It is all incredible nonsense, deceit and eavesdropping being the usual bedsprings of the thing.

CHAPTER 36.

Four masked men arrive at the inn accompanying a weeping lady. In a series of mutual unmaskings and recognitions, Luscinda, the lady, is reunited with Cardenio and Don Fernando with Dorotea, all this happening while Don Quixote is asleep upstairs.

CHAPTER 37.

At the beginning of chapter 35, the curate's reading of the tale was interrupted by Don Quixote's dream that he is slaying the giant who oppressed Dorotea; instead he only slashed wineskins hung on the wall. It is now decided that the deception of the Don should continue, and Dorotea, after some question whether she has or has not been enchanted into an ordinary damsel, is once more Queen of Micomicón. At the inn arrives a stranger, who had been a captive of the Moors, accompanying a veiled Moorish damsel. Don Quixote begins an elaborate discourse on knight-errantry.

CHAPTER 38.

Don Quixote continues his discourse. A commentator on the Spanish text, however, observes that "this discussion of the subject of arms and letters—who suffers more, the penniless scholar or the warrior, etc.—has its roots in the ancient literature of medieval times and comes to be a commonplace with the authors of the sixteenth century." In the present case, its importance is a structural one: it reinforces and causes to blossom at the right moment and in the right place the personality of Don Quixote. Note the hard words he directs against artillery, the introduction of which had done away with the type of knighthood and manner of fighting for which Don Quixote stood:

"Happy were the blessed ages that were free of those devilish instruments of artillery, whose inventor, I feel certain, is now in Hell paying the penalty for his diabolic device—a device by means of which an infamous and cowardly arm may take the life of a valiant knight, without his knowing how or from where the blow fell, when amid that courage and fire that is kindled in the breasts of the brave suddenly there comes a random bullet, fired it may be by someone who fled in terror at the flash of his own accursed machine and who thus in an instant cuts off and brings to an end the projects and the life of one who deserved to live for ages to come.

"And so, from this point of view, I could almost say that it grieves my soul that I have taken up the profession of knight-errant in an age so detestable as this one in which we now live. For, although no danger strikes terror in my bosom, I do fear that powder and lead may deprive me of the opportunity to make myself famous and renowned, by the might of my arm and the edge of my sword, throughout the whole of the known world. But

Heaven's will be done. If I succeed in carrying out my design, I shall be all the more honored for it, inasmuch as I shall have confronted greater perils than the knights-errant of old ever did."

CHAPTERS 39-41.

The Captive's Story begins after Don Quixote's discourse. As its background are the Allies (Flanders, Venice, and Spain) against the Turks (Turks, Moors, Arabs), the time being the 'sixties and 'seventies of the sixteenth century. Again the commentator on the Spanish text points out that this tale of a father sending out his three sons into the world to choose their careers is a common one in the folk literature of Europe. Here we have the "Church, the Sea, or the Royal Household," or, in simpler terms, Letters, Trade, Military Profession. The way the Captive (who chose the military) was captured is of interest since his story resembles Cervantes's own life story. At Lepanto "I leaped aboard the enemy galley, which, by veering off from the attacking vessel, prevented my men from following me. Thus I was alone among the enemy, who so greatly outnumbered me that any hope of resistance was vain; and the short of it is, after I had been badly wounded, they captured me." This interpolated story is of a completely different brand than those we had already encountered. But will the "realistic" tone last?

The author does appear himself, a Spanish soldier by the name of Saavedra: "for although this man had done things which will remain in the memory of that people for years to come, and all by way of obtaining his liberty, yet the Moor never dealt him a blow nor ordered him flogged; as a matter of fact, he never even gave him so much as a harsh word. And for the least of the many things that Saavedra did, we were all afraid that he would be impaled, and he himself feared it more than once. If time permitted, which unfortunately it does not, I could tell you here and now something of that soldier's exploits which would interest and amaze you much more than my own story."*

In this chapter 40 the story of the Captive takes a romantic turn for the worse. In fact, it becomes very poor. In chapter 41 the story of the beautiful Zoraida who helped the young Spaniard to escape and escaped with him

---

* Following this quotation, VN has a short paragraph, "The following reminds us vividly of the way many a Nazi used to plead his case when brought to court for his crimes." The reference appears to be to the Captive's account of the manner in which certain Christian renegades protected themselves by testimonials from captives in their charge in case they returned to their native country. This particular renegade helps the Captive and escapes with him.

drags on. [N.B. Her father's name is Hadji Morato.] It does gain some vitality, however, when the old Moor roundly curses his escaping daughter: "O infamous and ill-advised maiden! Where do you think you are going, so blindly and foolishly, with these dogs, our natural enemies? Cursed be the hour in which I begot you, and cursed all the luxury in which I have reared you!" But on the whole, at this stage, the tale is only a little above the level of the Italianate intrigues in the earlier interpolations. There are pleasing pictures, however, such as of the gallant French pirate: "It may have been around midday when they put us in the boat, giving us two kegs of water and some biscuit. And as the lovely Zoraida went to embark, the captain, moved by some sympathetic impulse or other, gave her as many as twenty gold crowns and would not permit his men to take from her those garments that she is now wearing." And the account is charming of the first countryman the narrator sees when they have landed in Spain: "We had gone, I imagine, a little less than a quarter of a league when there reached our ears the sound of a little bell, which showed plainly that we must be near some flock or herd, and as we all gazed about us attentively to see if we could discern any, we saw at the foot of a cork tree a young shepherd who very calmly and unconcernedly was engaged in whittling a stick with his knife."

CHAPTER 42.

Further happenings at the inn take place immediately after the soldier has finished his tale. A coach drives up and "At that moment there descended from the coach an individual whose garb plainly indicated the office and rank he held; for his long robe with the ruffled sleeves showed him to be a judge, as his servant had said. By his hand he led a damsel who looked to be around sixteen years of age. She was in traveling attire and was so beautiful, well bred, and elegant in appearance that all who beheld her were struck with admiration. Indeed, had they not seen Dorotea and Luscinda and Zoraida, who were now inside the inn, they would have regarded the maiden's loveliness as being of a sort that was hard to find."

Surprise, surprise! It is the soldier's brother and his daughter. The judge is bound for Mexico, of all places. Cervantes is heaping up events in a rather reckless way and forgets, when the company all sit down to supper, that in fact those at the inn have already eaten. The third of the three brothers is in Peru and enormously rich. Note how much ground the last chapters have covered—Belgium, France, Italy, Asia Minor, Africa, Central and South America. When the two brothers embrace, "The words which

[they] exchanged, the feelings they displayed, were such, I think, as could hardly be imagined, much less described." The author has sunk very low. An attempt, however, is made to come up to the Don Quixote level: "Don Quixote stood there all the while observing these happenings most attentively but saying not a word, for he associated them all with his chimerical fancies that had to do with knight-errantry." Later, as they retire for the night, "Don Quixote offered to stand guard over the castle lest they be attacked by some giant or wandering rogue of evil intent who might be covetous of the great treasure of feminine beauty within these walls."

While Don Quixote stands sentinel outside the slumbering inn, the chapter ends rather charmingly with a song in the darkness. "At times the singing appeared to come from the courtyard, at other times from the stable; and as [the damsels] were straining their ears and wondering about it, Cardenio came to the door of their room.

" 'Those of you who are not asleep,' he said, 'should listen, and you will hear the voice of a mule driver who sings most charmingly.'

" 'We hear it, sir,' replied Dorotea. And with this Cardenio went away."

CHAPTER 43.

The inn is becoming rather crowded. We shall also note that Cervantes has hit on the convenient "island" device which consists in grouping characters in some isolated limited locus—an island, a hotel, a ship, an airplane, a country-house, a railway car. As a matter of fact, it is also Dostoevski's device, in his completely irresponsible and somewhat antiquated novels, where a dozen of people have a tremendous row in a roomette on a train—a train that moves not. And to move still farther, the same trick of grouping people in one place is, of course, used in the modern mystery story where a number of potential suspects are isolated in a snowbound hotel, or in a solitary country-house, et cetera, so as to neatly limit possible clues in the little reader's mind.

Luscinda, Dorotea, Zoraida have settled their accounts with the reader, but there is still the judge's daughter, Clara. And sure enough, the mule driver who sings outside is her lover.* Ah, he is not a mule driver, but a gentleman's son. Clara tells her story into Dorotea's ear.

Maritornes, the servant girl, and the innkeeper's daughter play a prank on Don Quixote. This is an excellent scene from the artistic point of view

* Putnam notes that the second poem, the ballad, "is said to have been set to music by Don Salvatore Luis, in 1591, fourteen years before the *Don Quixote* appeared." VN

but its cruelty is appalling. Don Quixote gets to his feet on Rocinante's saddle in order to reach the window-sill where, as he imagined, a brokenhearted damsel stood. " 'Lady,' he was saying, 'take this hand. . . . The hand of no other woman has ever touched it, not even that of her who holds entire possession of my body. I extend it to thee, not that thou shouldst kiss it, but that thou mayest study the contexture of the sinews, the network of the muscles, the breadth and spaciousness of the veins, from which thou canst deduce how great must be the might of the arm that supports it.'

" 'That we shall soon see,' said Maritornes. And making a slip-knot of the halter [which she had taken from Sancho's ass], she put it over his wrist; then, getting down from the opening, she tied the other end to the bolt on the door of the loft." Then some horsemen approach, Rocinante moves, and Don Quixote is left hanging, we may suggest from the shadow of a cross.

CHAPTER 44.

The Clara-Luis romance continues, and the youth's story now runs concomitantly with a new event: the landlord is being beaten by two guests, a quarrel in which Don Quixote finally intervenes to settle it by mild and persuasive reasoning. Luis confesses his love for Clara to her father, who, though perplexed, is agreeble to the suit. In a recall from the past, the barber earlier met on the road appears and accuses Don Quixote of stealing his basin and Sancho Panza his packsaddle.

CHAPTER 45.

Don Quixote's barber friend, the curate, and the others, join Don Quixote for the sake of a little fun in declaring that the other barber's basin is a helmet. This is an excellent scene. " 'And if anyone states the contrary,' maintained Don Quixote, 'I will have him know that he lies, if he be a knight, and if he be a squire, that he lies a thousand times.'

"Our own barber, who had witnessed all this and who was well acquainted with Don Quixote's fancies, now decided to fall in with them and carry the joke a little further so that they might all have a good laugh.

" 'Master barber,' he said, addressing the other one, 'or whoever you may be, I may inform you that I also am of your profession and have held a license for more than twenty years, being quite familiar with each and every tool that a barber uses. And in my youth I was a soldier for some little while, and I likewise know what a helmet is, and a morion, and a closed helmet, along with other things having to do with a soldier's life. And I can tell you—standing always to be corrected by those of better judgment—that the piece we have before us here, which that worthy gentleman holds in his hands, is as far from being a barber's basin as white is from black or truth from falsehood; and I further assert that it is a helmet, though not a whole one.' "

All of the company support the first barber that it is indeed a helmet.

" 'God help me!' cried the barber of whom they were making sport. 'Is it possible that so many worthy folk can say that this is not a basin but a helmet? It is enough to astonish an entire university, however learned it may be. But enough; if this basin is a helmet, then this saddlebag must be a horse's trappings, as this gentleman has just stated.

" 'It looks to me like a saddlebag,' Don Quixote admitted, 'but as I have said, it is something that does not concern me.' " The company decides that Fernando should take a secret vote. "To those acquainted with Don Quixote's mad whims, all this was very amusing indeed, but to the rest it seemed utter nonsense. This was especially true of Don Luis's four servants, and of their master as well, so far as that was concerned; besides whom there were three other travelers who had just arrived at the inn and who had the appearance of being patrolmen of the Holy Brotherhood, as in fact they were. The one, however, who was the most desperately bewildered of all was the barber, whose basin, there in front of his eyes, had turned into Mambrino's helmet, and whose packsaddle, also, he had not the slightest doubt, was due to turn into the rich caparison of a steed."

Don Fernando announces the vote that the packsaddle is indeed a horse's caparison, but one of Don Luis's servants objects, and the troopers now coming in, one of them cries out angrily, " 'That is as much a packsaddle as my father is my father, and he who says anything else must be drunk.'

" 'You lie like a peasant knave!' replied Don Quixote. And, raising his pike, which he never let out of his hands, he aimed such a blow at the trooper's head that if the officer had not dodged, it would have left him stretched out on the ground." A free-for-all now takes place, which is suddenly quelled by Don Quixote, who admits that no one knows what the fight is all about. After peace is declared, the knight is almost arrested by a zealous member of the Brotherhood as a highwayman who had freed the galley-slaves. Don Quixote scorns the charge: "Who, I ask it again, is the stupid one who does not know that there are no letters-patent of nobility that confer such privileges and exemptions as those that a knight-errant acquires the day he is dubbed a knight and devotes himself to the rigorous duties of his calling? When did such a knight ever pay poll-tax, excise, queen's pattens, king's levies, toll, or ferry? What tailor ever took payment for the clothes he made for him? What castellan who received him in his castle ever made him pay his score? What king would not seat him at his board? What damsel but did love him, being ready to yield herself wholly to his will and pleasure? And, finally, what knight-errant was there ever, or ever will be in this world, without the mettle to deal singlehanded four hundred sturdy blows to any four hundred officers of the Holy Brotherhood that come his way?"

CHAPTER 46.

The disputes are finally settled when the curate convinces the troopers of Don Quixote's madness and gives the barber some money for his basin. Don Quixote still has the job of liberating Dorotea from the "giant," and he flies into a rage with Sancho who, having seen Don Fernando steal a kiss from Dorotea, tells Don Quixote that she is not a queen at all. Don Fernando, as peacemaker, reconciles the two by avouching that Sancho has been bewitched, an explanation that the knight readily accepts. His proffered services to Queen Micomicona are graciously accepted, but in the end it is decided that the curate and barber will take Don Quixote back to his village without incommoding Don Fernando and his bride. The company, disguising themselves, "very quietly entered the room where [Don Quixote] lay sleeping and resting from his recent frays, wholly unsuspecting of anything of this sort. Going up to him, they seized him firmly and bound him hand and foot, so that when he awoke with a start, he was unable to move or do anything except marvel at finding himself surrounded by so many strange faces. As a result, his disordered mind at once began to fancy that all these figures were phantoms of that enchanted castle and that he himself, without a doubt, was under a magic spell, seeing that he could not move nor defend himself. All of which was just as the curate, the originator of this scheme, had planned it." As they place him in a cage that has been constructed the barber in a sepulchral voice issues a prophecy that the imprisonment will only speed the mating of the Manchegan lion with the Tobosan dove. "Don Quixote was greatly consoled by these predictions, for he at once grasped their purport to the effect that he was to be united in holy and lawful bonds of matrimony with his beloved Dulcinea del Toboso, from whose fortunate loins should come forth whelps that were his sons, to the perpetual glory of La Mancha."

CHAPTER 47.

At last, and only here, the author manages to get rid of the puppets he had set in motion in chapter 23. "They all embraced one another and agreed to keep in touch by letter. . . ." None of them cares a jot for the poor Don Quixote at this point. As the cage is drawn along the highway with the enchanted knight inside, the curate meets a canon, whereupon there is a lengthy discourse about chivalry books as the cause of the Don's madness, in which both agree that the aesthetic sense cannot be accompanied by falsehood and nonsense. In a less detailed form we have heard this from the curate in the book burning chapter.

CHAPTER 48.

The canon continues to expatiate on the faults of chivalric romances and the conversation then drifts to the silly comedies of the time. "All of these pieces, or the greater part of them at any rate, whether purely fictitious or historical in character, are obviously nonsensical, without head or tail, yet the public takes pleasure in witnessing them and regards them as worthy productions, though they are far from good. And the authors who compose them and the actors who perform them tell us that plays have to be of this sort, since the public wants precisely that kind of thing and nothing else, whereas those pieces that have a plot and develop the story in an artistic fashion will appeal only to a handful of intelligent persons who are able to understand them, while all the others will fail to perceive the art that is in them." The curate joins in the canon's abuse by denouncing the sins against unity of time and place in plays: "I have witnessed a comedy in which the first act takes place in Europe, the second in Asia, and the third in Africa— and if there had been a fourth act, the scene would have been laid in America and thus they would have encompassed the four quarters of the globe." He is for truth in literature (as was Tolstoy). The curate criticizes Lope de Vega: "That this is so [i.e., that plays will not be bought unless they conform to the pattern] may be seen from the countless number of comedies composed by one of the most fertile minds in this realm, plays so full of brilliancy and grace, marked by such polished versification, admirable dialogue, and profound wisdom, and, finally, so full of eloquence and so elevated in style, that his fame has gone out to all the world; and yet, owing to the necessity he has been under of having to adapt them to the taste of the players, not all his productions have attained that degree of perfection that is to be desired." Finally, he proposes a type of censorship that is typical of modern police states, and stems from Plato.

CHAPTER 49.

Sancho tries to prove to Don Quixote that he is not enchanted since he must satisfy the humble and humdrum needs of nature. Don Quixote retorts that, perhaps, the fashion in enchantments has changed.

" 'I would ask your Grace [said Sancho], speaking with all due respect, if by any chance, since you have been in that cage and, as it seems to you, under a spell, you have felt the need of doing a major or a minor, as the saying goes.'

" 'I do not understand what you mean by "doing a major or a minor," Sancho. Speak more plainly if you wish me to give you a direct answer.'

" 'Is it possible that your Grace doesn't know what "a major or a minor" is? Why, lads in school are weaned on it. What I mean to say is, have you felt like doing that which can't be put off?'

" 'Ah, I understand you, Sancho! Yes, many times, and for that matter, right now. Get me out of this, or all will not be as clean here as it ought to be!'

" 'Ha!' cried Sancho [as chapter 49 opens], 'I have you there! That is what I wanted with all my life and soul to know! Come now, sir, can you deny the common saying around here when a person is out of sorts: "I don't know what's the matter with So-and-So; he neither eats nor drinks nor sleeps nor gives you a sensible answer to any question that you ask him; he must be bewitched?" From which we are to gather that while those that do not do any of these things or attend to those duties of nature that I have mentioned are under a spell, the ones like your Grace, on the other hand, who feel a desire to do them, who eat and drink what is set before them and answer all questions, are not enchanted.'

" 'You speak the truth, Sancho,' replied Don Quixote, 'but as I have told you before there are many ways of being enchanted, and it may be that the fashion has changed with the course of time and that today those who are in such a plight do everything that I do, although formerly such was not the case. So, there is no use arguing against custom or drawing inferences as you are doing. I know for a certainty that I am the victim of an enchanter, and that is all I need to know to set my conscience at rest, for it would hurt me sorely if I thought that, without being enchanted, I had slothfully and like a coward permitted myself to be put into a cage, thus cheating the wretched and the needy who at this very moment may be in great distress for want of my aid and protection.' "

Don Quixote argues with the canon about the reality of knights-errant and their adventures in books of chivalry, and "The canon as he listened was amazed at the manner in which Don Quixote jumbled truth and falsehood and also at the knowledge he possessed of everything touching upon and pertaining to those feats of knight-errantry of which he was so fond."

CHAPTER 50.

Don Quixote continues to defend the books of chivalry that he loves so dearly. "Do you mean to tell me that those books that have been printed with a royal license and with the approval of the ones to whom they have been submitted and which are read with general enjoyment and praised by young and old alike, by rich and poor, the learned and the ignorant, the gentry and the plain people—in brief, by all sorts of persons of every condition and walk in life—do you mean to tell me that they are but lies? Do they not have every appearance of being true? Do they not tell us who the father, mother, relatives of these knights were, the name of the country from which they came, their age, the feats that they performed, point by point and day by day, and the places where all these events occurred? Your Grace had best be silent and not utter such a blasphemy. . . ." He proceeds with the delightful description of the reception of the Knight of the Lake, quoted in Lecture III, and concludes: " 'As for myself, I may say that, since becoming a knight-errant, I am brave, polite, liberal, well-bred, generous, courteous, bold, gentle, patient, and long-suffering when it comes to enduring hardships, imprisonment, and enchantments; and although it was only a short while ago that I was shut up in a cage as a madman, I still expect, through the valor of my arm, with Heaven favoring and fortune not opposing, to find myself within a few days king of some realm or other where I may be able to display the gratitude and liberality that is in my heart. . . . I wish that fortune would speedily provide me with the opportunity of becoming an emperor in order that I might make manifest the virtues of my heart by doing good to my friends, and especially to this poor fellow, Sancho Panza, my squire, who is the best little man in the world; I should like to reward him by conferring upon him an earldom, which I promised him long ago. The only thing is I do not know if he has the ability to govern it.'

"These last words were no sooner out of his mouth than Sancho broke in upon his master. 'Just you see to it that I get that earldom, Señor Don Quixote,' he said, 'the one you promised me and which I have been waiting for all this time, and I give you my word that I'll be able to govern it all right; and if I should fail, I've heard them say that there are men in this world who rent such estates from their lords, giving them so much a year, while they themselves take over the government, in which case all the lord has to do is to stretch out his legs and enjoy his income without worrying about anything else. That's what I'll do. I'll not haggle over a penny here and a penny there. I'll get rid of all the bother and live like a duke on what's coming to me.' "

CHAPTER 51.

As the company is eating, a goatherd tells still another story about lovelorn shepherds and persecuted maidens. He has become a misogynist in contrast to the other shepherds who spend their time lamenting the fickle Leandra, now safely shut in a convent by her father after an escapade with a soldier.

CHAPTER 52.

If he can be released from his enchantment by a still more powerful magician, as he prays, Don Quixote offers his services to the goatherd Eugenio to rescue Leandra from the convent.

"The goatherd stared at him, observing in some astonishment the knight's unprepossessing appearance.

" 'Sir,' he said, turning to the barber who sat beside him, 'who is this man who looks so strange and talks in this way?'

" 'Who should it be,' the barber replied, 'if not the famous Don Quixote de la Mancha, righter of wrongs, avenger of injustices, protector of damsels, terror of giants, and champion of battles?'

" 'That,' said the goatherd, 'sounds to me like the sort of thing you read of in books of chivalry, where they do all those things that your Grace has mentioned in connection with this man. But if you ask me, either your Grace is joking or this worthy gentleman must have a number of rooms to let inside his head.'

" 'You are the greatest villain that ever was!' cried Don Quixote when he heard this. 'It is you who are the empty one; I am fuller than the bitch that bore you ever was.' Saying this, he snatched a loaf of bread that was lying beside him and hurled it straight in the goatherd's face with such force as to flatten the man's nose."

A fight between the two follows, in which Don Quixote gets the worst of it, interrupted by the appearance of a procession bearing the statue of the

Virgin, a sight that Don Quixote immediately takes for a group of brigands abducting a highborn lady. When he wades into them with his sword he receives a blow with a stick from one of the penitents that knocks him to the ground unconscious.

"At the sound of Sancho's cries and moans, Don Quixote revived, and the first thing he said was, 'He who lives apart from thee, O fairest Dulcinea, is subject to greater woes than those I now endure. Friend Sancho, help me onto that enchanted cart, as I am in no condition to sit in Rocinante's saddle with this shoulder of mine knocked to pieces the way it is.'

" 'That I will gladly do, my master,' replied Sancho, 'and we will go back to my village in the company of these gentlemen who are concerned for your welfare, and there we will arrange for another sally and one, let us hope, that will bring us more profit and fame than this one has.'

" 'Well spoken, Sancho,' said Don Quixote, 'for it will be an act of great prudence to wait until the present evil influence of the stars has passed.' "

This is the end of Cervantes's first part and of Don Quixote's second sally. He will stay at home, resting and dreaming for at least a month. Note, please, that in the course of these fifty-two chapters (more than four hundred pages) we have not yet met Dulcinea. After three epitaphs and some poorly translated sonnets supposedly written in praise of Don Quixote, Sancho, Rocinante, and Dulcinea, all of which end the first part, Cervantes half promises a third sally.

Defeat

Battle with Robbers - 82 -
abducting a Lady

Protector of Damsels in Distress
(Chivalry)

78

Chapter LII, p. 452 - 453

While the goatherd (who has been sarcastic about knight-
errantry) and Don Quixote fight, with the latter getting the
worst of it,

p.454. "The barber, however, so contrived it that the goatherd
came down on top of his opponent, upon whom he now showered
so many blows that the poor knight's countenance was soon
as bloody as his own.

As all this went on, the canon and the curate were
laughing fit to burst, the troopers were dancing with glee,
and they all hissed on the pair as men do at a dogfight."

The sound of a trumpet and a procession of people praying
for rain interrupt this scene. *the fight with the goatherd*

The score of Don Quixote's defeats and victories is 12 - 6.
The new adventures Don Quixote bears down upon *this a procession of* penitents
whom he mistakes for brigands carrying away a highborn lady,
in reality an image of the Virgin. Don Quixote suffers his *final defeat*
in the first part, when one of the bearers of the image almost kills him with a pole that
THIRTEENTH defeat. 13 - 6 is the final score. He is brought *Props the litter*
home in a daze. *with a [epitaphs (said*
to be found after a third sally Don Quixote made -- a vague
tradition of his having gone to Saragossa where he was present
at some famous tournaments. The author half promises an account
of his further adventures. Some sonnets (poorly translated)
are thrown in for good measure. Note please that in the course
of these 52 chapters (more than 400 pages) we have not yet
met Dulcinea.

discussed in other lecture

Note that First part ends with score 69-25, 5-6,

4-4

13 first to 13 defeat

*This is the end of his the first
part and of his second sally. He will stay at
home, resting and dreaming for at least a month.
Note that Cervantes [...]*

A page from Nabokov's notes and commentary revised for "Victories and Defeats"

Narrative and Commentary
Part Two (1615)

The grotesque "approbations" that preface this volume are in the spirit of modern Fascist or Soviet dictatorships and would have been approved by Plato, a fine artist-philosopher but a vicious sociologist.

Cervantes himself, an educated person, finds "droll" forms of cruelty that are absolutely impossible today in this country or in England and are, of course, censured by all civilized people in modern times. One suspects that now and then the author himself does not quite realize how disgustingly cruel the priests, barbers, innkeepers, etc. were in relation to Don Quixote.

CHAPTER 1.

When the barber and the curate come to visit Don Quixote, "they found their host seated upon the bed, clad in a green baize waistcoat and a red Toledo cap, and looking as withered and dried up as an Egyptian mummy. He received them very well and, when they made inquiries regarding his health, discussed with them this and other matters of a personal nature most sensibly and in words that were very well chosen." Even when they came to statecraft, "all the while Don Quixote displayed such good sound sense in connection with whatever topic was broached as to lead the two examiners to feel that he must undoubtedly be fully recovered and in his right mind." But to make the test complete, the curate remarks that the Turks are about to attack Christendom.

" 'Then, damn it, sir!' exclaimed the knight, 'what more need his Majesty do than command by public proclamation that all the knights-errant at present wandering over Spain shall assemble in the capital on a given day? Even if no more than half a dozen came, there well might be one among them who alone would be able to overthrow the Turk's mighty power. Pay attention, your Worships, and listen closely to what I am about to say. Is it by any chance an unheard-of thing for a single knight-errant to rout an army of two hundred thousand men, as if they all had but one throat or were made of sugar paste? Tell me, how many stories do we have that are filled with such marvels? If only, alas for me (I do not care to speak for any other), the famous Don Belianís were alive today, or any of the countless other descendants of Amadis of Gaul! . . .'

" 'Oh, dear,' wailed the niece at this point, 'may they slay me if my master doesn't want to go back to being a knight-errant!'

" 'A knight-errant I shall live and die,' said Don Quixote, 'and let the Turk come or go as he will, with all the strength he can muster. Again I say to you, God understands.' "

The barber tells a tale of a mad licentiate in Seville, who appears to have been cured and is about to be discharged from the madhouse when another madman, jealous of his departure, calls himself Jupiter and threatens never to permit any rain to fall on Seville.

"The bystanders all listened attentively to the madman's words and cries. Then our licentiate turned to the chaplain and seized his hands. 'Do not be disturbed, your Grace,' he pleaded, 'and pay no attention to what this fellow says. If he is Jupiter and will not rain, then I who am Neptune, father and god of the waters, will do so at any time that I feel like it or whenever it may be necessary.'

" 'For all of that, Sir Neptune,' the chaplain answered him, 'it would be as well not to annoy Sir Jupiter. Stay here, your Grace, and another day, when we have more time and it is more convenient, we will return for you.' "

Don Quixote sees but does not appreciate the point of the tale. "I, Master Barber, am not Neptune, god of the waters, nor would I have anyone take me for a wise man when I am not wise. My sole endeavor is to bring the world to realize the mistake it is making in failing to revive that happiest of times when the order of knight-errantry was in the field. But this degenerate age of ours does not deserve to enjoy so great a blessing as that which former ages knew, when wandering men of arms took upon themselves the defense of realms, the protection of damsels, the succor of orphans, the punishment of the proud, and the rewarding of the humble.

"The knights of the present time, for the most part, are accompanied by the rustling of damasks, brocades, and other rich stuffs that they wear, rather than by the rattling of coats of mail. There is none that sleeps in the field, exposed to the inclemency of the heavens and fully armed from head to foot. There is none who, as they say, snatches forty winks without taking foot from stirrup, merely by leaning on his lance. There is none who, sallying forth from a wood, will go up onto yonder mountain, and from there come down to tread the barren and deserted shore beside a sea that is almost always angry and tempest-tossed; or who, finding upon the beach a small craft, without oars, sail, mast, or rigging of any kind, will leap into it with intrepid heart and entrust himself to the implacable waves of the stormy deep, waves that now mount heavenward and now drag him down into the abyss. Such a one, breasting the irresistible tempest, may find himself more than three thousand miles from the place where he embarked; in which case, bounding ashore upon the soil of a remote and unknown land, he will meet with such adventures as are worthy of being recorded, not upon parchment but in bronze."

This is a very fine chapter.

CHAPTER 2.

Despite the outcries of the housekeeper and niece, Sancho Panza makes his way in to Don Quixote. They discuss their former adventures and then Don Quixote asks, "Sancho, my friend, tell me, what are they saying about me here in the village? What opinion do the people have of me, and what do the gentry think, the *hidalgos* and the *caballeros*? What do they say of my valor, of my exploits, of my courtesy? What kind of talk is there about my having undertaken to restore to the world the forgotten order of chivalry?"

After some urging, Sancho tells the truth. "Well, in the first place, the common people look upon your Grace as an utter madman and me as no less a fool. The *hidalgos* are saying that, not content with being a gentleman, you have had to put a 'Don' in front of your name and at a bound have made yourself into a *caballero*, with four vinestocks, a couple of acres of land, and one tatter in front and another behind."

Don Quixote's reply is dignified: " 'That,' said the knight, 'has nothing to do with me, since I always go well dressed and never in patches. Ragged I well may be, but rather from the wear and tear of armor than of time.' " (Putnam has a note of the Spanish proverb "An honored gentleman goes ragged rather than patched.")

Sancho also brings the news that a student at Salamanca who has just been made a bachelor, the son of Bartolomé Carrasco, has just come home with the news that Don Quixote and Sancho Panza have been put into a book. At the knight's request, Sancho goes in search of the young man.

CHAPTER 3.

The bachelor "Sansón, or Samson, was not very big so far as bodily size went, but he was a great joker, with a sallow complexion and a ready wit. He was going on twenty-four and had a round face, a snub nose, and a large mouth, all of which showed him to be of a mischievous disposition and fond of jests and witticisms." He confirms that such a book has indeed been published. Putnam has a note about this: "Only one month is supposed to have elapsed since Don Quixote's return from his wanderings, yet the story of his adventures has already been written and printed and, as we are soon to be told, has been distributed to the extent of some twelve thousand copies. Cervantes, however, is never concerned with discrepancies of this sort, and on the present occasion explains the matter by having resort to the magician's art." He is still the arch magician, the inventor of a Benengeli and his Arabian tale.

" 'But tell me, Señor Bachelor, what adventures of mine as set down in this book have made the deepest impression?.'

" 'As to that,' the bachelor answered, 'opinions differ, for it is a matter of individual taste. There are some who are very fond of the adventure of the windmills—those windmills which to your Grace appeared to be so many Briareuses and giants. Others like the episode at the fulling mill. One relishes the story of the two armies which took on the appearance of droves of sheep, while another fancies the tale of the dead man whom they were taking to Segovia for burial. One will assert that the freeing of the galley slaves is the best of all, and yet another will maintain that nothing can come up to the Benedictine giants and the encounter with the valiant Biscayan.' " Carrasco mentions that some criticism has been made of the inserted novella and of the author's forgetfulness about such matters as the theft of Sancho's ass.

CHAPTER 4.

Sancho tries to straighten out the matter but fails and finally confesses, "I don't know what answer to give you . . . except that the one who wrote the story must have made a mistake, or else it must be due to carelessness on the part of the printer."

Don Quixote inquires, " 'And does the author by any chance promise a second part?'

" 'Yes, he does,' said Sansón, 'but he states that he has not yet come upon it, nor does he know in whose possession it is, and accordingly there is a doubt as to whether it will appear or not. Indeed, there is some question as to whether a second part is desirable. There are those who say, "Sequels are never good," while others assert, "Enough has been written already about Don Quixote." But certain ones who are more jovially inclined and not of so morose a disposition will tell you, "Let us have more of these Quixotic adventures; let Don Quixote lay on and Sancho talk, and, come what may, we shall be satisfied.' "

" 'And how does the author feel about it?'

" 'If he finds the history he is looking for so diligently,' said Sansón, 'he will send it to the printer at once, being more interested in the profit that may come to him from it than in any praise it may earn him.' "

Sancho immediately puts in: " 'Let that Moorish gentleman, or whoever he is, pay attention, and my master and I will supply him with enough stuff, ready at hand, in the way of adventures and other happenings, to make not only one second part but a hundred of them. The good man thinks, no doubt, that we are asleep here in the straw, but let him hold up our hoofs to be shod and he will see which foot is the lame one. All I have to say is that if my master would take my advice, we would be in the field this minute, avenging outrages and righting wrongs as is the use and custom of good knights-errant.'

"No sooner had Sancho said this than they heard the whinnying of Rocinante, which Don Quixote took to be a very good omen; and he resolved then and there that they would sally forth again within the next three or four days."

CHAPTER 5.

This chapter consists entirely of the conversation between Sancho and his wife Teresa when she learns he is to accompany Don Quixote on further adventures. In what appears to be an afterthought, Cervantes opens the chapter thus: "As he comes to set down this fifth chapter of our history, the translator desires to make it plain that he looks upon it as apocryphal, since in it Sancho Panza speaks in a manner that does not appear to go with his limited intelligence and indulges in such subtle observations that it is quite impossible to conceive of his saying the things attributed to him. However, the translator in question did not wish to leave his task unfinished; and the narrative is accordingly herewith resumed."

Sancho's wife, by preface, tells him: "Listen to me, Sancho. . . . Ever since you joined up with a knight-errant, you've been talking in such a roundabout way that there's no understanding you."

After Sancho becomes a governor, he plans to marry his daughter to a count. " 'And now that luck is knocking at our door, we don't want to shut it out. Let us go with the favoring breeze that fills our sail.' (It was this way of speaking, and what Sancho has to say a little further on, that led the translator of the history to remark that he looked upon this chapter as apocryphal.)" Later, " 'If I remember rightly, [the padre] said that all present things which our eyes behold make much more of an impression on us and remain better fixed in our memories than things that are past.' (These remarks of Sancho's are another reason for the translator's saying what he did about the apocryphal nature of the chapter, since they are beyond the mental capacity of the squire.) '. . . And—these were the padre's very words—if the one that fortune has thus raised up out of the depths to the height of prosperity is well bred, generous, and courteous toward all and does not seek to vie with those that come of an old and noble line, then you may depend upon it, Teresa, there will be no one to remember what he was, but instead they will respect him for what he is, unless it be the envious, for no good fortune is safe against them.' "

But the special topic is Sancho's prospects. " 'It's not to a wedding that we're bound; we're out to roam the world and play give and take with giants, dragons, and other monsters. We'll be hearing hissings and roarings and bellowings and howlings. But all that would be lavender if we didn't have to count upon meeting with Yanguesans and enchanted Moors.'

" 'I know well, my husband,' said Teresa, 'that the squires of knights-errant have to earn the bread they eat, and so I will keep on praying to Our Lord to get you out of all this hard luck.'

" 'I can tell you one thing, wife,' said Sancho, 'that if I did not expect to see myself governor of an island before long, I would die right here and now.'

" 'No, not that, my husband,' Teresa protested. 'Let the hen live even though she may have the pip, and in the same way you should go on living and to the devil with all the governorships in the world. Without a governorship you came out of your mother's belly, without a governorship you've lived up to now, and without a governorship you will go, or they will carry you, to your grave when God so wills. There are plenty of folk in this world who manage to get along without being governors, yet they do not for that reason give up but are still numbered among the living. The best sauce in the world is hunger, and since this is something they never lack, the poor always have an appetite. But look, Sancho, if by any chance you do fall in with a governorship, don't forget me and your children. Remember that little Sancho is already turned fifteen, and it is only right that he should go to school, if his uncle, the abbot, means to have him trained for the Church. Remember, too, that your daughter, Mari-Sancha, would not drop dead if we married her off; for I have my suspicions that she is as anxious for a husband as you are to be a governor, and, when all is said and done, a daughter badly married is better than one well kept outside of marriage.' "

But Sancho's plan to make his daughter a countess and to marry her to a nobleman does not suit Teresa, who begins to weep in earnest. "Sancho consoled her by assuring her that, while he might have to make his daughter a countess, he would put off doing so as long as he could. Thus ended the conversation, and Sancho went back to see Don Quixote to make arrangements for their departure."

CHAPTER 6.

Don Quixote has a parallel conversation with his niece, who says, "your Grace must remember that all this you are saying about knights-errant is a fable and a lie. And as for those history books, if they are not to be burned, they ought all to wear the *sambenito** or some other sign to show how infamous they are and how they corrupt good manners." The Don's reaction is predictable:

" 'By the God who sustains me!' exclaimed Don Quixote, 'if you were not my flesh-and-blood niece, being the daughter of my own sister, I would so punish you for the blasphemy you have uttered that all the world would hear about it. How comes it that a lass who barely knows how to handle a dozen lace bobbins should set her tongue to wagging and presume to criticize these knightly histories? What would my lord Amadis say if he could hear such a thing? To be sure, he would pardon you, since he was the most humble and courteous knight of his age, and was, moreover, a great protector of damsels.' "

He points out that all the people in this world can be divided into four classes: (1) those who from humble beginning have attained greatness; (2)

* VN quotes Putnam's note: "The *sambenito* was the garment worn by those who, having been tried by the Inquisition, had confessed and repented. It was a yellow linen garment painted over with devils and flames and was worn by the condemned as they went to the stake."

those who were and remain great; (3) those who have from original greatness tapered to a pyramidal point; and (4) those who were and remain ordinary. Then he addresses his niece and housekeeper: "What brings happiness to the possessor of wealth is not the having but the spending of it, and by that I mean, spending it well and not simply to gratify his own whims. The gentleman who is poor, however, has no other means of proving that he is a gentleman than by following the path of virtue, by being affable, well bred, courteous and polite, and prompt to do favors for others; he will not be proud and haughty or a backbiter, and, above all, he will be charitable. . . . There are two paths, my daughters, by which men may succeed in becoming rich and honored. One is that of letters, the other that of arms. For my part, I am more inclined to the latter than to the former. Indeed, so strong is my inclination that it would seem that I must have been born under the influence of the planet Mars. And so I am practically compelled to follow that path, and I shall keep to it in spite of all the world. "

CHAPTER 7.

Don Quixote and Sancho discuss the matter of wages. " '[Teresa] said that I should get everything down in black and white with your Grace, to let papers talk and beards be still, since he who binds does not wrangle, and one "take" is worth a couple of "I'll give you's." And I can tell you that a woman's advice is of little worth and he who won't take it is a fool.'

" 'And so say I,' observed Don Quixote. 'Go on, friend Sancho, you are in rare form today.'

" 'The fact of the matter is, as your Grace well knows,' continued Sancho, 'we are all of us subject to death, we are here today and gone tomorrow, and the lamb goes as soon as the sheep, and no one can promise himself more hours of life in this world than God may see fit to give him, for death is deaf, and when it comes to knock at the door of our life it is always in a hurry, and neither prayers nor force nor scepters nor miters can hold it back, all of which is a matter of common talk and knowledge and we hear it from the pulpit right along.' "

The constant flow of proverbs coming from Sancho is a little boring. However, when Don Quixote, on purpose, counterattacks with a shower of proverbs, the fun is still quite fresh. "And so, my good Sancho, go back home and tell your Teresa how I feel about it, and if she and you are willing to depend upon my favors, *bene quidem*, and if not, we will be as good friends as we were before; for if there is no lack of food in the pigeon house, it will not lack pigeons. And remember, my son, a good hope is better than a bad holding, and a good complaint better than bad pay. If I speak in this manner, Sancho, it is to show you that I, too, can scatter proverbs like showers." The threat of taking Carrasco as squire brings Sancho to heel. He and Don Quixote embrace and with Carrasco's encouragement they start out after three days for El Toboso.

CHAPTER 8.

" 'Blessed be the mighty Allah!' exclaims [Cid] Hamete Benengeli at the beginning of this eighth chapter; and he repeats it three times: 'Blessed be Allah!' He goes on to tell us that the reason for the benediction is his thankfulness at seeing Don Quixote and Sancho together once more, and he wishes the readers of this pleasant chronicle to feel that the exploits and the drolleries of the knight and his squire really start at this point. Let them forget, he says, the chivalrous deeds which the Ingenious Gentleman has performed in the past and fix their eyes, rather, on those that are to come and that have their beginning here and now on the El Toboso highway just as the others began on the plains of Montiel."

Cervantes is taking no chances: he does not care to have the reader look back and notice all the discrepancies or repetitions. In this second part, also, Cervantes seems to have his eye fixed on the Church with more circumspection than in the first part. This may account for such speeches as the following by Don Quixote, as they ride along the highway toward Dulcinea:

"We Christians, Catholics, and knights-errant . . . are more concerned with the glory that, in ages to come, shall be eternal in the ethereal and celestial regions than we are with the vanity of that fame that is to be won in this present and finite time; for however long such fame may endure, it needs must finally end with the world itself, the close of which has been foreordained.

"And so, Sancho, our deeds should not exceed those limits set by the Christian religion which we profess. In confronting giants, it is the sin of pride that we slay, even as we combat envy with generosity and goodness of heart; anger with equanimity and a calm bearing; gluttony and an overfondness for sleep, by eating little when we do eat and by keeping long vigils; lust and lewdness, with the loyalty that we show to those whom we have made the mistresses of our affections; and sloth, by going everywhere in the world in search of opportunities that may and do make of us famous knights as well as better Christians. You may behold here, Sancho, the means by which one may attain the highest praise that the right sort of fame brings with it.' ". . .

"In talk of this kind they spent that night and the following day, without anything happening to them worthy of note, at which Don Quixote was not a little put out. On the day after that, at sunset, they sighted the great city of El Toboso. The knight was elated, but Sancho was downcast, for he did not know where Dulcinea lived nor had he ever in his life laid eyes upon her any more than his master had.* As a result, each of them was uneasy in his mind, the one being anxious to behold her while the other was worried because he had not already seen her. Sancho could not imagine what he was going to do when his master should send him into the town; but Don Quixote finally decided that they would wait until nightfall to make their entrance, and in the meanwhile they tarried amid some oak trees that grew round about."

CHAPTER 9.

When the two enter the city at midnight there is a stumbling search in the dark for a palace in a back alley. Sancho finally in desperation suggests that Don Quixote hide in a forest while he, Sancho, goes to find Dulcinea.

CHAPTER 10.

Don Quixote sends Sancho with a message to Dulcinea, a message that Sancho again does not deliver. He determines to take advantage of the knight's delusions: "And seeing that he is a madman, and that he is there can be no doubt—so mad that he takes one thing for another, white for black and black for white, like the time he insisted the windmills were giants and the monks' mules were dromedaries, and the flocks of sheep were enemy armies, and other things of the same sort—seeing that this is so, it will not be hard to make him believe that the first farm girl I fall in with around here is the lady Dulcinea. If he doesn't believe it, I'll swear to it. . . . Or maybe, and I imagine that this will more likely be the case, he will think that one of those wicked enchanters, who, he says, have it in for him, has changed her form just to spite and harm him."

Three farm girls ride by on jackasses, one of whom Sancho describes as Dulcinea in all her golden glory although to Don Quixote she is a snub-

* It will be remembered that Sancho had forgotten the letter that was to be carried to Dulcinea from Don Quixote in the Sierra Morena and as a consequence was forced to invent a story about its delivery and reception. Naturally, the knight expects Sancho to guide him to her palace. Ed.

nosed wench smelling of garlic. Don Quixote accepts the explanation that Dulcinea is enchanted and in great sadness they make their way toward Saragossa, Sancho inwardly laughing at the ease with which he had deceived his master. Henceforth throughout the second part Don Quixote will be worrying how to accomplish the disenchantment of Dulcinea: how to transform the ugly peasant girl whom he has seen back into a beautiful princess.

CHAPTER 11.

They ride toward Saragossa, Don Quixote in a troubled daydream allowing Rocinante to feed upon the abundant grass. Sancho spurs him on. He is much bigger, more cunning, and more evil than in the first part.* They meet with "a cart crossing the highway, filled with the most varied and weird assortment of persons and figures that could be imagined. He who drove the mules and served as carter was an ugly demon, and the vehicle was open to the heavens and had neither awning nor framework of branches on which to stretch it. The first figure that Don Quixote beheld was that of Death himself, with a human countenance. Next came an angel with large and painted wings. At one side was an emperor with what appeared to be a gold crown on his head, and at Death's feet was the god called Cupid, without a bandage over his eyes but with his bow, his quiver, and his arrows. There was also a knight in full armor, except that he had no morion or helmet but instead wore a hat decked with vari-colored plumes."

They are strolling players, and curiously enough Don Quixote, who had challenged the company, is satisfied with this explanation. A blow, however, frightens Rocinante—and only then does Don Quixote prepare to attack the "player demon," but is stopped by Sancho's wise advice and lets the "phantoms" go their way. A curious adventure when compared with former ones. But then the author warned the reader against such comparisons.

CHAPTER 12.

Don Quixote compares life to a comedy at the end of which emperors

* VN quotes Putnam's note: "These speeches of Sancho's may seem decidedly out of character, but this is something of which the author is by no means unaware. Cervantes in part one was never too greatly concerned with the matter, and in part two there can be no doubt that he definitely intends to portray a certain growth in character on the part of the squire as well as of the knight.... It is conceivable that Sancho, who, however simple-minded he may appear at times, is not dull-witted, may have picked up from his master a good deal of the cant of chivalry and some of Don Quixote's flowery language."

and merchants, knights and fools, take off the garb that differentiates them and become equal in the grave. Sancho Panza compares life to a game of chess, after which kings and pawns go back into a bag. This comparison is found in Edward Fitzgerald's *Rubaiyat of Omar Khayyam*, based on a Persian poem of the twelfth century:

> But helpless Pieces of the Game He plays
> Upon this Chequer-board of Nights and Days;
> Hither and thither moves, and checks, and slays,
> And one by one back in the Closet lays.

At last Don Quixote meets a "knight-errant" in the flesh and steel, and love-sick of course! We hear him intoning a love sonnet, for which Putnam quotes Ormsby: "The pieces of verse introduced in the second part are more or less burlesques, and sometimes, as here and in chapter 18, imitations of the affected poetry of the day. The verses in the first part (except, of course, the commendatory verses, and those at the end of the last chapter) are serious efforts, and evidently regarded by Cervantes with some complacency. The difference is significant."

The Knight of the Wood (later the Knight of the Mirrors) and Don Quixote have a solemn conversation.

CHAPTER 13.

In the meantime the squires of the two knights have their own talk. They both term their masters madmen and deplore their lot, though looking forward to promised riches. The Knight of the Wood's squire is better off in the way of food and drink than Sancho.

" 'Upon my word, brother,' said the other squire, 'my stomach was not made for thistles, wild pears, and woodland herbs. Let our masters observe those knightly laws and traditions and eat what their rules prescribe; I carry a hamper of food and a flask on my saddlebow, whether they like it or not. And speaking of that flask, how I love it! There is scarcely a minute of the day that I'm not hugging and kissing it, over and over again.'

"As he said this he placed the wine bag in Sancho's hands, who put it to his mouth, threw his head back, and sat there gazing up at the stars for a quarter of an hour. Then when he had finished drinking, he let his head loll on one side and heaved a deep sigh."

This is a fine description of an immemorial, but plumply localized, gesture.

CHAPTER 14.

As the Knight of the Wood tells of the commands laid on him by his lady, Casildea de Vandalia, and of the knights he has vanquished in her honor, he concludes: "But the one whom I am proudest to have overcome in single combat is that famous gentleman, Don Quixote de la Mancha; for I made him confess that my Casildea is more beautiful than his Dulcinea. . . ."

Don Quixote listens incredulously and finally assumes that the Knight of the Wood has vanquished some false knight raised up by an enchanter enemy and calling himself Don Quixote. He challenges the Knight of the Wood, who calmly persuades him to wait until daylight. At dawn they run their course, but by a mishap Don Quixote catches the Knight of the Mirrors (now so named) off guard when his sorry mount refuses to budge, and unhorses him. Undoing the straps of his helmet he is astonished to perceive the features of the bachelor Sansón Carrasco. In turn, the knight's squire turns out to be an old crony of Sancho's in disguise. Don Quixote believes that it is all enchantment, and that two strangers have at the last moment been transformed into the old friends of Don Quixote and Sancho Panza. This is in keeping with Don Quixote's gentle fancy but not with the shrewd Sancho Panza, a trickster in his own right. It is no use looking for any unity of structure in this book.

CHAPTER 15.

"Don Quixote went off very happy, self-satisfied, and vainglorious at having achieved a victory over so valiant a knight as he imagined the one of the Mirrors to be." This does not often happen to him—such victories (although never quite complete, not even this one, where the "spell" spoils a little the final pleasure). We then have the explanation that the barber and the curate and Carrasco had agreed that he should set himself up as a knight, conquer Don Quixote, and demand his return to his village where they hoped he could be cured. But we shall have to accompany Don Quixote on twelve encounters before Carrasco is fit after his battering to engage Don Quixote in battle again.

CHAPTER 16.

On the road they meet a horseman in green. "He impressed Don Quixote as being a man of good judgment, around fifty years of age, with hair that was slightly graying and an aquiline nose, while the expression of his countenance was half humorous, half serious. In short, both his person and his accouterments indicated that he was an individual of some worth.

"As for the man in green's impression of Don Quixote de la Mancha, he was thinking he had never before seen any human being that resembled this one. He could not but marvel at the knight's long neck, his tall frame, and the leanness and the sallowness of his face, as well as his armor and his grave bearing, the whole constituting a sight such as had not been seen for many a day in those parts."

His name is Don Diego de Miranda, a cultured country gentleman. He is one of the very few good men (really nice to Don Quixote) in the story. Don Quixote describes his profession as knight-errant, and the gentleman is amazed: "How can it be that there are knights-errant in the world today and that histories of them are actually printed? I find it hard to convince myself that at the present time there is anyone on earth who goes about aiding widows, protecting damsels, defending the honor of wives, and succoring orphans, and I should never have believed it had I not beheld your Grace with my own eyes. Thank Heaven for that book that your Grace tells me has been published concerning your true and exalted deeds of chivalry, as it should cast into oblivion all the innumerable stories of fictitious knights-errant with which the world is filled, greatly to the detriment of good morals and the prejudice and discredit of legitimate histories."

When the gentleman in green complains that his son cannot be persuaded to study law or theology but persists in writing poetry, Don Quixote launches into an eloquent defence: "In conclusion, then, my dear sir, my advice to you would be to let your son go where his star beckons him; for being a good student as he must be, and having already successfully mounted the first step on the stairway of learning, which is that of languages, he will be able to continue of his own accord to the very peak of humane letters, an accomplishment that is altogether becoming in a gentleman, one that adorns, honors, and distinguishes him as much as the miter does the bishop or his flowing robe the learned jurisconsult. . . . When kings and princes behold the marvelous art of poetry as practiced by prudent, virtuous, and serious-minded subjects of their realm, they honor, esteem, and reward those persons and crown them with the leaves of the tree that is never struck by lightning—as if to show that those who are crowned and adorned with such wreaths are not to be assailed by anyone."

And after this gentle speech delivered by Don Quixote (with Cervantes acting as prompter), the poor knight is about to encounter a dreadful and bewildering ordeal.

CHAPTER 17.

After the farcical scene of the curds in Don Quixote's helmet that Sancho
hands him, we have the adventure of the lions, a male and female that are
being transported as the gift of the Governor of Oran to the King of
Spain.* Don Quixote stops the cart and demands that the lions be turned
out of their cages to confront him. "Seeing Don Quixote posed there before
him and perceiving that, unless he wished to incur the bold knight's
indignation there was nothing for him to do but to release the male lion,
the keeper now opened the first cage, and it could be seen at once how
extraordinarily big and horribly ugly the beast was. The first thing the
recumbent animal did was to turn round, put out a claw, and stretch himself
all over. Then he opened his mouth and yawned very slowly, after which he
put out a tongue that was nearly two palms in length and with it licked the
dust out of his eyes and washed his face. Having done this, he stuck his head
outside the cage and gazed about him in all directions. His eyes were now
like live coals and his appearance and demeanor were such as to strike
terror in temerity itself. But Don Quixote merely stared at him attentively,
waiting for him to descend from the cart so that they could come to grips,
for the knight was determined to hack the brute to pieces, such was the
extent of his unheard-of madness."

Don Quixote shows real valor.

"The lion, however, proved to be courteous rather than arrogant and
was in no mood for childish bravado. After having gazed first in one
direction and then in another, as has been said, he turned his back and
presented his hind parts to Don Quixote and then very calmly and
peaceably lay down and stretched himself out once more in his cage. At
this, Don Quixote ordered the keeper to stir him up with a stick in order to
irritate him and drive him out" but is persuaded by the keeper that "Your
Grace's stoutheartedness has been well established; for no brave fighter, as
I see it, is obliged to do more than challenge his enemy and wait for him in
the field; his adversary, if he does not come, is the one who is disgraced and
the one who awaits him gains the crown of victory."

When the others, who had fled, are called back, Don Quixote exults,
"What do you think of that, Sancho? . . . Are there any spells that can
withstand true gallantry? The enchanters may take my luck away, but to
deprive me of my strength and courage is an impossibility." As they ride
along, Don Quixote again extols to Don Diego the virtues of knight-

* VN quotes Putnam's note that "lions coming from Oran would have been landed at Cartagena, and so would
not have been met by Don Quixote and his party on the road to Saragossa."

errantry: "Let the [knight-errant] seek out the nooks and corners of the world; let him enter into the most intricate of labyrinths; let him attempt the impossible at every step; let him endure on desolate highlands the burning rays of the midsummer sun and in winter the harsh inclemencies of wind and frost; let no lions inspire him with fear, no monsters frighten him, no dragons terrify him, for to seek them out, attack them, and conquer them all is his chief and legitimate occupation. Accordingly, I whose lot it is to be numbered among the knights-errant cannot fail to attempt anything that appears to me to fall within the scope of my duties, just as I attacked those lions a while ago even though I knew it to be an exceedingly rash thing to do, for that was a matter that directly concerned me."

He now wishes to be called the Knight of the Lions instead of the Knight of the Mournful Countenance.

CHAPTER 18.

Again, as they arrive at his house and Don Diego introduces Don Quixote to his wife, he is the first man to pay the knight a perfectly serious compliment: "I would have you receive with your customary kindness Señor Don Quixote de la Mancha, who stands before you here, a knight-errant and the bravest and wisest that there is in all the world"—although he doubts his sanity. Don Quixote explains to Don Diego's son, Don Lorenzo, why knight-errantry is a branch of learning—a very tree of learning, in fact. He is entertained for four days before taking his departure for the tournament to be held in Saragossa. Sancho Panza having filled his saddlebags, they leave, both the father and son marvelling "at the mixture of nonsense and wisdom that Don Quixote talked, as well as at the pertinacity he displayed in going through with his unfortunate adventures."

CHAPTER 19.

On the road they meet a party of students and peasants who invite them to attend the wedding of Quiteria the Fair and Camacho the Rich. One of the students explains that she is loved by a youth Basilio, who lives next door. " 'As the pair grew up, Quiteria's father decided to forbid Basilio the run of the house which the lad had previously enjoyed, and by way of relieving himself of fear and suspicion, he ordered his daughter to marry the wealthy Camacho, since it did not seem well for her to wed Basilio, whose fortune did not equal his native gifts; for to tell the truth without prejudice, he is the cleverest young fellow that we have, expert at throwing the bar, the finest of wrestlers, a great ball player; he runs like a deer, leaps better than a goat, and bowls over the ninepins as if by magic; he sings like a lark and can make a guitar speak, and, above all, he handles a sword with the best of them.'

" 'By reason of those accomplishments alone,' remarked Don Quixote, 'the lad deserves to wed not merely the fair Quiteria, but Queen Guinevere herself, if she were alive today, and this in spite of Lancelot and all those who might try to prevent it.'

" 'Tell that to my wife,' said Sancho Panza, who up to then had been listening in silence, 'for she insists that each one should marry his equal, according to the old saying, "Every ewe to her mate." I'd like to see the good Basilio—for I'm taking a liking to him already—marry this lady Quiteria, and eternal blessings—no, I mean just the opposite—on all those that would keep true lovers apart.' "

The student continues: "I have told you all there is, except that from the moment Basilio learned that the fair Quiteria was to wed Camacho the Rich, he was never again seen to smile or heard to utter a rational word but has remained sad and pensive and goes about talking to himself in a way that clearly shows he has lost his senses. He eats little and sleeps little. His diet is fruits, and as for sleep, if he sleeps at all, it is in the open, upon the hard earth like a brute beast. From time to time he will look up at the heavens, and again he will fasten his gaze upon the ground, with such an air of abstraction that he appears to be no more than a clothed statue whose draperies are stirred by the wind. In short, he gives evidence of being so heart-stricken that all of us who know him fear that when the fair Quiteria says 'yes' tomorrow, it will be his death sentence."

CHAPTER 20.

The wonderful display of meats at the wedding feast can be compared to the glutton's paradise in Gogol's *Dead Souls*. ("A steer spitted entire upon an elm tree"; "inside the steer's big belly, twelve delicate little suckling pigs gave it flavor and tenderness"; the "pots swallowed up and concealed in their insides whole sheep as if they had been pigeons"; "more than sixty wine bags, each holding more than two arrobas [six gallons], . . . filled with the best of vintages.") Sancho proves to be a good eater. "Three hens and a couple of geese" (just "skimmings" before the real feast) is what he is served from a gigantic jar. A masque is performed while Sancho attacks his food, which has quite won him over to Camacho's side. He bores the reader with his proverbs as much as he does Don Quixote.

CHAPTER 21.

A trick is played by Basilio to obtain his sweetheart. He plants a long rapier in the ground and "he swiftly, coolly, and resolutely threw himself upon it, and a moment later the crimson point and half the steel blade could be seen protruding from his back, as he lay there transfixed by his own weapon and bathed in blood." He persuades the priest, with Don Quixote's help, to marry him to Quiteria before he dies, after which she can marry Camacho. The priest, moved to tears, gives the pair his benediction "and no sooner had he done so than Basilio nimbly leaped to his feet and, with an unheard-of brazenness, drew the rapier from his body which had served as its sheath. The bystanders were dumfounded, and some of the more simple-minded and less inquisitive among them began shouting at the top of their voices, 'A miracle! A miracle!'

" 'No miracle,' said Basilio, 'but a trick.'

"Astounded and bewildered, the priest ran up and putting out both hands to examine the wound, discovered that the blade had passed, not through Basilio's flesh and ribs, but through a hollow iron tube filled with blood which he had placed there, the blood, as was afterward learned, having been especially prepared so that it would not congeal."

Don Quixote gains yet another moral victory when he breaks up the fight that ensues between the two sets of supporters. In a voice of thunder he shouts " 'What therefore God hath joined together, let no man put asunder; and whoever shall attempt it will first have to pass the point of this lance.'

"As he said this, he brandished his weapon with such strength and skill as to frighten all those that did not know him." So Camacho is reconciled and declares the rest of the feast will honor Quiteria and Basilio.

CHAPTER 22.

In Don Diego's house Don Quixote had declared his intention of exploring the Cave of Montesinos on his way to Saragossa. After being entertained by the newly married pair for three days he secures a guide and sets out. The guide reminds him that he will need ropes with which to lower himself into the depths. "To this Don Quixote's answer was that even if it was as deep as Hell, he proposed to see the bottom of it; and so they bought nearly a hundred fathoms of rope, and the following day, at two o'clock in the afternoon, they reached the cave, the mouth of which is broad and spacious, but clogged with boxthorn, wild fig trees, shrubs, and brambles, so dense and tangled an undergrowth as wholly to cover over and conceal the entrance. All three of them then dismounted, and Sancho and the guide bound Don Quixote very stoutly with the ropes.

" 'Look well what you do, master,' said Sancho, as they were girdling him. 'Don't go burying yourself alive or get yourself caught so you will hang there like a bottle that has been let down into the well to cool. If you ask me, I would say it is none of your Grace's affair to be prying into this cave, which must be worse than a dungeon.'

" 'Keep on tying and keep still,' Don Quixote admonished him. 'It is just such an undertaking as this, Sancho, that is reserved for me.' "

As he stands at the entrance, Don Quixote prays to Dulcinea: " 'What I ask of thee is nothing other than thy favor and protection, of which I so greatly stand in need at this moment. I am now about to sink, to hurl and plunge myself into the abyss that yawns before me here, simply in order that the world may know that there is nothing, however impossible it may seem, that I will not undertake and accomplish, provided only I have thy favor.' "

Don Quixote is let down eighty fathoms (480 feet), and after half an hour is pulled up in a blissful swoon.

CHAPTER 23

Don Quixote narrates his adventures. He came upon a recess in the cave, not far down, and fell into a deep sleep. When he awoke he was in the midst of a beautiful meadow. He then saw a sumptuous castle made of clear crystal from which Montesinos emerged to greet him. " 'It is a long time,' he said, 'O valiant knight, Don Quixote de la Mancha, that we in these enchanted solitudes have been waiting for a sight of you, that you might go back and inform the world of what lies locked and concealed in the depths of this cave which you have entered, the so-called Cave of Montesinos, an exploit solely reserved for your invincible heart and stupendous courage. Come with me, most illustrious sir, and I will show you the hidden marvels of this transparent castle of which I am governor and perpetual guardian; for I am Montesinos himself, after whom the cave is named.' "

Montesinos enlightens Don Quixote about his having cut out the heart of Durandarte, who fell at Roncesvalles, to take to his lady and brings him to the tomb where lay a knight with his right hand upon his heart. " 'This,' he said, 'is my friend Durandarte, flower and mirror of the brave and enamored knights of his age. Merlin, that French enchanter, who they say was the devil's own son, holds him here under a spell as he does me and many other knights and ladies. How or why he did it to us, no one knows; but time will tell, and it is my belief that the time is not far off.' " Although they have all been held for over five hundred years by Merlin's spell, no one has died. Many more marvels are seen, including a procession of the lady Belerma, Durandarte's beloved, with his heart in her hand. Grief has impaired her beauty. " 'If it were not for that [Montesinos continues], even the great Dulcinea del Toboso, so famous in these parts and throughout the world, would scarcely equal her in beauty, grace, and dashing manner.'

" 'Hold there, Señor Don Montesinos!' said I [Don Quixote] at this point. 'Your Grace should tell your story in the proper way for, as you know, all comparisons are odious. There is no reason for comparing anybody with anybody. The peerless Dulcinea del Toboso is who she is and has been, and let the matter rest there.' " Montesinos apologizes.

Although Don Quixote was in the cave for only half an hour, he spent three days without eating or sleeping in the magic land ruled by Montesinos. In a meadow he sees the three peasant girls Sancho had pointed out as Dulcinea and her attendants. "I asked Montesinos if he knew them and he replied that he did not, but that he thought they must be some highborn ladies with a spell upon them. He added that they arrived but a few days ago, which to me was not surprising in view of the fact that many other ladies of the present time as well as of past ages were to be found there in various strange and enchanted shapes, among whom he said he recognized Queen Guinevere and her duenna Quintañona, she who poured the wine for Lancelot 'when from Britain he came.' "

Don Quixote relates how one of the peasant girls came to him, to borrow money for her lady Dulcinea, and he gave her what he had and added that " 'I mean to take no rest but to roam the seven parts of the world more faithfully than did the prince Dom Pedro of Portugal until I shall have freed her from this spell.'

" 'All this and more you owe my lady,' was the damsel's answer; and, taking the four reales, in place of dropping a curtsy she cut a caper, leaping more than two yards into the air.' "

CHAPTER 24.

Other fantastic episodes are always explained realistically by someone deceiving Don Quixote or by his rearranging impressions in such a way as to deceive himself. But here the time element and the space element are difficult to dismiss; and, after all, even Don Quixote ought to know if he dreams or not. This chapter begins with the translator's attempt to explain things.

"He who translated this great history from the original manuscript left by its author, Cid Hamete Benengeli, states that when he came to the chapter dealing with the adventure in the Cave of Montesinos, he found in the margin, in Hamete's own handwriting, these words:

" 'I cannot bring myself to believe that everything set down in the preceding chapter actually happened to the valiant Don Quixote. The reason is that all the adventures that have taken place up to now have been both possible and likely seeming, but as for this one of the cave, I see no way in which I can accept it as true, as it is so far beyond the bounds of reason. On the other hand, it is impossible for me to believe that Don Quixote lied, since he is the truest gentleman and noblest knight of his age and would not utter a falsehood if he were to be shot through with arrows; and, furthermore, I must take into account that he related the story in great detail and that in so brief a space of time as that he could not have fabricated such a farrago of nonsense. Accordingly, I would state that if the episode has the appearance of being apocryphal, the fault is not mine, and so, without asserting that it is either false or true, I write it down. You, wise reader, may decide for yourself; for I cannot, nor am I obliged, to do any more. It is definitely reported, however, that at the time of his death he retracted what he had said, confessing that he had invented the incident because it seemed to him to fit in well with those adventures that he had read of in his storybooks.' "*

At the end of the chapter they arrive at an inn "and Sancho was pleased to see that his master took it for a real inn this time and not for a castle as was his wont."

CHAPTER 25.

At the inn arrives the puppet master Pedro, with a patch of green taffeta over one eye and the whole side of his face. He brings with him a divining ape.

" 'Señor,' he said, 'this animal does not answer any questions concerning things that are to come, but he knows something concerning the past and more or less about the present.'

*Don Quixote's deathbed recantation of chivalry books contains no mention of the Cave of Montesinos. Ed.

" 'Pshaw!' exclaimed Sancho, 'I wouldn't give a penny to be told my past, since who can know it better than I? It would be foolish to pay you for that. But since he knows the present also, here are my two reales, and let this Sir Ape of Apes tell me what my wife, Teresa Panza, is doing right now and how she is amusing herself.'

"Master Pedro, however, declined to take the money. 'I accept no fees in advance,' he said; 'you can pay me when the service has been rendered.' Saying this, he slapped his left shoulder a couple of times, and with a single bound the ape was there and with his mouth close to his master's ear began chattering his teeth very rapidly. Having kept this up for the time it takes to say a Credo, he gave another leap and was back on the ground once more. In great haste Pedro then ran over and threw himself upon his knees before Don Quixote, embracing the knight's legs.

" 'I embrace these legs as I would the columns of Hercules, O illustrious reviver of the now-forgotten profession of knight-errantry, O Don Quixote de la Mancha, thou who canst never be praised enough, bringer of courage to the faint of heart, support of those that are about to fall, arm of the fallen, staff and counsel of all the unfortunate!'

"Upon hearing these words, Don Quixote was astounded, Sancho was amazed, . . . the landlord was bewildered, and all present were filled with wonder.

" 'And thou, O worthy Sancho Panza,' the puppet master went on, 'the best squire to the best knight in the world, be of good cheer, for your good wife Teresa is well and at this moment is engaged in hackling a pound of flax. What is more, she has at her left hand a jug with a broken spout that holds a good sip of wine to cheer her at her work.' "

As Pedro begins preparation for putting on his puppet show, Don Quixote surmises that he has a pact with the devil.

CHAPTER 26.

A young lad narrates the events which the puppets enact.

" 'The true story,' he said, 'which your Worships are about to witness, is taken word for word from the French chronicles and Spanish ballads that you hear in the mouths of people everywhere, even the young ones in the street. It tells how Señor Don Gaiferos freed his wife, Melisendra, who was held captive by the Moors in Spain, in the city of Sansueña, for that was the name then given to what is now known as Saragossa.'

" 'There was no want of idle eyes of the kind that see everything; and, seeing Melisendra descend from the balcony and mount her husband's horse, these persons notified King Marsilio, who at once ordered the call to arms to be sounded. Observe with what haste they go about it. The entire city is now drowned in the sound of bells, pealing from the towers of all the mosques.'

"At this point Don Quixote interrupted him. 'No,' he said, 'that won't do. In this matter of the bells Master Pedro is far from accurate, for bells are not in use among the Moors; instead they employ kettledrums and a kind of flute somewhat like our flageolet. So, you can see that this business of bells ringing in Sansueña is beyond a doubt a great piece of nonsense.'

"Hearing this, Master Pedro stopped ringing the bells. 'Don't be looking for trifles, Señor Don Quixote,' he said, 'or expect things to be impossibly perfect. Are not a thousand comedies performed almost every day that are full of inaccuracies and absurdities, yet they run their course and are received not only with applause but with admiration and all the rest? Go on, boy, and let him talk; for so long as I fill my wallet, it makes no difference if there are as many inaccuracies in my show as there are motes in the sun.' "

The boy continues, and then the sudden madness seizes Don Quixote, who leaps up beside the stage and slashes with his sword at the Moorish puppets until he has knocked the entire theater to the ground. Pedro is sickened at his loss and Sancho suggests to Don Quixote that he should be paid for the damage. " 'I am now coming to believe,' said Don Quixote, 'that I was right in thinking, as I often have, that the enchanters who persecute me merely place figures like these in front of my eyes and then change and transform them as they like. In all earnestness, gentlemen, I can assure you that everything that took place here seemed to me very real indeed, and Melisendra, Don Gaiferos, Marsilio, and Charlemagne were all their flesh-and-blood selves. That was why I became so angry. In order to fulfill the duties of my profession as knight-errant, I wished to aid and favor the fugitives, and with this in mind I did what you saw me do. If it came out wrong, it is not my fault but that of my wicked persecutors; but, nevertheless, I willingly sentence myself to pay the costs of my error, even though it did not proceed from malice. Reckon up what I owe you, Master Pedro, for those figures I have destroyed, and I will reimburse you in good Castilian currency.' " They all sup together after Don Quixote has paid for the puppets one by one. Master Pedro was up earlier in the morning and had departed before they took to the road again.

CHAPTER 27.

It transpires that the puppet master Pedro with the green patch was really Ginés de Pasamonte, one of the galley slaves that Don Quixote had freed in part one, chapter 22. His divining ape was, of course, a fraud, for his master would seek out information before coming to a town and then pretend that the ape had communicated it. He had, of course, recognized Don Quixote and Sancho when he entered the inn and thus was able to astonish them both. On the road Don Quixote makes peace, by a long oration, between two towns whose inhabitants had jeered at each other over a braying match. The peace is broken, however, by Sancho illustrating his own braying accomplishments, whereupon he is beaten and the Don forced ignominiously to flee.

CHAPTER 28.

Sancho Panza is so badly battered that he wants to go home. He and Don Quixote start to reckon up the wages he is due, but Sancho is overcome with remorse. " 'Master,' he said in a weak and sorrowing voice, 'I will grant you that all I lack is a tail and I would be an ass; and if your Grace wants to put one on me, I'll look upon it as well placed and will serve you as a beast of burden all the days of my life that are left me. Forgive me, your Grace, have mercy on my foolishness. Remember that I know little, and if I talk much, that is due to weakness rather than to malice. But he who sins and mends his ways, commends himself to God.' "

CHAPTER 29.

When they reach the River Ebro, Don Quixote supposes that an empty bark is inviting him to give succor to some knight in trouble. "With this, he leaped into the boat, followed by Sancho, and severed the rope that held it. The bark then began drifting slowly away from the bank, and when Sancho found himself some two yards out in the river, he started trembling all over, fearing that he was lost. What pained him most of all was the braying of the ass and the sight of Rocinante struggling to get loose."*

They see some big watermills moored in the middle of the river, "and no

* VN interjects the comment that Don Quixote says to the frightened Sancho, " 'Are you perchance tramping barefoot over the Riphaean Mountains. . . .?' The curious point is that about fifty (?) years later a real exile, the unfortunate and persecuted priest Avvakum, the first major Russian prose writer, was tramping across these Riphaean Mts., i.e., *the Oural Mts*."

sooner did Don Quixote catch sight of them than he called out to Sancho in a loud voice, 'Do you see that, my friend? There is the city, castle, or fortress where they must be holding some knight in captivity, or some sorely wronged queen, infanta, or princess, to rescue whom I am being brought there.'

" 'What the devil city, fortress, or castle is your Grace talking about?' said Sancho. 'Can't you see, master, that those are nothing but watermills on the river, where they grind corn?'

" 'Be quiet, Sancho,' Don Quixote admonished him, 'for though they may appear to be watermills, they are not. I have already explained to you how enchanters change and transform things from their natural shape. I do not mean that they actually change them from one shape to another, but they appear to do so, as experience has taught us in connection with the transformation of Dulcinea, sole refuge of my hopes.'

"By this time the bark was in midstream and was not moving as gently as it had been up to then. The millers, seeing this boat coming down the river and perceiving that it was about to be sucked in by the millwheels, came running out in all haste to stop it. Many of them carried poles, and, as their faces and their clothes were covered with flour, they presented a sinister appearance."

Don Quixote hurls threats at them and brandishes his sword, but the millers succeed in rescuing the knight and Sancho, though not without tipping them into the river. The owner of the boat demands damages, which Don Quixote eventually pays. Then, raising his voice, "he continued speaking as he gazed at the mills. 'Friends,' he said, 'whoever ye may be who are locked within these prison walls, forgive me. It is my misfortune and yours that I am unable to rescue you from your dire peril. This emprise must doubtless be reserved for some other knight.' "

It is curious that in this episode of the watermills, neither Don Quixote nor his squire recalls the episode of the windmills in part one.

CHAPTER 30.

Don Quixote comes upon a Duke and his Duchess hunting. They recognize him and invite him to their castle where for their amusement they will treat him with all the customary ceremonies due a knight-errant.

CHAPTER 31.

Don Quixote warns Sancho to bridle his tongue. But the Duchess intervenes. " 'By the life of the duke,' exclaimed the duchess, 'I am not going to part with Sancho for a moment. I am extremely fond of him, for I know him to be very discreet.' " A commonsensical churchman at the Duke's table rebukes Don Quixote. "The ecclesiastic, upon hearing this talk of giants, rogues, and enchanters, decided that their guest must be none other than Don Quixote de la Mancha whose story the duke was always reading—he had reproved him for it many times, telling him it was nonsensical to waste his time on such nonsense—and now, becoming convinced that his suspicions were correct, he turned to the duke and addressed him angrily.

" 'Your Excellency, *Señor mío*,' he said, 'will have to give an account to the Lord for what this good man does. This Don Quixote, or Don Simpleton, or whatever his name is, surely cannot be such a dunce as your Excellency would make him out to be by thus lending encouragement to his foolish carryings-on.' Addressing himself, then, to Don Quixote, he continued, 'And as for you, addlepate, who ever put it into your head that you are a knight-errant who conquers giants and captures malefactors? I say to you: go your way and Heaven be with you; return to your home, see to bringing up your children if you have any, look after your property, and stop wandering about the world like a gaping ninny, making a laughingstock of yourself in the eyes of all, whether they know you or not. Where in the name of goodness did you ever come upon any knights-errant living or dead? Where are there giants in Spain, or bandits in La Mancha, or enchanted Dulcineas, or any other silly things they tell about in connection with you?' "

CHAPTER 32.

Don Quixote answers the churchman, eloquently. "Is it, perchance, a vain occupation or a waste of time to wander over the earth, seeking not the pleasures of this life but those hardships by which the virtuous may mount to the seat of immortality?" He discusses Dulcinea with the Duke and Duchess. He says, "God knows whether or not there is a Dulcinea in this world or if she is a fanciful creation. This is not one of those cases where you can prove a thing conclusively. I have not begotten or given birth to my lady, although I contemplate her as she needs must be, seeing that she is a damsel who possesses all those qualities that may render her famous in all parts of the world, such as: a flawless beauty; dignity without haughtiness; a tenderness that is never immodest; a graciousness due to courtesy and a courtesy that comes from good breeding; and, finally, a highborn lineage, for beauty is more resplendent and more nearly perfect in those of lofty extraction than in creatures of humbler origin."

The Duchess intervenes by stating her belief in Dulcinea: "But, for all of that, there is still some small doubt in my mind, and here I hold a grudge against Sancho Panza; for the story that I have mentioned states that when Sancho brought the lady Dulcinea a message from your Grace, he found her winnowing a bag of wheat, and red wheat at that, a circumstance that leads me to question her exalted lineage."

Don Quixote responds: " What I think is that when my squire brought her my message, those same enchanters transformed her into a country wench and set her at so low a task as is that of winnowing wheat. But I have already said that the wheat in question was not red, nor was it wheat, but oriental pearls; and, in proof of this, I may inform your Highnesses that when I came to El Toboso not long ago, I was able to find Dulcinea's palace; and the very next day Sancho, my squire, beheld her in her proper form, which is the most beautiful of any on earth, while to me she appeared as a coarse and ugly peasant girl and very rude in her speech, though she herself is the soul of propriety. And seeing that I am not enchanted and, it stands to reason, cannot be, she must be the one who has suffered this injury and has been thus altered, changed, and transformed. That is to say, my enemies through her have had their revenge on me, and it is on account of her that I live amid ceaseless tears until I shall once more have beheld her in her pristine state."

Sancho is mocked by the servants but petted by the Duchess, who enjoys the situation. The Duke promises him the governorship of an island.

CHAPTER 33.

A very tedious chapter of Sancho talking with the Duchess. He lets her in on the secret of how he deceived Don Quixote about the delivery of the letters and his trick of identifying Dulcinea with one of the three peasant girls whom they met.

CHAPTERS 34-35.

At night in the forest the Duke and Duchess play an elaborate joke. One of their servants dressed as the devil appears to inform Don Quixote that Dulcinea is being escorted by six troops of enchanters who will inform him how she may be disenchanted.

" 'If you are a devil as you say and as your appearance shows you to be [replied Don Quixote intrepidly], you would have recognized Don Quixote de la Mancha, for he stands here before you.'

" 'In God's name and upon my conscience,' said the devil, 'I did not take a good look at him. I have so much on my mind that I am forgetting the chief thing for which I came.'

" 'There is no doubt about it,' said Sancho, 'this demon must be a good man and a good Christian, for if he wasn't, he wouldn't swear by God and his conscience. For my part, I'm convinced now that there are good people even in Hell.'

"Then without dismounting, the demon fastened his gaze upon Don Quixote. 'O Knight of the Lions,' he said, 'for I can see you between their claws at this very moment, it is that ill-starred but valiant knight, Montesinos, who has sent me to you to inform you that you should wait for him in whatever place you chance to be, as he is bringing with him the one who is known as Dulcinea del Toboso in order that he may show you what you must do to disenchant her. And since I came for no more than that, I need tarry no longer. May demons like me be with you, and good angels with these gentle folk.'

"Saying this, he blew upon that monstrous horn of his and turned his back and went away without waiting for an answer from anyone.

"They were more astonished than ever now, especially Sancho and Don Quixote: Sancho at seeing how, in spite of the truth, they would have it that Dulcinea was enchanted; while Don Quixote was unable to make up his mind as to whether what had happened to him in the Cave of Montesinos was real or not. He was immersed in these thoughts when the duke spoke to him.

" 'Does your Grace intend to wait, Señor Don Quixote?'

" 'Why not?' was the reply. 'I will wait here, strong and intrepid, though all Hell should come to attack me.' "

A tempest of sound breaks out, and three enchanters pass by in carts, announcing their names. Then, "To the sound of the pleasing strains they saw coming toward them a cart, one of the kind known as triumphal chariots, drawn by six gray mules with white linen trappings, and on each of them rode a penitent, likewise clad in white, with a lighted wax taper in his hand. This car or chariot was twice, and even three times, as big as those that had gone before, and on top and along the sides of it stood twelve other penitents, in snow-white garb and with their tapers. It was an astonishing and at the same time an awe-inspiring sight. Seated upon an elevated throne was a nymph [Dulcinea] who wore countless cloth-of-silver veils, all of them glittering with a countless number of embroidered gold spangles, which gave her, if not a sumptuous, at least a showy appearance. Her face was covered with a fine, transparent sendal, the warp of which did not prevent the features of a most beautiful maiden from being discovered. In the light of the many tapers her comeliness was revealed, and her age as well; she was apparently not older than twenty nor younger than seventeen.

"Beside the maiden was a figure wearing what is known as a robe of state, which fell all the way down to its feet, while its head was covered with a black veil. When the cart was directly opposite Don Quixote and the ducal pair, the music of the flageolets ceased, and then that of the flutes and harps on the car; whereupon the figure rose up, parted the robe, and, removing the veil from its face, disclosed for all to see the ugly, fleshless form of Death itself, which startled Don Quixote, filled Sancho with terror, and even made the duke and duchess a little afraid. Having risen to its feet, this living Death, in a somewhat sleepy voice and with a tongue that was not quite awake, began reciting the following verses:

> Merlin am I, who, so the histories say,
> had the devil for a sire (it is a lie
> that with the course of time hath stronger grown.)
> . . . .
>   In Pluto's murky pit I was absorbed
> in contemplation of the mystic shape
> of geometric figures, when there came a voice
> the grief-filled voice of the ever beauteous
> Dulcinea del Toboso without peer.
> 'Twas then I learned of her enchantment foul
> and heard how she had been vilely transformed
> from highbred lady into rustic wench.
> My pity was aroused, I turned the leaves
> of a hundred thousand books of demonic art,
> then wrapped my spirit in the frightful shell
> of this grisly skeleton and hied me here
> to announce the remedy that must be had
> for such a sorrow, such a dreadful wrong."

The upshot is that Sancho has to promise to take three thousand lashes on his bare behind. Else "Dulcinea goes back to the Cave of Montesinos and her former peasant-girl state, or she will be conveyed as she is to the Elysian Fields, there to wait until the requisite number of lash strokes has been administered." Sancho vigorously protests, whereupon Dulcinea removes her veil and "With a masculine assurance and voice that was not precisely feminine," she abused Sancho to no avail until under the Duke's threat to withdraw the offer of the governorship he finally consents with great reluctance. The whole show was put on by the Duke's major-domo, who had impersonated Merlin and secured a page-boy to act the part of Dulcinea.

CHAPTER 36.

Sancho writes to his wife that she is now a governor's lady and that he is sending her a green hunting suit given him by the Duchess in order to make a fine petticoat and bodice for their daughter. "And so, one way or another, you are going to be a rich woman and a lucky one. . . . From this castle, the twentieth of July 1614.

Your husband, the governor,
SANCHO PANZA."

Another ridiculous show is put on by the major-domo. A gaunt old man, Trifaldin of the White Beard (after the Truffaldin of Boiardo's *Orlando Innamorato* and Ariosto's *Orlando Furioso*), begs that Don Quixote aid his mistress, the Countess Trifaldi, otherwise known as the Distressed Duenna.

CHAPTER 37.

A short and superfluous chapter in which duennas are discussed, with Sancho upholding the view that they are busybodies and nuisances.

CHAPTER 38.

Accompanied by a dozen duennas, the Countess Trifaldi enters. As the chief duenna of the beautiful young Infanta Antonomasia, heiress to the kingdom of Candaya, she was won over by the charms of a young private gentleman Don Clavijo, to admit him to Antonomasia's chamber as her lawful husband. The intrigue went on for some time until Antonomasia's growing pregnancy threatened to reveal the situation. It was decided that Don Clavijo should appear before the Vicar to ask her hand in marriage, since there was a written contract, and Antonomasia was put into protective custody.

CHAPTER 39.

The marriage took place, but the Queen, the young girl's mother, was so overcome with grief that she died within three days and was buried. Then "over the queen's grave there appeared, mounted upon a wooden horse, Malambruno, Maguncia's [the queen's] first cousin, who is not merely a cruel being but an enchanter as well. In order to punish Don Clavijo for his rashness and avenge his cousin's death, and also out of spite over Antonomasia's stubbornness, Malambruno thereupon, by the exercise of his magic arts, proceeded to cast a spell upon the two of them and left them there upon the grave itself, the infanta having been transformed into a female ape, while her lover had become a crocodile made of some unknown metal, with a pillar, also of metal, standing between them, bearing an inscription in Syriac characters that, translated into the Candayan, and now into the Castilian, read as follows:

" 'These two rash lovers shall not regain their former shape until the valiant Manchegan shall come to meet me in singlehanded encounter, since it is for his great valor alone that the fates have reserved this unheard-of adventure.' "

In addition, as a punishment to the duennas who had failed in their duty, he inflicted a long-drawn-out penalty: "With this, the Distressed One and all the other duennas raised their veils, revealing faces covered with heavy beards, some red, some black, some white, and some grizzled, at sight of which the duke and duchess and all the others present were filled with wonder."

CHAPTER 40.

The chapter opens with Cervantes's paean of praise: "Really and truly, all those who enjoy such histories as this one ought to be grateful to Cid Hamete, its original author, for the pains he has taken in setting forth every detail of it, leaving out nothing, however slight, but making everything very clear and plain. He describes thoughts, reveals fancies, answers unasked questions, clears up doubts, and settles arguments. In short, he satisfies on every minutest point the curiosity of the most curious. O author celebrated above all others! O fortunate Don Quixote! O famous Dulcinea! O droll Sancho Panza! May all of you together and each of you separately live for unnumbered centuries, for the delight and general pastime of your fellow-men!"

The Distressed Duenna then informs the company that Malambruno will send his wooden horse Clavileño to fly Don Quixote and Sancho, on the crupper, through the air the three thousand leagues to Candaya, and Don Quixote accepts the quest.

CHAPTER 41.

Four savages bring in the wooden horse. Before they are to mount the magic steed, Don Quixote "led the squire to one side, among some of the garden trees, and there, taking both of his hands, spoke to him as follows.

" 'You are aware, brother Sancho, of the long journey that awaits us. God knows when we shall return or how much leisure it will allow us; and so I wish you would retire to your room as if you were seeking something that is needed for the road, and there in a twinkling pay something on account toward those three thousand three hundred lashes that you are supposed to give yourself, even if it be no more than five hundred for the present. It will be just so many of them out of the way, and a thing well begun is half done.'

" 'By God,' exclaimed Sancho, 'your Grace must be out of your mind! As the saying has it, you see me pregnant and you want me a virgin. Here, I'm supposed to go seated on a bare board and you'd have me skin my backside before I start! No, no, your Grace is all wrong. Let us go now and see to shaving those duennas, and when we come back, I give you my word, I'll make such haste to fulfill my obligation that your Grace will be more than satisfied. That is all I have to say.'

" 'Well, my good Sancho,' replied Don Quixote, 'I shall console myself with that promise; and I believe you will keep it, too, for while you may be a simpleton, you are really a trusty fellow.'

" 'I'm not rusty,' said Sancho, 'only sunburned; but even if I was a little of each, I'd still keep my word.' "

Blindfolded, the two mount the wooden horse, twist the peg in its neck, and aided by various devices of the ducal pair, such as bellows for wind and burning tow for fire, they imagine they are being transported through the air until at the end the horse is exploded and they tumble to the ground, half scorched.

"By this time the entire band of bearded ladies, La Trifaldi and all the others, had disappeared from the garden, and those that remained lay stretched out on the ground as if unconscious. The knight and his squire rose, rather the worse for wear, and glancing about them in all directions, were very much astonished to find themselves back in the same garden from which they had started, with all those people prostrate on the earth.

And their wonder grew as, at one side of the garden, they caught sight of a long lance that had been thrust into the ground, with a smooth white parchment hanging from it by two silken cords. Upon the parchment, written in large gilt letters, was the following inscription:

"*The renowned knight, Don Quixote de la Mancha, merely by undertaking it, has finished and concluded the adventure of the Countess Trifaldi, otherwise known as the Distressed Duenna. Malambruno is satisfied in every way, the faces of the duennas are once more smooth and clean, King Clavijo and Queen Antonomasia have been restored to their former state, and as soon as the squirely flogging shall have been completed, the white dove shall be set free of the annoying gerfalcons that persecute it and shall return to the arms of its beloved mate. For it is so ordered by Merlin the Sage, proto-enchanter of enchanters.*"

CHAPTERS 42-43.

To continue the jest, the Duke instructs his retainers how to behave toward Sancho in his governorship, and informs Sancho that the next day but one he is to set out to govern his island. Don Quixote gives Sancho advice at length, chiefly classical precepts, while Sancho spouts proverbs.

CHAPTER 44.

Sancho having departed, Don Quixote feels lonely, not so much because he misses his squire as because his solitude is now full of melancholy dreams of Dulcinea. Under his window that night the Duchess's waiting woman Altisidora, on instructions, sings a love song. "There came then the sound of an instrument very gently touched, hearing which Don Quixote was deeply moved; for at that moment all the innumerable adventures of a like sort, at windows, gratings, and in gardens, to the accompaniment of serenades, love-making, and fainting fits, that he had read of in those vapid books of chivalry of his, came back to mind. He at once fancied that one of the duchess's waiting women must be enamored of him but was compelled by her modesty to conceal her passion. He feared that he would yield to temptation, but took a firm resolve not to permit himself to be overcome; and, commending himself with all his heart and soul to his lady Dulcinea del Toboso, he decided that he would listen to the music, giving as a token of his presence a feigned sneeze which pleased the maidens very much, since their one desire was for him to hear them." After the song he expostulates with himself and reaffirms his entire devotion to Dulcinea.

"With this, he banged the window shut and, gloomy and out of sorts, as if some dire misfortune had befallen him, went to bed."

CHAPTER 45.

Sancho enters his governorship, a village of about a thousand inhabitants, one of the best in the Duke's domain, with a wall around it. Relying on his good memory, he proves himself to be quite a Solomon in his judgments. He tries three cases, and we are treated to all sorts of medieval fun and samples of horse sense as old as horses.

CHAPTER 46.

The next night when Don Quixote retires to his room, he finds a guitar. "He first tried it out, then opened the window, and, perceiving that there was someone in the garden, once more ran his hands over the frets, tuning the instrument as well as he could. Having done this, he spat and cleared his throat and in a voice that was a little hoarse but well modulated began singing the following ballad, which he had composed that very day" in honor of his Dulcinea. The Duke and Duchess torment him, interrupting the song by letting down from the gallery above a multitude of cats with bells attached to their tails, which create a pandemonium when Don Quixote attacks them with his sword, and he suffers a wound when one sinks its teeth in his face and must be pulled off by the Duke.

CHAPTER 47.

Back again to Sancho Panza. Cervantes caricatures a custom that actually existed in Spain: that of having a physician present at the table of princes to advise what foods should be eaten and to see that royal appetites were restrained. Sancho's physician, as part of the jest, removes every morsel that Sancho loves and keeps him half-starved. We have the idiotic episode of the farmer who petitions for six hundred ducats for his son's marriage and whom Sancho—still oozing healthy peasant horse sense—drives away.

CHAPTER 48.

We have been confronted with a double pattern of enchantments— those coming from the ducal pair and those coming from the servants.

Now, in this chapter, we find a waiting-woman, Doña Rodríguez, who actually believes in Don Quixote and complains to him in earnest. "The door opened, and he immediately stood up in the bed, wrapped from head to foot in a yellow satin coverlet, with a nightcap on his head and with his face and mustaches swathed in bandages—his face by reason of the scratches and his mustaches to keep them from drooping and falling down—all of which gave him the most extraordinary and fantastic appearance that could possibly be conceived. Watchfully he kept his eyes fastened on the door, expecting to see Altisidora enter, in tears and ready to yield herself; but, instead, he beheld a most dignified duenna in a long, white-bordered veil, so long that it enveloped her entire body like a cloak all the way down to her feet. In her left hand she carried a half-burned candle, while with her right hand she shaded it to keep the light out of her eyes, which were concealed behind a pair of huge spectacles. She came treading softly and cautiously."

She tells him that the son of a rich farmer under promise of marriage seduced her daughter and is now unwilling to keep his word. Moreover, the Duke will not interfere since the rich farmer often lends him money that he needs. "What I would ask of you, then, my good sir, is that you take it upon yourself to undo this wrong, either by entreaties or by force of arms; for everyone says that you were born into the world for that purpose: to redress grievances and protect the wretched."

Unfortunately, she also divulges the curious fact that the legs of the beautiful Duchess are covered with boils; and at this moment in the darkness the door bursts open and fiends give the woman a thorough drubbing. Then the silent executioners fall upon the knight. "Stripping the sheet and coverlet from him, they pinched him so hard and fast that there was nothing for him to do but defend himself with his fists; all of which took place in a silence that was truly astonishing.

"The battle lasted for something like half an hour, at the end of which time the phantom figures departed. Pulling down her skirts and bemoaning her ill fortune, Doña Rodríguez went out the door without a word to Don Quixote. Here [says Cervantes] we shall leave him to his solitude, sorely pinched, bewildered, and downcast, wondering who the perverse enchanter could be who had placed him in such a predicament."

CHAPTER 49.

Says Sancho: "It is my intention to rid this island of all kinds of trash, of all good-for-nothing loafers and vagabonds; for I would have you know, my friends, that the lazy and idle are to a state what drones are to a hive, which eat the honey that the worker bees have made. I propose to aid the farmer, to preserve the privileges of gentlemen, to reward the virtuous, and above all, to respect religion and to honor those in holy orders."

Sancho Panza is here voicing Cervantes's own views on society and government. The wisdom of his maxims surprises the perpetrators and participants of the hoax. In the case where money is involved, Sancho has some of it disbursed for the poor prisoners. The episode of the boy and girl brought before him (brother and sister who have swopped clothes) is *not* staged as the others are. The girl is the daughter of a rich man who has kept her so secluded that she becomes unhappy and wants to see the life around her. "My misfortune is that I asked my brother to dress me up like a man in one of his suits and to take me out some night to see the town while our father was asleep. I insisted so strongly that he finally agreed to humor me, and so I put on his clothes and he dressed in mine—for he has no hair on his face and looks like a very pretty girl—and tonight, about an hour ago, we left the house and, led on by a youthful and foolish impulse, roamed the entire town." Seeing the watch they turned to flee but she was captured and brought into the court. "The truth of what she had said was now confirmed by the arrival of constables with her brother, one of them having overtaken the lad as he ran away from his sister. He had on nothing but a skirt of rich material and a short blue damask cloak with a fine-gold border; he had no bonnet on his head nor adornment of any kind other than his blond curly hair, which resembled golden ringlets." Sancho orders the two to be returned to their father's house without disturbing him, and secretly he plans to marry the young man to his daughter, a plan that the overthrow of the government prevents.

CHAPTER 50.

Curious as to what her serving woman wanted of Don Quixote, the Duchess and her maid had "tiptoed along very cautiously to the door of the knight's room and took up a position near by where they could hear all that was said. As the duchess listened to Doña Rodríguez making public property of her mistress's ailments, she was unable to bear it, and Altisidora felt the same way about it [she had been said to have bad breath], and so, filled with rage and thirsting for vengeance they burst into the chamber, where they spanked the duenna and punished Don Quixote."

Again we have the familiar intonation of ending one prank and planning another. Now the ducal pair send the page (who had

VLADIMIR NABOKOV

impersonated Dulcinea) with presents, a kind note from the Duchess, and Sancho's letter to Teresa Panza, who is quite overcome with the news.

" 'Señor Curate, I wish you would find out if there is anyone going to Madrid or Toledo who could buy me a hoop skirt, the best there is and in the latest fashion; for I certainly mean to be as much of an honor as I can to my husband in his government, that I do, and if I get my pride up I intend to go to court and set up a coach like all the other ladies, for she who is the wife of a governor may very well keep one.'

" 'And why shouldn't you, mother!' cried Sanchica. 'Would to God it was today instead of tomorrow, even though they said, when they saw me seated in the coach with my mother, "Just look at that little nobody, that garlic-eater's daughter, how she rides around at her ease as if she were a female pope!" But let them tramp in the mud and let me go in my carriage, with my feet off the ground. Bad luck to all the gossips in the world. So long as I go warm, let the people laugh! Am I right, mother?'

" 'Indeed you are, my daughter,' replied Teresa. 'My good Sancho prophesied all this luck and even better, and you'll see, my child, I'll not stop until I've become a countess. For luck is all in the way you begin; as I've heard your father say many times—and he's the father of proverbs as well—when they offer you a heifer, run with the halter, and when they offer you a government, take it; when they give you an earldom, grab it, and when they say *tus, tus* to you with some nice present, snap at it. It would be just as if you were to go on sleeping and not answer when fortune and good luck stand knocking at the door of your house.'

" 'And what do I care,' added Sanchica, 'if somebody or other says, when they see me holding my head up like a fine lady, "The dog saw himself in hempen breeches," and so forth?' "

CHAPTER 51.

Sancho receives a letter full of advice from Don Quixote and again sits in judgment where he is posed with the old chestnut about the telling of the truth. "That law was the following: 'Anyone who crosses this river shall first take oath as to whither he is bound and why. If he swears to the truth, he shall be permitted to pass; but if tells a falsehood, he shall die without hope of pardon on the gallows that has been set up there.'. . . And then it happened that one day, when they came to administer the oath to a certain man, he swore and affirmed that his destination was to die upon the gallows which they had erected and that he had no other purpose in view.

"The judges held a consultation. 'If,' they said, 'we let this man pass without hindrance, then he has perjured himself and according to the law should be put to death; but he swore that he came to die upon that scaffold, and if we hang him that will have been the truth, and in accordance with the same law he should go free.' And now, my Lord Governor, we should like to have your Grace's opinion as to what the judges should do with the man; for up to now they have been very doubtful and perplexed, and, having heard of your Grace's keen understanding and great intellect, they have sent me to beseech your Grace on their behalf to tell them what you think regarding this intricate and puzzling question."

After some discussion Sancho delivers himself: " 'See here, my good sir,' said Sancho, 'either I am a blockhead or this man you speak of deserves to die as much as he deserves to live and cross the bridge; for if the truth saves him, the lie equally condemns him. And this being the case, as indeed it is, it is my opinion that you should go back and tell those gentlemen who sent you to me that, since there is as much reason for acquitting as for condemning him, they ought to let him go free, as it is always more praiseworthy to do good than to do harm. I would give you this decision over my signature if I knew how to sign my name; and in saying what I do I am not speaking on my own account but am remembering one of the many pieces of advice which my master Don Quixote gave me the night before I came here to be governor of this island. When justice was in doubt, he said, I was to lean to the side of mercy; and I thank God that I happened to recollect it just now, for it fits this case as if made for it.' " This decision was acclaimed as worthy of Lycurgus.

Sancho spent the afternoon drawing up a number of ordinances for the proper administration of his island. "He decreed that there were to be no peddlers of provisions in the state, and that wine might be imported from any region whatever so long as its place of origin was declared in order that a price might be put upon it according to its reputation for quality and the esteem in which it was held, while anyone who watered wine or put a false name on it was to pay for it with his life. He reduced the cost of all shoes and stockings, but especially of shoes, as it seemed to him that the prices being charged for them were exorbitant. He put a tax on servants' wages which were out of all proportion to the service rendered. He prescribed an extremely heavy fine for those who sang lewd and lascivious songs, either by night or by day, and ordained that no blind man should go about singing verses having to do with miracles unless he could produce trustworthy evidence that the miracles had actually occurred; for it was his opinion that most of the events that formed the burden of their lays were trumped up, to the detriment of the truly miraculous ones.

"He created and appointed a bailiff for the poor, not for the purpose of harassing them but to make an investigation of their real status, since many a thief or drunkard of sound body goes about as a make-believe cripple or displaying false sores. In brief, he ordered things so wisely that to this day his decrees are preserved in that town, under the title of *The Constitutions of the Great Governor, Sancho Panza*."

CHAPTER 52.

Doña Rodríguez and her daughter petition Don Quixote to right their wrongs and he proposes to seek out the young man to challenge him. But the Duke accepts the challenge on his behalf and promises that a combat will be arranged six days hence. Letters arrive from Teresa Panza to the Duchess and to Sancho, the latter containing the news of the village, among this that "The curate, the barber, the bachelor, and even the sacristan cannot believe that you are a governor and say it is all some kind of humbug or enchantment like everything that concerns your master, Don Quixote; and Sanson says they are coming to look for you as they mean to get that government out of your head and the madness out of Don Quixote's noodle, but I only laugh and look at my string of beads and go on planning the dress that I am going to make for our daughter out of your suit. I sent some acorns to my lady the duchess and wish they had been of gold. Send me a few strings of pearls if they have any in that island. . . . There are no olives this year, nor is there a drop of vinegar to be had in all the town. A company of soldiers passed this way, taking with them three village girls; I would rather not tell you who they are, for it may be they will come back and will not fail to find those who will marry them with all their faults, for better or for worse. Sanchica is making bone-lace . . . but now that you are a governor, you will give her a dowry without her having to work. The fountain in the public square dried up and lightning struck the pillory (it would suit me if that was where it always hit)."

CHAPTER 53.

The culminating trick on Sancho is to report the invasion of the island by an enemy. Sancho is badly trampled in the tumult. Stiff and sore, he walks to the stable, saddles his gray, and addresses the company: " 'And so, your Worships, God be with you. Tell my lord the duke that naked was I born and naked I find myself, and so I neither win nor lose. By this I mean I came into this government without a penny and I leave it without one, which is just the opposite of what generally happens with the governors of other islands.'" After some discussion, "They all agreed to this [to accept his resignation] and allowed Sancho to depart, having first offered to provide him with company and anything that he needed in the way of comfort or conveniences for the journey. He replied that all he wanted was a little barley for his gray and half a cheese and half a loaf of bread for himself, adding that since the distance was so short there was no necessity for him to carry any more or better provisions than that. They all embraced him then, and he, weeping, embraced them all in turn after which he rode away, leaving them filled with admiration at the words he had spoken and at the firmness and wisdom of his resolve."

CHAPTER 54.

Beginning with this chapter the shuttling between Don Quixote and Sancho is performed within chapters and not by alternation. "The duke and duchess resolved to go ahead with the challenge which Don Quixote, for reasons already set forth, had given their vassal; and inasmuch as the young man was in Flanders, whither he had fled to escape having Doña Rodríguez for a mother-in-law, they decided to substitute for him a Gascon lackey by the name of Tosilos, whom they first instructed very carefully in all that he had to do."

On his way back to his master Sancho meets Ricote, a Moorish shopkeeper from his village, now a beggar disguised as a Dutchman (the Moors had been expelled to Africa by royal decrees, 1609-1613). The group of mendicants were all fine young fellows and their saddlebags were well provided. "They stretched out on the ground and, making a tablecloth of the grass, set out upon it bread, salt, knives, nuts, bits of cheese, and clean-picked ham-bones which, if they could not be gnawed any longer, could still be sucked. There was also a black substance called caviar, which is made of fish eggs and is a great awakener of thirst. There was no lack of olives, and although they were dried and without seasoning, they were very palatable."

The old Moor Ricote is returning in disguise to reclaim some treasure buried in the ground near his village, after which he will bring his family from Algiers and settle in Germany where he has found freedom. His story is not important.

CHAPTER 55.

On his way, because of the delay in hearing Ricote's narrative, Sancho is overtaken by darkness and he and the ass fall into a deep pit. His cries are heard the next morning by Don Quixote, who is out practicing for his coming single combat.

"It sounded to Don Quixote like Sancho Panza's voice, at which he was greatly astonished. 'Who is it down below?' he shouted as loudly as he could. 'Who is it that is lamenting in that manner?'

" 'Who should it be,' came the answer, 'or who should be lamenting, if not the wretched Sancho Panza, who as a punishment for his sins has the misfortune to be governor of the island of Barataria, and who was formerly squire to the famous knight Don Quixote de la Mancha.'

"Upon hearing this Don Quixote was doubly astonished, and his amazement grew as the thought came to him that Sancho Panza must be dead and his soul in torment down there. Carried away by this idea, he called out once more, 'I conjure you by all that, as a Catholic Christian, I well may conjure you by, tell me who you are and whether or not you are a soul in torment. Tell me, also, what it is that you would have me do for you; for it is my calling to aid and succor those who are in trouble in this world, and those in the other world as well who are not able to help themselves.' "

There is mutual recognition, aided by the bray of Sancho's ass, whereupon Don Quixote returned to the castle and the Duke's retainers with ropes and tackle drew Sancho and the gray out of the pit. Sancho secures the pardon of the ducal pair for giving up his governorship without first informing the Duke. " 'And so, my lord and lady, the Duke and Duchess, your governor, Sancho Panza, who stands before you here, in the ten days, no more, that he has held the governorship, has come to learn that he would not give anything whatever to rule, not alone an island, but the entire world. Now that I've made this clear, I kiss your Highnesses' feet; and like the small lads who say "Leap and let me have it," I give a leap out of my government and pass over to the service of my master Don Quixote; for with him, even though I eat my bread with fear and trembling, at least I get my fill, and in that case it's all the same to me whether it be of carrots or of partridges.' "

CHAPTER 56.

Don Quixote arrives on the field of battle, and then "Shortly afterward, accompanied by many trumpets, the big lackey Tosilos hove in sight at one side of the square. He was mounted upon a powerful steed that shook the whole place and was clad in a suit of stoutly wrought and gleaming armor. . . . This brave fighter had been well schooled by his master the duke as to how he was to behave toward Don Quixote de la Mancha, and he had been warned that under no circumstances was he to slay the knight; rather, he was to endeavor to shun the first clash in order to avoid killing him, as he certainly would if he met him in full tilt. He now rode slowly across the square to where the duennas were and remained there for some little while gazing at the one who was asking that he take her as his bride. . . . By this time the duke and duchess had taken their places in a gallery overlooking the enclosure, which was filled with a vast multitude waiting to witness this most extraordinary conflict. In accordance with the conditions that had been laid down, if Don Quixote won, his opponent was to have to marry Doña Rodríguez's daughter; and if he was vanquished, the other was to be free of the promise that was claimed of him, without having to give any further satisfaction."

As the lackey awaited the signal for the conflict and as he gazed upon the daughter, "she had impressed him as being the most beautiful woman he had seen in all his life," and Cupid pierced his heart with an arrow at least two yards long. "Accordingly, when they came to give the signal for the charge, our lackey was rapt in ecstasy. Thinking of the beauty of her whom he had made the mistress of his liberty, he paid no attention to the sound of the trumpet, but Don Quixote, the moment he heard it, was off on the run, bearing down on his enemy at Rocinante's top speed." Tosilos did not stir, but called out to the master of ceremonies: "I would have you know that my conscience hurts me, and I'd be laying a heavy burden on it if I went through with this battle. I therefore yield myself as vanquished and am willing to marry the lady at once." When his helmet is unlaced, the countenance of the lackey is revealed.

" 'It's a trick! A trick!' screamed Doña Rodríguez and her daughter. 'They've put Tosilos, lackey to my lord the duke, in the place of the true husband! Justice from God and the King against such cunning as this, not to say villainy!'

" 'Do not distress yourselves, ladies,' said Don Quixote. 'This is neither cunning nor villainy, or if it is, it is not the duke who is to blame but those wicked enchanters that persecute me. Enviously fearful that I might win a glorious victory, they have converted your husband's face into that of one who, so you say, is the duke's lackey. Take my advice and despite the malice of my enemies, go ahead and marry this man, for undoubtedly he is the one you wanted to marry all the time.' "

The Duke's anger at his betrayal by Tosilos now changes to laughter. " 'The things that happen to Señor Don Quixote,' he said, 'are so extraordinary that I am ready to believe this is not my lackey.' " He then proposes that the lackey be confined for several weeks to see if he will return to his former shape, " 'for the grudge the enchanters hold against Don Quixote cannot last as long as that, especially when they see that these tricks and transformations are doing them so little good.' " Doña Rodríguez's daughter announces her intention to marry him, whether or not he is changed, and so the adventure ends with laughter and satisfaction on all sides.

CHAPTER 57.

Don Quixote takes leave of the Duke and Duchess in order to continue his way to Saragossa. Altisidora, as a last jest, accuses him of stealing her garters and sings an impudent song of farewell.

CHAPTER 58.

On the road the two meet a group of workmen eating in a meadow, with objects beside them under white sheets. These are carved images in relief that are being carried to their village. Don Quixote correctly identifies each warrior saint and discourses on his deeds. He regrets that Dulcinea's enchantment prevents him from better fortunes and a sounder mind than he has, a consciousness of his madness that prepares the mood of the final chapter. Nevertheless, his meeting with these images seems to Don Quixote a happy omen, and Sancho Panza also appreciates the sweet adventure.

Continuing their journey, "they entered a wood alongside the road, when suddenly, without his expecting it, Don Quixote found himself entangled in some nets of green cord [note the *green*, Cervantes's favorite color] that had been strung between the trees." Taking this to be another enchantment perhaps in revenge for his stern treatment of Altisidora, "He was about to ride on and burst through them all when without warning there appeared before him from among the trees two most beautiful shepherd lasses—or, at least, they were dressed like shepherdesses, save for the fact that their jackets and peasant skirts were of fine brocade. . . ." The shepherd theme now returns. "It is our intention [they say] to set up here a new pastoral Arcadia, with the maidens dressing as shepherdesses and the lads as shepherds. We have been studying two eclogues . . . but we have not as yet acted them." The nets of green cords are to catch birds.

The girls and their brothers have read about Don Quixote and Sancho Panza, and they make much of them both. To reciprocate, Don Quixote posts himself in the middle of the highway and announces: "O ye travelers and wayfarers, knights and squires, those on foot and those on horseback, who pass along this road within the next two days, know that Don Quixote de la Mancha, knight-errant, stands here to maintain that the nymphs who inhabit these groves and meadows excel in beauty and in courtesy all others in the world, leaving aside the lady of my heart, Dulcinea del Toboso. And so, let anyone who holds the contrary come on, for I await him on this spot."

A large number of men with lances, riding in close formation, come galloping, and the foremost cries to Don Quixote, "Out of the way, devil take you, or these bulls will trample you to pieces!" When Don Quixote refuses, the herd of wild bulls and the leading-oxen knock down the knight and Sancho, with Rocinante and the ass, and leave them badly battered. (This is a reversion to part one, chapter 18, where Don Quixote fought the sheep he had mistaken for armies.) Bruised and hurt, "Then master and man mounted once again, and without turning to bid farewell to the imitation Arcadia they continued on their way with more of shame than pleasure in their mien."

CHAPTER 59.

They sit down beside the bright clear water of a spring. " 'Eat, friend Sancho,' said Don Quixote, 'and sustain life, since that is of more importance to you than it is to me. Leave me to die of my thoughts and my misfortunes; for you may know, Sancho, that I was born to live dying and you to die eating. That you may see how true this is, look at me now. Here I am with my name in the history books, a famous man of arms, courteous in my conduct, respected by princes, sought after by damsels, and just when I was expecting palms, triumphs, and crowns, I find myself this morning, as a climax to it all, trodden underfoot, battered, and kicked by a herd of filthy animals. When I think of this, my teeth are blunted, my jaws are numbed, my hands are paralyzed, and I lose all appetite to such an extent that I've a mind to die of hunger, which is the cruelest death there is.' " But Dulcinea being still bewitched, he recovers enough to ask Sancho Panza to give himself three or four hundred lashes as a payment on account of the three thousand and some still left. Sancho, as usual, promises future payment.

A little later they stop at an inn. Don Quixote hears voices in the next room mentioning his name. " 'Upon your life, Señor Don Jerónimo,' someone was saying, 'while they are bringing our supper, let us read another chapter of the *Second Part of Don Quixote de la Mancha.*'*

"No sooner did he hear his name mentioned than Don Quixote rose to his feet and began listening intently to what they were saying about him.

" 'Why should your Grace have us read such nonsense as that, Señor Don Juan,' came the reply, 'seeing that he who has read the First Part of the history of Don Quixote de la Mancha cannot possibly find any pleasure in this second one?'

" 'For all of that,' said Don Juan, 'it would be well to read it, since no book is so bad that there is not some good to be found in it. What displeases me most about it is that it depicts Don Quixote as no longer in love with Dulcinea del Toboso.'"**

In anger and resentment Don Quixote challenges them in his own name. The two gentlemen enter the room, "one of whom threw his arms about Don Quixote's neck.

" 'Your appearance,' he said, 'does not belie your name, nor can your name fail to suggest your appearance. You, sir, are undoubtedly the true Don Quixote de la Mancha, north pole and morning star of knight-errantry despite the one who has sought to usurp your name and obliterate your achievements, as the author of this book which I hand you here has done.' "

Don Quixote leafs through the book and hands it back after a short time saying that he has seen enough. There are certain phrases in the preface that would not have been used, the language is Aragonese and not Castilian, and the author thinks that the name of Sancho's wife is Mari Gutiérrez when the name should be Teresa Panza.† "And it is greatly to be feared that one who errs in so important a matter as this will be wrong in all the other particulars throughout the history."

When Sancho asks how he is portrayed, the answer is, " 'Faith, then,' said the gentleman, 'this new author does not treat you with that decency that your person displays. He portrays you as a glutton and a simpleton, not

---

* VN quotes Putnam's note, "Allusion is to the spurious continuation of Part I by Fernandez de Avellaneda. Rodriguez Marin: 'Cervantes was thinking of writing this chapter when there came to hand the *Second Volume of the Ingenious Gentleman, Don Quixote de la Mancha,* supposedly written by Alonso Fernandez de Avellaneda, and published at Tarragona in 1614.' See the Prologue to Part II."

** VN quotes Ormsby from Putnam's note: "Avellaneda in chap. II of his continuation makes Aldonza Lorenzo write to Don Quixote threatening him with a beating for calling her Princess and Dulcinea, and Don Quixote, stung by her ingratitude, resolves to look out for another mistress."

† VN quotes Putnam's note: "It was Cervantes himself who, in Part I, Chapter VII, called Sancho's wife Mari Gutiérrez; a few lines above, in the same chapter, he had referred to her as Juana Gutiérrez, and in Part I, Chapter LII: she is Juana Panza."

at all droll—in short, quite different from the Sancho described in the first part of your master's history.' "*

As usual with the positive characters in the book, the two gentlemen are amazed at the combination of wisdom and madness in Don Quixote's speech (just as others had been amazed by the combination of common sense and rusticity in Sancho Panza).

Don Quixote decides not to go to the tournament at Saragossa as he had intended and gives the following amazing reason: "Don Juan informed him that this new history told how Don Quixote, whoever he might be, in that same tournament had participated in a tilting at the ring but that the description given had shown a sorry lack of inventiveness, especially with regard to the mottoes of the knights and their liveries, in which regard it was impoverished in the extreme though rich in foolishness.

" 'For that very reason,' said Don Quixote, 'I will not set foot in Saragossa but will let the world see how this new historian lies, by showing people that I am not the Don Quixote of whom he is speaking.' "

CHAPTER 60.

"The morning was cool and gave promise of the same kind of day to follow as Don Quixote sallied forth from the inn, having made inquiries as to which was the most direct route to Barcelona without passing through Saragossa; for he was determined to give the lie to that new historian, who, so they told him, had heaped so much abuse upon him." They travel for six days without incident, and then at nightfall make themselves as comfortable as they can in a dense grove of oak or cork trees "(on this point Cid Hamete is not as precise as he usually is)." While Sancho sleeps, "Don Quixote, on the other hand, kept awake by his thoughts rather than by hunger, was unable to close his eyes as his mind wandered here and there through a thousand different places. Now it seemed that he was in the Cave of Montesinos and was beholding Dulcinea, transformed into a peasant maid, skipping about and mounting her she-ass; and again the words of Merlin the sage were ringing in his ears, setting forth the conditions to be observed and what was to be done in order to accomplish the lady's

* VN quotes Putnam's note: "In this chapter the author clearly reveals his own conception of Sancho's character, and we can see the respect that he had for the squire and the peasant type in general. This is a point that Aubrey F. G. Bell [who tends to idealize Sancho—VN] stresses throughout in his *Cervantes*. Sancho is neither a glutton nor a drunkard nor a vulgar buffoon; he is 'graci'oso'—'droll,' which is something quite different. This is one of the chief sins of Motteux and certain other English-language translators who would make him out to be a cockney clown."

disenchantment. He fell into a mood of despair as he thought of the laxness and want of charity displayed by his squire Sancho, who, to his master's knowledge, had given himself but five lashes in all, a very small proportion indeed of the countless number that remained to be administered." The knight then attempts to administer some of the lashes himself but Sancho resists, and so violently that he trips up Don Quixote and holds him pinned to the ground until he swears that he will never again attempt to flog Sancho with his own hand.

They are taken prisoner by a Robin Hood sort of bandit named Roque Guinart when Don Quixote is surprised without his lance and can put up no resistance. Roque, who has heard of Don Quixote but could not believe that his adventures were true, takes a great fancy to him. A girl disguised as a young man in green arrives at a gallop with the usual story: man promised to marry her, now is about to marry another. She shoots him, but it transpires that the rumors were wrong and she falls fainting on his dead body as he breathes his last. Idiotic.

The bandits capture two captains of Spanish infantry and some pilgrims on their way to Rome. Also some women. Usual stuff.

CHAPTER 61.

Roque sends word ahead and then escorts Don Quixote and Sancho to Barcelona, where he leaves them on the beach to await dawn. They marvel at their first view of the sea. "But at this point the liveried horsemen with cheers, cries, and Moorish war whoops came galloping up to where Don Quixote waited in astonishment and some alarm.

"And then one of them—the one to whom Roque had sent word—raised his voice and cried out to the knight, 'Welcome to our city, O mirror, beacon, and north star of all knight-errantry, in the full sense of the word. You are, I repeat, very welcome indeed, O valiant Don Quixote de la Mancha—not the false, not the fictitious, not the apocryphal one that we read of in mendacious histories that have appeared of late, but the true and legitimate one, the real one that Cid Hamete Benengeli, flower of historians, has portrayed for us.' " The horsemen escort Don Quixote to the house of Don Antonio Moreno, there to be his guest.

CHAPTER 62.

Don Antonio, who was fond of amusing himself albeit in what is described as an innocent and kindly way, exhibits Don Quixote to the populace on his balcony and takes him for a ride with a sign pinned to his back, unknown to the knight, who is astonished at the number of people who call him by name. Don Antonio shows Don Quixote a magic head carved by a great sorcerer, which is able to answer all questions. (It is later revealed that an alert young man is placed below the table, whose voice coming up through a tube, appears to issue from the bronze head.) Various of Don Antonio's friends ask questions and receive answers.

"Don Quixote now came forward. 'Tell me,' he said, 'you who do the answering, with regard to my story of what happened to me in the Cave of Montesinos, did it really happen or was it a dream? Will my squire Sancho be sure to receive the lashes that are his due? And will Dulcinea finally be disenchanted?'

" 'With respect to the cave,' the head replied, 'there is much to be said on both sides; Sancho's lashes will proceed apace; and the disenchantment of Dulcinea will ultimately be accomplished.'

" 'That is enough,' said Don Quixote. 'Let me but see Dulcinea freed of the magic spell and it will seem to me that all the good fortune I could wish for has come to me at once.' "

After revealing how the voice was produced by the trick, "Cid Hamete further tells us that this marvelous contrivance lasted for ten or a dozen days, but as the news spread through the city that Don Antonio had in his house an enchanted head that answered all queries put to it, he, fearing lest word of this should reach the alert ears of those reverend gentlemen, the sentinels of our faith, had explained the matter to the Inquisitors, who had ordered him to smash the mechanism and carry the jest no further, in order that the ignorant rabble might not be scandalized."*

Don Quixote visits a printing shop where proofs are being corrected, and when he asks the title, he is told it is the *Second Volume of the Ingenious Gentleman, Don Quixote de la Mancha*, composed by a certain native of Tordesillas. " 'I have heard of this work,' he said, 'and, in all truth and upon my conscience, I think it ought to be burned to ashes as a piece of impertinence; but Martinmas will come for it as it does for every pig. Fictional tales are better and more enjoyable the nearer they approach the truth or the semblance of the truth, and as for true stories, the best are those that are most true.'

"Saying this, he stalked out of the printing shop with signs of considerable displeasure."

* VN adds a note: "NB. this: it is doubtful that any such remark could be made today in Russia regarding the political police."

CHAPTER 63.

Don Quixote is taken to inspect a galley and is ceremoniously welcomed by its commander. As they make ready for sea, "the boatswain piped them to weigh anchor, and, leaping upon the middle of the gangway, he began flaying the backs of the rowers as they little by little put out to sea." Don Quixote, seeing how attentively Sancho was watching, remarked, "Ah, friend Sancho, . . . how quickly you could finish with the disenchantment of Dulcinea if you would only strip down to the waist and take your place among these gentlemen! For amid the pain and misery of so many you would not feel your own to any great extent; and it might be that the wise Merlin would count each one of these lashes, lustily laid on, as equivalent to ten of those which you must give yourself anyway, sooner or later."*

A Turkish brigantine is captured, and we have yet another disguise (count them!). The captured crew point out their captain, a fine young fellow, whom the commander proposes to hang from the yardarm.

"The viceroy looked the prisoner over and saw how handsome he was, how gallant and modest his bearing, and, the young man's comeliness being his letter of recommendation, he at once felt a desire to spare his life.

" 'Tell me, Captain,' he asked, 'are you a Turk by nationality, a Moor, or a renegade?'

"To this the youth replied, also in Spanish, 'I am neither a Turk, nor a Moor, nor a renegade.'

" 'Then what are you?'

" 'A Christian woman.'

" 'A woman and a Christian, in such a costume and in such a plight? Why, it is astonishing—scarcely to be believed.'

" 'If you gentlemen,' replied the youth, 'will suspend my execution while I tell you the story of my life, you will not have to wait too long for your revenge.'

The girl is the Christian daughter of Ricote, the Moor, beloved by a neighbor Don Gregorio, but carried off at an early age to Algiers, with Gregorio accompanying her. While he lives in Algiers disguised as a woman, she has been allowed to return to Spain under supervision to recover the family treasure for the King of Algiers. Ricote, who has come aboard disguised as an old pilgrim, recognizes his daughter and there is a tearful reunion. The story is not worth reading, but it may be said that plans are laid to rescue Don Gregorio and all will end happily.

* In pencil VN notes in the margin of this speech, "DQ the Righter of Wrongs surrenders here to DQ the champion of an Imaginary Lady—he forgets that he liberated slaves and egotistically concentrates on his fading dream."

"And then, one morning, as Don Quixote went for a ride along the beach, clad in full armor—for, as he was fond of saying, that was his only ornament, his only rest the fight, and, accordingly, he was never without it for a moment—he saw approaching him a horseman similarly arrayed from head to foot and with a brightly shining moon blazoned upon his shield.

"As soon as he had come within earshot the stranger cried out to Don Quixote in a loud voice, 'O illustrious knight, the never to be sufficiently praised Don Quixote de la Mancha, I am the Knight of the White Moon, whose incomparable exploits you will perhaps recall. I come to contend with you and try the might of my arm, with the purpose of having you acknowledge and confess that my lady, whoever she may be, is beyond comparison more beautiful than your own Dulcinea del Toboso.' "

It is really Carrasco who had once already fought with Don Quixote. The brief encounter is described. A very poor scene. The author is tired. He might, I suggest, have squeezed much more fanciful fun and interest out of this. It ought to have been the climax, the most furious and elaborate battle in the whole work! But all we get is "And then, without blare of trumpet or other warlike instrument to give them the signal for the attack, both at the same instant wheeled their steeds about and returned for the charge. Being mounted upon the swifter horse, the Knight of the White Moon met Don Quixote two-thirds of the way and with such tremendous force that, without touching his opponent with his lance (which, it seemed, he deliberately held aloft) he brought both Rocinante and his rider to the ground in an exceedingly perilous fall. At once the victor leaped down and placed his lance at Don Quixote's visor.

"You are vanquished, O knight! Nay, more, you are dead unless you make confession in accordance with the conditions governing our encounter."

Don Quixote yields and promises to return to his village for a year or until released from his word, but he will not confess that Dulcinea has a peer. Carrasco, as the Knight of the White Moon, accepts the pledge, and allows Dulcinea's beauty to remain unchallenged. Don Quixote is nursed back to health at Don Antonio's house, where he is brought the news of the recovery of Don Gregorio and the happy ending to the tale of the Christian girl. No longer a knight-errant, Don Quixote starts the journey back to his village.

CHAPTER 66.

Sancho settles a dispute between two groups of peasants. He meets Tosilos, the lackey, carrying letters from the Duke to the viceroy at Barcelona. Tosilos recounts how, after Don Quixote had left, the Duke gave him a hundred blows with a club for disobeying orders about the combat with Don Quixote, Doña Rodríguez has returned to Castile, and her daughter has entered a nunnery.

CHAPTER 67.

As Don Quixote and Sancho jog along, they come to the place where they had been trampled by the bulls. Don Quixote recognized it at once.

" 'This,' he observed, 'is the meadow where we fell in with those gallant and gaily bedecked shepherds and shepherdesses who were endeavoring to imitate and restore the Arcadia of old, a novel idea and an inspired one; and if you approve, Sancho, I would suggest that, at least for the time that I have to live in retirement, we likewise turn shepherds. I will purchase some sheep and all the other things that are necessary to the pastoral life, taking for myself the name of "the shepherd Quixotiz," while you will be "the shepherd Pancino." Together we will roam the hills, the woods, and the meadows, now singing songs and now composing elegies, drinking the crystal water of the springs or that of the clear running brooks or mighty rivers. The oaks will provide us with an abundance of their delicious fruit, the hardwood trunks of the cork trees will furnish us a seat, the willows will give us shade, the roses will lend their perfume, and the spacious meadows will spread a myriad-colored carpet for our feet; we shall breathe the clean, pure air, and despite the darkness of the night the moon and stars will afford us illumination; song will be our joy, and we shall be happy even in our laments, for Apollo will supply the inspiration for our verses and love will endow us with conceits and we shall be everlastingly famous—not only in this age, but for all time to come.' "

Sancho accepts the idea with enthusiasm and hopes that the barber and curate and even Sansón Carrasco may be persuaded to join them.

CHAPTER 68.

Again Don Quixote suggests that Sancho Panza flog himself, and again he is put off. They are trampled by a herd of swine, and then are captured by disguised horsemen and brought to a place that they recognize as the Duke's castle.

CHAPTER 69.

They are escorted into the courtyard where the beautiful maiden Altisidora lies as if dead upon a rich bier surrounded by burning tapers, above which two kings, Minos and Rhadamanthus, sit as judges. After a certain amount of mumbo-jumbo it is disclosed that she can be revived only if Sancho will allow himself to have his face given twenty-four smacks, and his body a dozen pinches and half a dozen pinpricks. He objects violently. "At this moment a procession of as many as six duennas was to be seen crossing the courtyard. Four of them wore spectacles and all had their right hands raised with four inches of wrist showing, by way of making them seem longer as is the present fashion. As soon as he caught sight of them, Sancho began bellowing like a bull.

" 'I might allow myself to be manhandled by anybody else,' he said, 'but to think that I am going to let duennas touch me—nothing of the sort! Cat-claw my face as they did my master's in this very castle, run my body through with burnished dagger points, nip my arms with red-hot pincers—I'll bear it all patiently to please these gentlefolk; but the devil take me if I let duennas lay hands on me!'

"It was Don Quixote's turn to break silence now. 'Be patient, my son,' he said. 'Comply with the wishes of these gentlemen, and thank Heaven there is lodged in your person such virtue that through the martyrdom of your flesh you are able to disenchant the enchanted and resurrect the dead.'

"As the duennas approached him Sancho became more quiet and tractable, and, settling himself comfortably in his chair, he held up his face and beard to the firstcomer, who gave him a resounding smack, followed by a low bow. . . .

"To make a long story short, all the duennas slapped him and many other members of the household pinched him, but the thing he could not stand was the pinpricks. When it came to that, he rose from his chair with a show of anger and, seizing a lighted torch that stood near by, began laying about him among the duennas and all his other tormentors, crying, 'Away with you, ministers of Hell! I am not made of brass so that I do not feel such unusual torture as this!' "

Altisidora comes to life and is greeted with shouts of acclaim.

"When Don Quixote saw Altisidora stirring, he fell on his knees before Sancho.

" 'O son of my loins,' he said, 'for I will not call you squire, now is the time for you to give yourself a few of those lashes that you owe toward Dulcinea's disenchantment. Now, I repeat, is the time, when the virtue that is in you is ripe and may efficaciously accomplish the good that is expected of you.'

" 'That,' said Sancho, 'to my mind, is trick upon trick and not honey on pancakes. It would be a fine thing to have lashes on top of pinches, slaps, and prickings! . . . Leave me alone or by God I'll throw everything over, no matter what happens.' "

CHAPTER 70.

Altisidora comes to Don Quixote and Sancho's bedroom that night to reproach him for his cruelty to her. She recounts that while she was under the spell and imagined herself as partly in Hell, she saw a dozen devils playing tennis with books. "To one of the brand-new volumes, which was very well bound, they gave such a whack that they knocked the insides out of it and sent the leaves flying in all directions. 'Just see what book that is,' said a devil to his companion, and the other devil replied, 'This is the *Second Part of the History of Don Quixote de la Mancha*, written not by Cid Hamete, the original author, but by an Aragonese who, according to his own account is a native of Tordesillas.'

" 'Take it away,' said the other. 'Throw it into the bottomless pit so that I shan't have to see it.'

" 'Is it as bad as all that?'

" 'It is so bad,' said the first devil, 'that if I had deliberately set myself to write a worse one, I shouldn't have been able to achieve it.'

"They then went on with their game, batting about other books, but, for my part, on hearing the name of Don Quixote whom I so adore, I made up my mind then and there to remember this vision I had seen."

CHAPTER 71.

Leaving the castle on his way back to his village, "As the vanquished and deeply afflicted Don Quixote went his way, he was, on the one hand, overly sad, and, on the other, very happy. His sadness was due to his defeat, while his happiness lay in thinking of the virtue his squire had shown he possessed by resurrecting Altisidora, although it must be admitted he had some difficulty in persuading himself that the lovelorn maiden had really been dead."

He permits Sancho to pay himself from the Don's purse for each lash, and Sancho promises to begin that night. After giving himself some six or eight strokes, with Don Quixote counting, Sancho retired to the woods and there laid about him on the trees, all the time moaning as if in great pain until Don Quixote in pity joined him and snatched the donkey's reins (which had played a part twice before in enchantments) and bade him cease for that night. Resuming their journey they come to a village and "Dismounting at a hostelry, the knight recognized it for what it was and did not take it to be a castle with a deep moat, turrets, portcullis, and a drawbridge, for ever since he had been overcome in combat he had talked more rationally on all subjects. . . ."

CHAPTER 72.

After meeting one of the characters from Avellaneda's spurious *Second Volume*, Don Quixote has a notary draw up a document stating that the real Don Quixote and Sancho Panza are not the ones referred to in Avellaneda's book. That night among the trees, which suffer instead of his shoulders (or behind), Sancho completes his lashings and Don Quixote now expects to meet the disenchanted Dulcinea at every turn.

CHAPTER 73.

Although he sees what he takes to be some ill omens on entering his village, Don Quixote informs the curate and Carrasco of his pledge to remain at home for a year, and invites his friends to join him in the Arcadian life he has promised himself. "Both his listeners were dismayed at the new form which his madness had assumed. However, in order that he might not go faring forth from the village on another of his expeditions (for they hoped that in the course of the year he would be cured), they decided to fall in with his new plan and approve it as being a wise one, and they even agreed to be his companions in the calling he proposed to adopt. . . . With this, they took their leave of him, advising and beseeching him to take care of his health and to eat plentifully of the proper food."
However, Don Quixote does not feel well and takes to his bed.

CHAPTER 74.

On his deathbed Don Quixote's mind clears. When his friends come to visit him, " 'I have good news for you, kind sirs,' said Don Quixote the moment he saw them. 'I am no longer Don Quixote de la Mancha but Alonso Quijano, whose mode of life won for him the name of "Good." I am the enemy of Amadis of Gaul and all his innumerable progeny; for those profane stories dealing with knight-errantry are odious to me, and I realize how foolish I was and the danger I courted in reading them; but I am in my right senses now and I abominate them.'

"Hearing this, they all three were convinced that some new kind of madness must have laid hold of him.

" 'Why, Señor Don Quixote,' exclaimed Sansón. 'What makes you talk like that, just when we have received news that my lady Dulcinea is disenchanted? And just when we are on the verge of becoming shepherds so that we may spend the rest of our lives in singing like a lot of princes, why does your Grace choose to turn hermit? Say no more, in Heaven's name, but be sensible and forget these idle tales.'

" 'Tales of that kind,' said Don Quixote, 'have been the truth for me in the past, and to my detriment, but with Heaven's aid I trust to turn them to my profit now that I am dying. For I feel, gentlemen, that death is very near; so, leave all jesting aside and bring me a confessor for my sins and a notary to draw up my will. In such straits as these a man cannot trifle with his soul. Accordingly, while the Señor Curate is hearing my confession, let the notary be summoned.' . . . When the confession was over, the curate came out.

" 'It is true enough,' he said, 'that Alonso Quijano the Good is dying, and it is also true that he is a sane man. It would be well for us to go in now while he makes his will.' . . .

"Death came at last for Don Quixote, after he had received all the sacraments and once more, with many forceful arguments, had expressed his abomination of books of chivalry. The notary who was present remarked that in none of those books had he read of any knight-errant dying in his own bed so peacefully and in so Christian a manner. And thus, amid the tears and lamentations of those present, he gave up the ghost; that is to say, he died. Perceiving that their friend was no more, the curate asked the notary to be a witness to the fact that Alonso Quijano the Good, commonly known as Don Quixote, was truly dead, this being necessary in order that some author other than Cid Hamete Benengeli might not have the opportunity of falsely resurrecting him and writing endless histories of his exploits.

"Such was the end of the Ingenious Gentleman of La Mancha, whose birthplace Cid Hamete was unwilling to designate exactly in order that all the towns and villages of La Mancha might contend among themselves for the right to adopt him and claim him as their own, just as the seven cities of Greece did in the case of Homer. . . ."

Cid Hamete (otherwise Cervantes) concludes: "For me alone Don Quixote was born and I for him; it was for him to act, for me to write, and we two are one in spite of that Tordesillesque pretender who had, and may have, the audacity to write with a coarse and ill-trimmed ostrich quill of the deeds of my valiant knight. . . . For the two sallies that he did make to the delight and approval of all who heard of them, in foreign countries as well as our own, are sufficient to cast ridicule upon all the ridings forth of knights-errant in times past. . . . I have had no other purpose than to arouse the abhorrence of mankind toward those false and nonsensical stories to be met with in the books of chivalry, which, thanks to this tale of the genuine Don Quixote, are already tottering and without a doubt are doomed to fall. *Vale*."

VLADIMIR NABOKOV

Appendix

Sample passages from romances of chivalry mimeographed and distributed to Vladimir Nabokov's students as background reading.

From Le Morte d'Arthur *by Sir Thomas Malory, The Book of King Arthur and of his Noble Knights of the Round Table, 1469-1470.*

FROM VOL. I, BOOK IV, CH. 22:

So it was then in the Month of May that [Lady Ettard, Sir Pelleas' lady] and Sir Gawaine went out of the castle and supped in a pavilion and presently Sir Pelleas found them clipped in sleep and he left his naked sword overthwart both their throats and made marvellous dole and sorrow....*

FROM VOL. I, BOOK V, CH. 23:

How Sir Pelleas loved no more Ettard by means of the damosel of the lake, whom he loved ever after.

---

* VN's redaction of Malory.

213

Sir knight Pelleas, said the damosel of the lake, take your horse and come forth with me out of this country, and ye shall love a lady that shall love you. I will well, said Sir Pelleas, for this Lady Ettard hath done me great despite and shame, and there he told her the beginning and the ending, and how he had purposed never to have arisen till that he had been dead.—And now such grace God hath sent me, so that I hate her as much as ever I loved her, thanked be our Lord Jesus! Thank me, said the damosel of the lake. Anon Sir Pelleas armed him, and took his horse, and commanded his men to bring after his pavilions and his stuff where the damosel of the lake would assign. So the Lady Ettard died for sorrow, and the damosel of the lake rejoiced Sir Pelleas, and loved together during their life days.

FROM VOL. I, BOOK V, CH. 4:

And as the king lay in his cabin in the ship, he fell in a slumbering and dreamed a marvellous dream: him seemed that a dreadful dragon did drown much of his people, and he came flying out of the west, and his head was enamalled with azure, and his shoulders shone as gold, his belly like mails of a marvellous hue, his tail full of tatters, his feet full of fine sable, and his claws like fine gold; and an hideous flame of fire flew out of his mouth, like as the land and water had flamed all of fire.

FROM VOL. I, BOOK V, CH. 5 (Description of the giant):

... saw where he sat at supper gnawing on a limb of a man, baking his broad limbs by the fire, and breechless, and three fair damosels turning three broaches whereon broached twelve young children late born, like young birds. . . .

FROM VOL. I, BOOK V, CH. 5:

And so weltering and wallowing they rolled down the hill till they came to the sea mark, and ever as they so weltered Arthur smote him with his dagger.
    [And then, panting, he says:]
This was the fiercest giant that I ever met with, save one in the mount of Araby, which I overcame, but this was greater and fiercer.

FROM VOL. I, BOOK VI, CH. 3:

Thus as they rode they heard by them a great horse grimly neigh, then were they were ware of a sleeping knight, that lay all armed under an apple-tree; anon as these queens looked on his face, they knew it was Sir Launcelot....

FROM VOL. I, BOOK VI, CH. 10:

Now turn we unto Sir Launcelot, that rode with the damosel in a fair highway. Sir, said the damosel, here by this way haunteth a knight that distressed all ladies and gentlewomen, and at the least he robbeth them or lieth by them. What, said Sir Launcelot, is he a thief and a knight and a ravisher of women? he doth shame unto the order of knighthood, and contrary unto his oath; it is pity that he liveth. But, fair damosel, ye shall ride on afore, yourself, and I will keep myself in covert, and if that he trouble you or distress you I shall be your rescue and learn him to be ruled as a knight.

FROM VOL. I, BOOK VIII, CH. 6:

So to shorten this tale, when Sir Tristram was arrived within the island he looked to the farther side, and there he saw at an anchor six ships nigh to the land; and under the shadow of the ships upon the land, there hoved the noble knight, Sir Marhaus of Ireland. Then Sir Tristram commanded his servant Gouvernail to bring his horse to the land, and dress his harness at all manner of rights. And then when he had so done he mounted upon his horse; and when he was in his saddle well apparelled, and his shield dressed upon his shoulder, Tristram asked Gouvernail, Where is this knight that I shall have ado withal? Sir, said Gouvernail, see ye him not? I weened ye had seen him; yonder he hoveth under the umbre of his ships on horseback, with his spear in his hand and his shield upon his shoulder. That is truth, said the noble knight, Sir Tristram, now I see him well enough.

FROM VOL. I, BOOK VIII, CH. 7:

Then they began to feutre [set in socket] their spears, and they met so fiercely together that they smote either other down, both horse and all. But Sir Marhaus smote Sir Tristram a great wound in the side with his spear, and then they avoided [quit] their horses, and pulled out their swords, and threw their shields afore them. And then they lashed together as men that were wild and courageous. And when they had stricken so together long, then they left their strokes, and foyned [thrust] at their breaths [breathing holes] and visors; and when they saw that that might not prevail them, then they hurtled [dashed] together like rams to bear either other down. Thus they fought still more than half a day, and either were wounded passing sore, that the blood ran down freshly from them upon the ground. By then Sir Tristram waxed more fresher than Sir Marhaus, and better winded and bigger; and with a mighty stroke he smote Sir Marhaus upon the helm such a buffet that it went through his helm, and through the coif of steel, and through the brain-pan, and the sword stuck so fast in the helm and in his brain-pan that Sir Tristram pulled thrice at his sword or ever he might pull it out from his head; and there Marhaus fell down on his knees, the edge of Tristram's sword left in his brain-pan. And suddenly Sir Marhaus rose grovelling, and threw his sword and his shield from him, and so ran to his ships and fled his way, and Sir Tristram had ever his shield and his sword.

From Amadis of Gaul, *by Vasco Lobeira, a Portuguese of the second half of the fourteenth century, written originally either in French or in Portuguese. Translated from a Spanish version of Garciodonez de Montalvo by Robert Southey, the English poet. London: John Russell Smith, 1872.*

FROM VOL. I, CH. 27: *How Amadis delivered the damsel from the knight who mistreated her, and how afterwards when he was sleeping another knight carried her away.*

Such speed made Amadis, that, having overthrown the knight who would have known whither he went, he overtook him who misused the damsel and cried to him, Sir knight, you have been committing great wrong: I pray you do so no more.—What wrong?—The shamefullest that could be devised, in striking that damsel.—And you are come to chastise me?—Not so: but to counsel you for your own good. It will be more for yours to turn back as you came, said the knight.—Thereat was Amadis angered: and he went to the squire and said, Let go the damsel, or thou diest! and the squire in fear put her down. Sir knight, you shall dearly abide this, quoth his master. Amadis answered, We shall see! and ran his career and drove him from his saddle, and was about to ride over him, but he cried out for mercy!—Swear then never to wrong dame or damsel. And, as he approached to receive the oath, the traitor stabbed his horse. Amadis recovered from the fall, and with one blow paid him for the treason.

The damsel then besought him to compleat his courtesy by accompanying her to a castle whither she was going. He took the horse of the slain, and they went on together, and by the way he learnt from her the story of Antebon. About midnight they came to a river-side, and, because the damsel would fain sleep, they stopt. Amadis spread Gandalin's cloak for her bed, and he laid his head upon his helmet, and they all slept. There came up a knight as they were sleeping, and he seeing the damsel, gently wakened her with the end of his lance. She seeing an armed knight, thought it was Amadis, and said, Do you wish us to depart? He answered, It is time! In God's name, then, quoth she; and, being still drowsy, she suffered the stranger to place her before him; but then recollecting, What is this? she cried: the squire should have carried me. And when she saw it was a stranger, she shrieked out and called to Amadis, Let not a stranger carry me off! But the knight clapt spurs to his horse, and galloped away [with her].

FROM VOL. I, CH. 44: *How Don Galaor and Glorestan, going towards the kingdom of Sobradisa, met three Damsels at the Fountain of the Elm Trees.*

Four days they rode without adventure; on the fifth at evening they came to a tower. A knight, who stood at the court-gate, courteously invited them for the night; and there were they worshipfully entertained. The knight their host was a fair knight and a wise, and of goodly stature; but oftentimes he appeared so lost in thought and sadness, that the brethren asked each other what it might mean, and Don Galaor at last said to him, Sir, methinks you are not so cheerful as you should be! if your sadness is for any cause which our aid can remedy, tell us, and we will do your will. Many thanks replied he of the tower: I believe you would do so like good knights; but my sadness proceeds from the force of love, and I will not tell you more now, for it would be to my own great shame. The hour of sleeping came on; their host went to his apartment, and the brethren remained in a handsome chamber where there were two beds. In the morning he rode to bear them company, but unarmed; and, that he might see whether they were such in arms as their appearance bespoke them, he led them not along the high road, but through bye ways, till they came to a place called the fountain of the Three Elms, for there were three great and lofty elm-trees above the fountain. Three fair damsels and well apparelled, were by the fountain, and there was a dwarf aloft in the trees. Florestan went first and saluted them gently, as a courteous man, and one who had been gently bred. God save you, sir knight, quoth the one; if you are as brave as you are handsome, God hath gifted you well. Damsel, he replied, if my beauty pleaseth you, my courage would please you more if it were put to proof. You answer well, quoth she; see now if your courage be enough to carry me from hence.—Certes, quoth Florestan, little goodness is enough for that; since it is your pleasure, I will do it.—He then bade his squires place her upon a palfrey which was tied to one of the elms: when the dwarf, who was sitting up in the tree, cried out aloud, Come forth, knight, come forth! they are carrying away your mistress! At these words a knight well armed and on a great horse, came up from the valley, and cried out to Florestan, Knight! who bid you lay your hands upon that damsel? I do not think she can be yours, replied Florestan, seeing of her own will she desired me to carry her hence.

FROM VOL. II, BOOK III, CH. 6 (The Dumb Damsel): *How the Knights of the Serpents embarked for Gaul, and fortune led them where they were placed in great peril of their lives by treachery, in the power of Arcalaus the Enchanter; and how being delivered they embarked and continued their voyage; and also how Don Galaor and Norandel came by chance that way seeking adventures, and of what befell them.*

Some days King Perion abode in the forest to rest, then seeing that the wind was fair they put to sea, thinking soon to be in Gaul; but the wind soon changed and made the sea rage so that after five days the storm obliged them to return back to Great Britain, to a distant part of the coast; there, while the weather continued, and while their men took in fresh water, they rode into the country to learn where they were, taking three squires with them, but leaving Gandolin to wait for them in the galley because he was well known. They rode up a glen and reached a plain, and proceeded not far before they came to a fountain, whereat a damsel was letting her palfrey drink. Richly clad was she, and over her garments she wore a scarlet cloak with gold buttons, and the button-holes worked with gold. Two squires and two damsels were in her company with falcons and dogs for sport. She seeing their arms knew that they were the Knights of the Serpents, and went towards them with a shew of much joy, and saluted them courteously, making signs that she was dumb, whereat they were grieved seeing how fair she was, and of what courteous demeanour. She went up to him of the golden helmet and embraced him, and would have kissed his hand, and then by signs she invited them to be her guests that night, but they not understanding her signs she tokened to her squire to explain them. They seeing her good will, and that it was now late, rode with her in full confidence, and came to a goodly castle, so that they held the damsel as very rich seeing she was mistress thereof. When they entered they found enough servants to welcome them, and sundry dames and damsels, who all regarded the dumb damsel as their lady. Their horses were taken from them, and they were led up to a rich chamber about twenty cubits from the ground [some thirty feet], and then they were disarmed and rich garments brought them, and after they had talked to the dumb damsel and with the others, supper was brought and they were well served. The damsels then retired, but presently they returned with many candles and with stringed instruments to delight them; and when it was time to sleep they again retired. The dumb damsel had ordered three rich and goodly beds to be prepared in that chamber, and their arms were laid by the bed side, so they lay down and fell asleep like men who were fatigued.

Now you must know that this chamber was made with great cunning, for the floor did not fasten into the walls but was supported upon an iron screw like a wine-press, and fitted onto a frame of wood, so that it could be lowered or raised from below by turning an iron lever. So when they awoke in the morning they had been let down twenty cubits low, and perceiving no light, but yet hearing the stir of people above them, they marvelled greatly and rose from bed and felt for the door and windows, but when they found them and put their hands through they felt the wall of the castle, and knew that they were betrayed. Being in this great trouble a knight appeared at a window above, who was huge of stature and limb, and of a sullen countenance, and in his beard and hair more white hairs than black; he wore a mourning dress, and upon his right hand a glove of white cloth that reached to his elbow. You are well lodged there, cried he, and according to the mischief ye have done me shall be the mercy ye shall find, which shall be a cruel and bitter death, and even with that shall I not be revenged for what you did in battle with the false King Lisvarte. Know that I am Arcalaus the Enchanter, if you have never seen me before, learn to know me now; none ever injured me without my taking vengeance, except only one, whom I yet hope to have where I have you, and to cut off his hands for the hand which he lopt from me. The damsel was by him, and she pointing to Amadis said, Good uncle, that young one is he of the golden helmet. But they hearing they were in the power of Arcalaus were in great fear of death, and much were they surprised to hear that dumb damsel speak. This damsel was Dinarda, the daughter of the Ardan Canileo, who was expert in all wickedness, and had come to that land to contrive the death of Amadis, and for that cause had feigned herself dumb.

E

DUE DATE